DISCARDED

860.9
P34s   89448

DATE DUE			
~~Oct 24 7~~			
~~Dec 8 74~~			
May 19 75			

STUDIES IN HISPANIC LITERATURES

General Editor : E. ALLISON PEERS

SPANISH GOLDEN AGE POETRY AND DRAMA

LIVERPOOL STUDIES IN SPANISH LITERATURE : SECOND SERIES

EDITED BY

E. ALLISON PEERS

PHAETON PRESS

NEW YORK

1974

CARL A. RUDISILL LIBRARY
LENOIR RHYNE COLLEGE

Originally Published 1946
Reprinted 1974

Published by Phaeton Press, Inc.

860.9
P34s
89448
July 1974

Library of Congress Cataloging in Publication Data

Peers, Edgar Allison.
  Spanish golden age poetry and drama.

  (Liverpool studies in Spanish literature, 2d ser.)
(Studies in Hispanic literatures)
  Reprint of the 1946 ed. published by Institute of
Hispanic Studies, Liverpool, Eng.
  1. Spanish poetry—Classical period, 1500–1700—
Addresses, essays, lectures. 2. Spanish drama—
Classical period, 1500–1700—Addresses, essays,
lectures. I. Title. II. Series. III. Series:
Studies in Hispanic literatures.
PQ6065.P43 1974   860'.9   74–5001
ISBN 0–87753–060–2

LENOIR RHYNE COLLEGE

PREFACE

Four years have passed since the bulk of the material presented in this volume was ready for publication, for which reason, and also because two of the three authors have for nearly the whole of that time been away from all books, no reference has been possible to publications later in date than 1940. Once normal conditions of life return, I hope it may be practicable to develop and extend this series of studies, but our first duty was to these three authors who had waited so long for their work to appear in print and this volume is therefore being published at the first opportunity.

The individual authors alone are responsible for the opinions expressed in their contributions. It will be seen that they are not always in agreement with each other: no attempt, however, has been made to bring them into harmony. My own part in the book has been limited to the preparation of it for press.

E. A. P.

NOTE ON REFERENCES AND ABBREVIATIONS

The principal editions used are specified in footnotes near the beginning of each study. The following abbreviations are used throughout :

Ac. Ed.—Spanish Academy edition of the works of Lope de Vega.

B.A.E.—Biblioteca de Autores Españoles.

B.S.S.—Bulletin of Spanish Studies, Liverpool.

H.R.M.S.—E. Allison Peers : *A History of the Romantic Movement in Spain.* Cambridge, 1940. 2 vols.

Montoliu.—Manuel de Montoliu : *Manual de historia de la literatura castellana.* Barcelona, 1930.

Vossler.—Karl Vossler : *Lope de Vega y su tiempo.* Madrid, 1933.

CONTENTS

I

SENTIMENT AND ARTISTRY IN THE WORK OF THREE GOLDEN AGE POETS

(i) FRANCISCO DE MEDRANO

Medrano has received little attention from the critics. He is mentioned by Nicolás Antonio and L. J. Velázquez ; half a dozen of his poems figure in Böhl von Faber's *Floresta* ;[1] but only in 1854 did Adolfo de Castro include all that are known of them in the *Biblioteca de Autores Españoles*.[2]

Scarcely anything is known of his life. A Sevilian of the sixteenth century, he spent some time in Italy ;[3] his poems, published at Palermo in 1617, show an intimate knowledge of the country around Seville ;[4] among the people to whom he dedicates verses is the Archbishop of Seville, and he refers in friendly terms to such leading Sevilian men of letters as Arguijo, Rioja and Juan Antonio del Alcázar, brother of the witty Baltasar. Several allusions suggest a connection with Salamanca, where he may have studied,[5] and he certainly stayed at Madrid and Rome.[6] More than that cannot be said.

As obscure as the details of his life are his literary affinities. Menéndez y Pelayo calls him a Sevilian of the Salamancan School[7] and later critics attach him, now to Salamanca, now to Seville. And no wonder, for he is akin to poets of each. Like Luis de León, he is a lover of Horace, though, unlike him, he adds nothing original to his model. His links with Garcilaso, though less obvious, are perhaps stronger, for he follows him as a poet of emotion. With the

[1] Vol. I, Hamburg, 1821, Nos. 102–6, 312.
[2] Vol. XXXII.   All references to Medrano's work are from this volume.
[3] B.A.E., XXXII, xxiii.
[4] *E.g.*, Sonetos 20, 26, 27, 38 ; Oda 30.
[5] Oda 4 ; Soneto 9.
[6] Soneto 4 ; Oda 30.
[7] *Horacio en España*, Madrid, 1885, I, 43.

Andalusian poets he shares a fondness for plastic imagery and a feeling for colour and light ; the mannered elegance of one or two amorous sonnets may also be ascribed to these influences.

But the really original part of Medrano's work lies, not in its artistry, but in its sentiment. He writes with a subjectivity not common in Golden Age poetry, and reacts with intense personal emotion to the three lyric themes : God, Love and Nature. He is almost always an interesting poet : at his best he attains a perfect equilibrium of feeling and expression.

In considering Medrano's poetic personality, we shall examine in turn his range of sensibility, his reactions towards religion, his patriotism and his attitude to love and Nature. Subsequently we shall discuss his artistry.

No less than twenty-two of Medrano's thirty-four odes are acknowledged imitations of Horace ; three more are partially imitated from him, and a further three are close, though unacknowledged, renderings. It is natural, then, that the interpretation of life found in his original poems should also be largely Horatian. Life is transience and mutability, change and decay ; beauty is a " breve tiranía " ; human greatness, " humo vano " : glory resembles the Guadalquivir emptying itself into the sea.[1] The simple life is the only happy one : if earthly possessions are sources of evil, a restriction of needs should produce contentment and virtue.[2] But the *aurea mediocritas*, as preached by Medrano, remains an ethical rather than a lyrical conception : whereas Horace's Sabine farm is the constant background of his verse, Medrano's ancestral retreat, the Mirar-Bueno of Oda 31, is no more than an elusive shadow and scarcely seems to enter into his poetic consciousness.

In arguing the futility of worldly possessions from the insignificance of the earth compared with the entire universe, Medrano follows Horace less closely. Like Luis de León, in

[1] Oda 2 ; Sonetos 11, 20, 21, 47, 50.
[2] Sonetos 20, 48.

his " Noche serena," he sees the world as a " punto breve,"
and of this speck only a fifth is habitable. So,

> pues tal es, y a éstos llaman bienes,
> en el quinto de un punto, que es la tierra,
> para te envanecer ¿ qué parte tienes ? [1]

Man, who inhabits this miserable planet, is the most helpless
of created things. Despite his illimitable ambition, his
activities and pleasures pass away, leaving no trace. That
lesson is driven home by the ruins of Itálica, in the desolation
of which Medrano sees the destiny of all man's creation :

> ¡ Cómo feneció todo ! [2]

The melancholy here is far more poignant than in Horace,
whose hedonism is an elegant and urbanely complacent pose.
For Medrano life is more complex and tragic. He seems to
shrink from it, as though personal disillusion had reinforced
his temperamental melancholy. His philosophy is that of
the timid hyper-sensitive recluse. [3]

But in his interior life he is more violent. We shall see
later with what passion he can react to God and human
love. For the moment, let us look, not at the philosopher,
with his ideal of contented equanimity, but at the man—
restless, introspective, the prey of every mood :

> Yo quedo en tierra firme y mal cons'anʇe ;
> de dolor embestido y de alegría,
> altero por momentos el semblante ;
>   Mas si un mar brama dentro en la alma mía,
> No fuera, no, cual tú lo ves delante.
> Júpiter ¿ cuántas formas mudaría ? [4]

Resignation and hope, the philosophic nostrums, are useless
to him :

> ¿ Aguardaré ?   La muerte antes que el tedio
> de una esperanza. [5]

Patience is folly.   Nothing but violent action will resolve his
depression :

> Osar sólo es el medio.
> Osemos ; que es dichosa la osadía. [6]

[1] Soneto 25.   [2] Soneto 26.
[3] Sonetos 4. 24, 26 ; Oda 30.   [4] Soneto 23.
[5] Soneto 45.   [6] Ibid.

Only death can end his restless melancholy.[1] Such turbulence could never be deduced from his calm Classical verses. He is a true precursor of the nineteenth-century Romantics and reveals a degree of introspectiveness unusual in his age.

A very different aspect of his personality is revealed in the difficult but interesting Sonnet 29, which shows a strong strain of mysticism. Here he describes an experience that lies outside the ken of the senses :

> que es bien pequeño
> el que puede abarcar solo el sentido.

He grasps the essential truth that in these intuitive glimpses of reality ignorance is the only knowledge, and describes his vision of Beauty, not in intellectual terms, but in suggestive images. He feels like one struck motionless on a dark night, unable to comprehend his experiences and conscious only of a supreme calm :

> No sé cuándo ni cómo ni qué ha sido,
> que lo sensible todo puso en calma.

This unusual sonnet illustrates Medrano's sensitive perception and shows how far he was from the many poets of Andalusia who were limited by the senses.

Contrasting with the tendencies of his age and country, the religion of Medrano is emotional rather than dogmatic. Religion is no integral part of his philosophy, but rather a spirit informing all his work. It is inherent in his inability to accept the hedonism of Horace, and in his sensitiveness to the tragedy of life ; it is seen at its purest in his intimate personal approach to God, an attitude which finds its closest parallel in some of the *Rimas sacras* of Lope de Vega.

We have seen how Medrano's spontaneous emotional reactions exist alongside his rationally acquired philosophy. In a similar way subjective feeling invades religious themes that most poets would treat objectively. In his sonnet on St. Peter, for example, the description of the traditional

[1] *Ibid.*

attributes of the Saint leads up to an entirely personal application. He asks St. Peter :

> Los ojos vuelve al mar enfurecido ;
> y pues tal vez osó mojar tu planta
> aun siendo hollado de tu fe animosa,
>   su hinchazón rompe, acalla su ruido,
> y, enseñado discípulo, levanta
> mi fe y mis pies con mano poderosa.[1]

When, however, his religious feeling is centred on God, he is capable of the very deepest emotion. He rejects the pious platitudes of conventional religion : with a deep consciousness of his sins and shortcomings, his is not an easy faith or love. He has no doubts as to the greatness and power of God, Who alone can still the tempest and deliver when human help has failed.[2] Yet he is always aware of the insurmountable barrier of his own unworthiness. He turns from earthly joys in search of interior rest, but his tragedy is that he can never lay hold upon his soul's desire— and, furthermore, he is ashamed of his hypocrisy in praying to be freed from the sin in which he still takes pleasure.[3] Yet, through all his confusion of soul, he has an instinctive trust in God's forgiveness ; in spite of himself, he will be saved.[4] Religious feeling is not Medrano's main inspiration, but his questionings, doubts, perplexities and final intuitive glimpses of faith reveal another phase of his adaptation to the great problems of life. Here, as in other spheres, his reactions are sensitive and complicated ; his introspection tends to make him self-distrustful ; but he never loses his fundamental idealistic faith.

How does Medrano react to his environment and what is his attitude to the political system and social organization of his country ?

He has an immense pride in Spain's past and his panegyrics of her great monarchs are suggestive of an old man who finds consolation in the past for the failures of the present.

---

[1] Soneto 3.   [2] Sonetos 32, 40.   [3] Sonetos 10, 46, 54.
[4] Sonetos 10, 54. Other testimony to this instinctive feeling will be found in Sonetos 12, 17, 18.

Internal evidence would place Medrano's work at about the beginning of the reign of Philip III, when Spain was in the early stages of political, economic and social decadence. That Medrano could remember better times is evident from his references to the preceding reigns as standards of comparison. But a clearer indication that he is no longer young is the tone in which he addresses the young King, urging him to fulfil the obligations laid upon him by his illustrious predecessors, to be more warlike and at the same time to cultivate the arts of peace. In Herreran language he paints a glowing picture of the glorious day when Spain's enemies—the " inconstante galo e inglés pirata "—shall incline before the conquering banners of St. James, and Philip shall be

> aunque Tercero, sin segundo,
> para favor y emulación del mundo.[1]

But Medrano can diagnose Spain's ills and sees that leadership in peace and war will not suffice to heal them. He boldly adapts the odes in which Horace bewails the condition of his own country. Spain, like Rome, had attained greatness only through self-discipline and sacrifice ; and the accusations of immorality, lawlessness, corruption of justice and breaches of faith are made by Horace and by Medrano against a similar background. In the sense that the criterion of his judgments is the solid achievement of the past, Medrano is a traditionalist. He is no fulsome panegyrist, however, and his democratic conception of kingship unites him still more closely to those Spaniards of past ages for whom he has so great an admiration.

Medrano's love-poems—twenty-one sonnets and two odes—form the largest section of his original work and reveal perhaps more clearly than any other group the wide range of his sensibility. Besides being extremely varied in technique, they present many interesting problems, the clues to which are lost ; and the Arcadian dedications confuse rather than enlighten, since no consistency can be discovered

---

[1] Oda 4.

in the assignment of names to particular poems. There is every reason, however, to suppose that real persons are involved. A poem like Soneto 53 is woven in so complicated an emotional pattern that it seems inconceivable that the whole can be an artistic fabrication, for art defeats its own purpose when, through over-elaboration, it becomes incomprehensible.

Many of these poems adopt the commonplaces of that conception of Neoplatonic love which was popularized in Spanish verse by Herrera. They constantly exalt the soul and the spirit above the body,[1] and elevate the loved object to a supernatural plane.

> Vine y vi, y sujetóme la hermosura
> de un serafín que en apariencia humana
> a los mortales ojos tal se allana,
> que, aunque flacos, sostengan su luz pura.[2]

Neither age nor decay of beauty, distance nor absence, can affect love, since it is an affinity of souls and eternally binding ;[3] indeed, it can triumph over the longer absence of death.[4]

There are two symbols of Neoplatonic love of which Medrano makes some use. One is the fire of love[5]— Castiglione's " foco santissimo nelle anime (che) distrugge e consuma ciò che v'è di mortale, e vivifica e fa bella quella parte celeste, che in esse prima era dal senso mortificata e sepulta "[6]—which had been one of the favourite symbols of Herrera. The other is the wound of love[7]—delectable and never-healing—a mediaeval figure intimately connected with the language of mysticism.

But, notwithstanding these affinities of Medrano's love-poetry with Neoplatonism, there is much in him that is strictly personal. He accepts the atmosphere of idealization because it is congenial to him but he is far from limiting himself by any rigid code. His love, while no less chaste and noble than Herrera's, is far more human. When he

---

[1] Sonetos 2, 11.   [2] Soneto 5.   [3] Sonetos 11, 42, 34, 41.
[4] Soneto 12.   [5] Sonetos 38, 42.
[6] Il Cortegiano, IV, lxix (Florence, 1894, p. 429).
[7] Sonetos 11, 41.

breaks loose from the fetters of artificiality, he reveals a spontaneity and a variety of emotion that seem more characteristic of the Romantic Movement than of the Golden Age. He uses the sonnet form to express the whole range of human reaction to the stimulus of love. He heightens the dramatic effect by juxtaposing the elements of love and death.[1] He himself seems to be speaking, not when he idealizes love in the Neoplatonic sense, but when he exalts it in the modern Romantic sense—that is, in its purely human attributes. Soneto 39, perhaps, best describes his own conception of love. It is an affinity of spirits ; once present, it can never be eradicated ; it thrives on obstacles ; it is unaffected by time, violence, difference in station, or any other condition.

> Que si nuestras dos almas son a una,
> ¿ en quién, si no ya en Dios, habrá potencia
> que las gaste o las fuerce o las desuna ?

Where there is such a love, life is meaningless without the loved one, and absence assumes an importance which it could never have in Neoplatonic theory. It is an angry sea, and the lover's only hope is to reach his mistress' side and die.

> Yo lucho con la ausencia ; y sostenido
> de mi esperanza, ¿ llegaré seguro,
> Flora, a tus ojos ? [2]

But the lovers do not fear death provided they are together.

This is the passion, at once ideal and human, which Medrano describes with such sincere simplicity. Though often conventional, the apt disciple of Herrera, he is not content to use love as a decorative element, or as a stock theme on which to compose variations. He gives it a poetic value which it has in scarcely any other Golden Age poet save Lope de Vega and which it will not have again till centuries later. If tentatively, and with many lapses into conventionality, Medrano opens up an important sphere of lyrical inspiration.

---

[1] Sonetos 13, 14, 43.

[2] Soneto 14.

In one of his sonnets, Medrano describes the beauties of wild scenery—

> aquel descuido soberano
> de la naturaleza—[1]

its abundance, its variety and its grandeur, in terms which would seem to indicate a feeling for Nature far in advance of his age. But this almost Wordsworthian delight in meadow, stream and mountain he scarcely ever parallels elsewhere. Occasionally a phrase suggests sympathetic insight or keen observation : in the " ricas plantas de fértiles racimos,"[2] for example, he describes exactly the lush vegetation of the river bed. His pleasure, too, in the natural beauties of his beloved Mirar-Bueno seems genuine, though not unmixed with other emotional elements. But, generally speaking, little interest in Nature is to be expected in a Golden Age poet whose aim is avowedly moral. He will always show the greatest interest in those aspects of it which offer the most profitable lessons. The most we can hope to find is some personal element in his choice.

It is more than chance, for example, that sent him so often for his illustrations to sea and river. Living in Seville, he could not fail to be conscious of the part played in its life by the sea : he must have caught some of the atmosphere of that great port, the clearing-house for the Old and New Worlds. He could see how the magnetic lure of the ocean drew Spaniards in search of gold and adventure, and watch their ships return with the almost fabulous products of the Indies.[3] The sea, in his work, is never considered as a subject for contemplation, but only as it affects humanity, bearing or wrecking the ships of men that carry them away from what they love, towards unknown shores. Thus, though he says that he loves the sea whether calm or rough :

> Turbio me place y pláceme sereno.[4]

[1] Soneto 30.

[2] Oda 25.

[3] In his renderings of Horace he makes repeated references to America and the " riqueza de los ingas " (e.g., Odas 1, 10, 18, 24) and testifies clearly to the attraction which the Americas held for Spaniards of his day.

[4] Soneto 4.

2

he presents it only in angry mood, for a hostile ocean best reveals the intimate relationship between man and the sea.

Metaphorically, the sea stands for restlessness, changeableness, and hostility. The " mar falso " represents the world's turmoil, greed, ambition and insubstantial glory.[1] More subjectively, Medrano relates the sea to the adverse forces of fate.[2] He himself is the rock that withstands its " furia inmensa." [3] In curiously dramatic symbols the stormy sea stands for the poet's absence from his beloved and the dangers that attend the frail bark of their love, and, on a yet more subjective plane, for his own incurable restlessness. A sea rages within his soul. And, when love has gone, the agitation of mind that remains is like the sea after a storm, when the waves still beat against each other and moan.[4]

The sea is obviously the aspect of Nature which appealed to Medrano most ; and the development which he gives to sea-images, far transcending the needs of merely conceptual comparison, suggests that they were more to him than a source of moralizing reflections. Sometimes, indeed, the descriptive part forms the main body of the poem, and the application to human life seems almost an after-thought— the poet's tribute to the prevailing poetic convention.

Yet there is little to show that Medrano viewed the sea with an artist's eye. His is always the emotional approach ; he appreciates the inner spiritual significance of the conflict of wind and wave rather than the sea's exterior plastic beauty. So there is monotony in his seascapes—the monotony of continuous storm. No favouring breezes ever blow him into port and the conflict-motif is always completed by the presence of man—the pilot, the captain, the " impío marinero," the " pasajero humilde." [5] It is this symbolic aspect of the sea which chiefly interests Medrano and occupies so large a place in his work.

Only less inspiring does Medrano find rivers. His river-images, however, are far more particularized than his sea-images. He writes with more affection of that " sacro rey

---

[1] Sonetos 4, 50 ; Oda 30.   [2] Soneto 44.   [3] Soneto 34.
[4] Sonetos 23, 16.   [5] Sonetos 4, 14.

de ríos"[1] so much beloved of Herrera and Góngora, than of
the "dulce y claro río" of Garcilaso's Second Eclogue.
He seems to find most pleasure in the dynamic aspect of
rivers, their ceaseless flow from source to mouth. Among
the spectacles of Nature which he particularly singles out as
worthy of admiration is :

> Ver cómo corre eternamente un río.[2]

And if he isolates one characteristic as symbolizing all rivers
it is that of their movement. The endless course of their
waters is like the endless course of his miserable days :

> ¿ Quién aguarda a mañana mal prudente ?
> Que acabe de correr espera un río,
> y él corre y correrá perpetuamente.[3]

But his observation is not confined to a river's movement.
He must have noticed how the Guadalquivir had changed its
course, leaving a sandy bed which was later brought under
cultivation ; and he uses his observations to form an image
expressing his belief in the return of happiness after sorrow.[4]
Generally speaking, his references to rivers, though less
frequent than his references to the sea, show a more intrinsic
interest in Nature. The connection with human activities
is always there, but less prominently.

Little as he says of his life at Mirar-Bueno, it is clear that
he was familiar with the life of the farmer and enjoyed
rustic pastimes. One sonnet is built up round the opera-
tions of pruning and sowing. Another illustrates the
transience of human life from the growth of crops. A third
shows a knowledge of fishing, while an ode reveals his love for
the "robusta caza."[5] In wild life he has little interest, and
his references to it are conventional.

Medrano also uses Nature as a decorative background—
notably in his amatory verse—and as a source of moral
symbols. The Nature he evokes when writing of his love is,

---

[1] The phrase is Herrera's. Cf. Góngora, Soneto 70 (B.A.E., XXXII, 435) :
"rey de los otros ríos caudaloso."

[2] Soneto 30.   [3] Soneto 45.   [4] Oda 25.

[5] Sonetos 24, 47, 44, Oda 18.

as in Herrera and Góngora, highly stylized. As Herrera
commands Betis to adorn itself in honour of the bride of the
Marquis of Tarifa,[1] so Medrano would have Tormes make
itself worthy of the surpassing beauty of Margarita. All
nature and art are called into service : the river must
embroider its banks of emerald sward with pearls, Flora
must rob Dawn of the roses in her cheeks, the dryads must
pour forth the " turquesadas maravillas "of the " rica gruta "
in their shining white baskets. And all this

> para que pise Margarita ufana,
> tierra y agua llenando de favores ; [2]

Individual elements are employed in a similar way.
Neoplatonism had thrown a special stress upon light ; and
by Medrano's day certain of the light-images which he uses
had already become clichés.[3] His twelfth sonnet, however,
in which the stars betoken his dead Flora's immortality,
makes an entirely satisfying fusion of emotion and back-
ground. References to flowers and animals, on the contrary—
such as the wounded stag and the swan[4]—do little more
than provide an atmosphere of beauty.

Conventional, and of little interest, are the symbolic
uses of Nature made by Medrano in his moral reflections.
Often he shows slight awareness of the intrinsic meaning of
an image and employs it merely as a convenient synonym.
The sun denotes the universe, universality, brilliance ; the
stars, loftiness, inaccessibility, fame. Flowers symbolize
life's fragility and transience—and this is especially true of
the rose, which, in his version of Horace's ode on the fair
lady grown old, he substitutes for the concluding image of
the sere leaf. Young men despise

> rosas que desmayó una tarde fría ;

and delight only in the newly-opened buds :

> de las que hoy apenas abrió el día
> se coronan de grado.[5]

These images have hardly more reality than those of the

---

[1] Herrera, Elegía 7 (*Poesías*, ed. Diego, Madrid, 1914, p. 217).
[2] Soneto 8.   [3] Cf. Sonetos 5, 22, 28, 38.
[4] Sonetos 41, 42.   [5] Oda 22.

phoenix, the lion and the eagle. [1] It is only when Medrano's personal experience touches Nature that we occasionally see the glimmerings of disinterested appreciation.

It might be deduced from what has been said that purely artistic considerations find little place in Medrano's poetry. His chief aim is didactic ; matter interests him more than manner ; and ideas and sentiments are never sacrificed to form. His verses have not the sensuous appeal, or the profusion of light and colour, of those of Herrera and Rioja. The concrete seldom intrudes itself in the shape of images and of these very few have pictorial value. Like Luis de León, with whom he has a certain affinity, Medrano tends to starkness of style and his imagery strikes one more as a concession to literary convention than as an expression of his own poetic personality.

Many of his images, drawn from the common poetic stock, are completely unobtrusive. The descriptions of age in terms of the seasons, [2] of love as a conflict, a bondage or a fire, [3] are trite and meaningless. Occasionally Medrano shows a slightly Baroque tendency to extend and complicate such familiar metaphors. If love is a wound, then his lady's beauty is a knife, whose edge, though blunted by age, still produces an incurable wound. Or it is a flame which, even when death has stolen the breath of life from his mistress, cannot be extinguished. [4]

Medrano's attempts to express complicated ideas by means of images are seldom successful. Even where he has found a suitable figure for his thought he neglects that interior bond of harmony that unites idea and image into a poetic whole. Of this class is his comparison of man's fortune with a toga :

> Quiero, a fuer de la toga, la fortuna
> limpia, de mi medida y concertada,
> ni con grandeza pródiga sobrada
> ni corta y miserablemente ayuna. [5]

Here there is an exact parallel between the idea and its

[1] Soneto 17 ; Odas 4, 13.
[2] Sonetos 7, 42 ; Oda 4.
[3] Sonetos 2, 32, 51.
[4] Soneto 11.
[5] Soneto 19.

figurative equivalent, yet the whole process is intellectual, and the result lacks both imaginative and sensuous appeal.

Here and there, as in Soneto 6, he can produce a forceful comparison, reinforcing the thought on both the intellectual and the emotional plane. Occasionally, as in the comparison of the pleasures of the youthful Philip III with nightingales,[1] he produces an image both unusual and evocative. The best of the images are drawn from Nature—especially from river or sea.

Perhaps because of its very restraint, one of Medrano's most successful artistic effects is his use of light and colour. He has not the Andalusian's passion for brilliance of effect. If, as is believed, he was a painter, this careful use of pictorial elements would be natural.

Generally speaking, there is but little colour in his work : he can, on occasion, use it lavishly, as in Sonnet 8, which glows with whites, greens, reds, blues and golds, but his more usual method is to brighten a poem with a flash of colour where it is least expected. Thus the " melena roja "[2] of Philip III comes as rather a surprise in a patriotic ode and two sonnets on the tomb of Rodrigo de Castro[3] have more colour than the subject would appear to warrant. On the other hand, Medrano does not slip into the facile use of conventional colour where this was most used by his contemporaries. In a sonnet on his lady's beauty[4] (a subject which, as we may see in Herrera, lends itself to a profusion of colour) there is no colour at all, save the glowing ruby of her lips (" el rubí de tu boca ").[5] Góngora, in similar circumstances, introduces a range of colours from " blanco nácar y alabastro duro " and " coral preciado " to the " verde puro " of a fine emerald.[6]

Not only are Medrano's methods of introducing colour different from those of most poets of his day, but the very colours he chooses are different. In this respect he stands closer to Garcilaso than to Herrera and Góngora. For he prefers clear bright colours used with an exact appreciation

[1] Oda 4.   [2] *Ibid.*   [3] Sonetos 17, 18.
[4] Soneto 22.   [5] *Ibid.*
[6] Góngora, Soneto 56 (B.A.E., XXXII, 433).

of their value against a dull or neutral background.   Garci-
laso loved the delicate contrast of the most elementary natural
colours, and did not seek to add to them :

> por ti la verde yerva, el fresco viento,
> el blanco lyrio y colorada rosa,
> y dulce primavera desseava. [1]

Medrano has greater richness than this, but he retains closer
kinship with the earlier poet than with the Góngora who
could thus describe a sunrise :

> Tras la bermeja aurora el sol dorado
> por las puertas salía del oriente,
> ella de flores la rosada frente,
> y él de encendidos rayos coronados. [2]

Here colours lose their individual values and become merged
in a general brilliance.

Most striking is Medrano's use of red, particularly in
conjunction with white.   The " birreta roja " [3] of a cardinal
makes a focal spot in a sonnet that contains no other colour ;
mention of the " fiero jabalí " hunted by Philip III is made
more striking by reference to the " púrpura caliente " [4] of
its blood.   Even conventional colour-images take on new
meaning when used to give contrast.   Compare this sunrise
with that by Góngora quoted above :

> Así mirarse deja con segura
> vista el temprano sol de la mañana,
> y entre nubes de nieve, tinta en grana,
> permite a nuestra vista su figura. [5]

The sonnet in which he describes his love in old age, her hair
whitened and the colour gone from her cheeks, is a delicate
interplay of red and white, with perhaps an undertone of
gold suggested by the word " dora " and intensified by the
rhyme :

> Veré al tiempo tomar de ti, Señora,
> por mí venganza, hurtando tu hermosura ;
> veré el cabello vuelto en nieve pura,
> que el arte y juventud encrespa y dora.
> Y en vez de rosas, en que tiñe ahora
> tus mejillas la edad ¡ ay ! mal segura,
> lilios sucederán en la madura,
> que el pesar quiten y la envidia a Flora. [6]

[1] Égloga I (*Works*, ed. Keniston, New York, 1925, p. 84).
[2] Góngora, Soneto 49 (B.A.E., XXXII, 432).
[3] Soneto 4.   [4] Oda 4.   [5] Soneto 5.   [6] Soneto 11.

Against the dead-white background of the " mármol sacro " composing the tomb of Rodrigo de Castro he sets the glow of " topacios rojos " to contrast with " perlas " and the " senos de alabastro " of the Archbishop's effigy.[1] And, describing the swans of Tormes, he picks out the vivid colour of their " pies . . . rojos " contrasting with the " cándida plata " of their " blancas plumas."[2] Red, besides being actually mentioned, is often suggested to a greater or a lesser degree in such words as " llama," " incendio," " fuego," " herida," " rosa." In a sonnet such as Soneto 11, in which there are explicit colour-values, words merely suggesting colour will have little more than their conceptual import. But we cannot deny the colour in such lines as :

> Arde la llama, y a la oscura y fría
> noche el festivo incendio vence. . . .[3]

where the effect of glowing red is as strong as if the poet had been more specific.

Although red and white are his prime favourites, Medrano also likes clear cold colours, such as green and blue, generally used in conjunction with red, or white, or both. The banks of the Tormes are covered with " yerbas de esmeralda," while round about are white flowers and roses, golden reeds in the blue waters (" turquesadas maravillas ")[4] ; a delicate and beautiful effect is obtained by the contrast of the pearly ears of corn within their green sheaths :

> Éstas vi que hoy son pajas más ufanas,
> sus hojas desplegar para que vieses
> vencida la esmeralda en sus enveses,
> las perlas en su haz por las mañanas.[5]

One colour of a different type, much used by Medrano, provides a link between his treatment of colour and of light. This is the shade he calls " rubio," and employs to describe both people and aspects of Nature. Besides having the conventional meaning of " blonde " (as when the brow of Philip III is described as " rubio " and the attacking

---

[1] Soneto 18. [2] Oda 4. [3] Soneto 38.
[4] Soneto 8. [5] Soneto 47.

French are characterized as the " franco rubio ") it is the adjective generally used of ripe corn :

> . . . . estas de mieses hoy rubias campiñas.[1]

This epithet is found in Garcilaso, but generally applied to hair.[2] Medrano gives it a wider application and it connects the simple colour-scheme we have been discussing with the more complex light and colour harmonies which are typical of him.

Throughout his work there is a marked sensitiveness to light. Indeed, he sees colour in terms of light—that is to say, he seldom writes of a colour as opaque, but as shot through with light, like a jewel.

Red is the most notable exception : we have seen several examples of it as a flat colour (" rojo," " grana," " púrpura ") but even this can be luminous, as in " el rubí de tu boca,"[3] and the " topacios rojos " referred to above. Other colours are almost consistently transparent or radiant ; white is only called " nieve " on occasions consecrated by convention ; clouds are " nubes de nieve,"[4] and his lady's hair is " vuelto en nieve pura."[5] Apart from these examples white for Medrano is something that gleams : a swan's plumage is " cándida plata."[6] Most often he sees it as pearls—precious stones he particularly seems to favour : they are the chosen gift of Neptune,[7] and accompany the topaz as adornment :

> No por las perlas y topacios rojos,
> de las manos adorno y de las sienes.[8]

When he commands the Tormes to cover its banks with flowers he uses the words :

> Borde Tormes de perlas sus orillas . . .[9]

---

[1] Oda 25. Cf. the " rubias mieses " of Soneto 47.

[2] *E.g.*,   Alce una de vosotras, blancas deas,
    del agua su cabeça rubia un poco,
    . . . .
    ¡ O dryades . . . .
    Con los cabellos rubios . . . ! Garcilaso, Égloga II. (*Ed. cit.*, p. 124).

[3] Soneto 22.   [4] Soneto 5.   [5] Soneto 11.   [6] Oda 4.

[7] Soneto 17.   [8] Soneto 18.   [9] Soneto 8.

And he describes the grains of wheat in the ear as " las perlas en su haz." [1]

Green is always " esmeralda," whether as grass (" yerbas de esmeralda " [2]) or as the corn sheath : [3] the waters of the Tormes are turquoise-coloured. [4]

Among Medrano's subsidiary light-effects may be counted the use of metals. Of silver he makes striking use as a term of comparison, as well as of other substances with smooth, light-reflecting surfaces like those of metals :

> Tus ojos, bella Flora, soberanos,
> y la bruñida plata de tu cuello,
> y ése, envidia del oro, tu cabello,
> y el marfil torneado de tus manos . . . [5]

But silver is also used, somewhat artificially, to describe a lady's neck, a swan's plumage and the sea. Gold adds richness to the poet's colour-schemes, as in the " junquillos dorados " of Soneto 8 and the golden beaks of the swans of Tormes (Oda 4) which soften the abrupt transition from red to white. Other rich, glowing substances used by Medrano are porphyry and alabaster, [6] and, like many poets of his day, he depicts the effect of light gleaming on armour. [7]

In the figurative sphere, the attributes of light are conventionally applied to reason, faith, love and beauty, [8] to the eternal Truth sought by his restless soul [9] and to immortality. [10]

Little need be said of Medrano's metre and diction. In one sense he has no peculiar poetic style, for expression in his work is subordinated to thought and sentiment, and varies with changes in emotional tone. Mental agitation produces the broken lines of Sonnets 46 and 53 and balanced, evenly accented lines reflect the calm philosophical mood of Sonnet 20. Occasionally, however, he reproduces current literary styles. The elaborately symmetrical arrangement and richness of diction of Sonnet 8 are reminiscent of

[1] Soneto 47.   [2] Soneto 8.   [3] Soneto 47.
[4] Soneto 8.   [5] Soneto 2.   [6] Sonetos 3, 18.
[7] Oda 4.   [8] Sonetos 28, 32, 38, 42. Oda 4.
[9] Soneto 46.   [10] Sonetos 12, 17.

Herrera's love-sonnets, while Sonnet 3 reveals traces of *conceptismo*.

But Medrano generally expresses himself with the greatest simplicity, his aim being to communicate the thought of a poem as clearly as possible. To this end he makes extensive use of *enjambement*, and this, coupled with a freedom from inversions and most other devices of the so-called " poetic " style, produces an almost prose-like effect. At his best, and under the influence of strong emotion, he writes in a concentrated emphatic style. The very repetition with which Sonnet 39 begins seems rather the spontaneous expression of sentiment than the result of any consciously rhetorical intent :

> Las almas son eternas, son iguales,
> son libres, son espíritus, María ;
> si en ellas hay amor, con la porfía
> de los estorbos crece y de los males.
> Nacimos en fortuna desiguales,
> no en gustos ; la violencia nos desvía ;
> el tiempo corre lento, y deja el día
> de sí hasta en los mármoles señales.[1]

The one type of inversion—probably a Latinism—which he uses repeatedly results from his anxiety to be concise :

> Ésta que te consagro fresca rosa . . . [2]
> Éstos de pan llevar campos ahora . . .[3]
> Reserva esas en risa envueltas iras.[4]

Medrano's vocabulary is singularly free from the elevated terms so dear to Herrera. Only when he is consciously imitating him, as in the grandiose ode addressed to Philip III in Salamanca, does he indulge in such intolerable periphrases as " portátiles torres " for ships, and " golfo de crespada plata," or " salobre plata," for the sea. Apart from these examples it is significant that he is almost always content with the simple word " mar," unlike such poets as Rioja who can only refer to the sea as " piélago," " ponto " or " golfo." With the exception of an occasional Latinism such as " pro común " or " proceloso," Medrano's vocabulary is very little different from the vocabulary of prose.

In view of his comparative indifference to poetic technique

---

[1] Soneto 39.   [2] Soneto 21.   [3] Soneto 26.   [4] Soneto 28.

it is a little surprising to find that he is master of a large
variety of verse-forms.   In his translation of Horace he
expresses the varied range of subject-matter and tone in a
remarkable series of modifications of the *lira* and four-lined
stanza, as well as in longer strophes.   By far the largest
number of translations from Horace are adaptations of the
four-lined verse-form used by Francisco de la Torre.   Many
are in the latter poet's favourite combination of three
heptasyllabic lines followed by a pentasyllabic line, the
only difference being, as Menéndez y Pelayo notes,[1] that
Medrano's version is " aconsonantada."   Other examples
vary the order of the heptasyllabic and pentasyllabic lines,
and alter the rhyme system.   Medrano also produces some
interesting varieties of the *lira*, which he manages with a
considerable amount of skill.

Longer strophes include the *sextilla* and many types of
unclassified verse form.   Some of these, such as the four-
teen-line strophe of the original Oda 4, are clearly modi-
fications of the famous " estancia lírica " used by Garcilaso
for his First Eclogue.   Other stanzas are original arrange-
ments of heptasyllabic and pentasyllabic units, varying in
length from seven to twelve lines.   On the whole, however,
these more complicated arrangements are not as successful
as the shorter and more flexible stanzas of four and five lines,
which are especially suited to Medrano's direct simplicity
of diction.   It is interesting to compare, for example, Oda 4,
mentioned above, with one of his almost perfect renderings
of Horace.   One can hardly believe that the same poet
could produce the heavy, monotonously accented lines of
the former, and the airy grace and skilful blending of
rhythm to sense of the latter.

But the verse-form most used by Medrano in his original
work is the sonnet.   Like Herrera, who regarded it as the
most flexible of poetic forms, Medrano adapts it to many
subjects and moods.   He has written sonnets on love, on
religion, on philosophy, and on contemporary events, and
has expressed in them his most intimate emotions.

The construction of his sonnets depends largely on the

[1] *Horacio en España, ed. cit.*, II, 64-5.

subject-matter. The traditional division into eight and six lines is more obvious in a stylized sonnet of the Herreran type, such as Soneto 8, than in one expressing personal feelings, such as Soneto 10. But, on the whole, the separation of the tercets from the first eight lines is preserved, and even in a sonnet like 53, which has the effect of an unpremeditated outburst, there is a break between the jealous rage of the first eight lines and the calmer tone of the ending.

It is difficult to trace any one influence in Medrano's sonnets. His frequent practice of devoting the last three or six lines to an image describing what has preceded resembles the technique of Rioja, but in the absence of definite evidence it is impossible to know whether Rioja influenced Medrano or *vice versa*. Medrano owes a more general debt to Herrera, in that he has taken over many of his Neoplatonic themes and images. And in some of his sonnets (*e.g.*, 5, 39) he returns directly to the manner of Garcilaso. The emotional pitch rises slowly in the first eight lines, and finds its full expression in the tercets, which usually culminate in a last line striking either for its emotional force or pathos. Herrera attached great importance to the value of a good last line in a sonnet, but scarcely ever succeeded in carrying out his own precepts. Medrano shows a similar desire for an effective ending in the concluding lines of Soneto 6 (a rhetorical question) and Soneto 9 (balanced antithesis), as well as in the series of proper names which concludes Soneto 18. And he rarely produces the pitifully weak last lines that mar so many sonnets by Herrera. Even when adding no new thought to the poem, he usually ends with a line both apt and harmonious.

Technically, Medrano's sonnets show a certain advance on those of Garcilaso and Herrera. He has more variety and force than the former, and a greater mastery of construction than the latter. Though he seldom achieves the linguistic perfection and rhythmical smoothness of the best sonnets of Garcilaso, Medrano reveals a nicely balanced consciousness of the relative value of individual lines and of the poem as a whole. He must certainly be placed high in the second class of Spanish sonneteers.

(ii) FRANCISCO DE RIOJA.

In Rioja we have a poet of a very different type from Medrano. His life was spent in the shadow of great men and great events. He was a protégé of Olivares, sharing both the favourite's eminence and his disgrace, an Inquisitor, a Canon of Seville and Court Librarian. He was famous as a poet during his lifetime—the chief literary figure in Seville, praised by Lope de Vega and Cervantes.

His poetic affinities, however, are less sharply defined than the details of his life. Though related to the Andalusian group by his preoccupation with form, he inclines more to sentiment and subjectivity than Herrera, Arguijo and Góngora. Critics have tried to resolve this contradiction by considering the emotional elements in his work as characteristic of the Baroque ; but his melancholy is as far from the deliberately induced emotion of the typical Baroque as are Herrera's ingenious analyses of his emotions from the spontaneous feelings of a Medrano ; in the same way his essentially emotional response to Nature is quite unlike Góngora's intense aesthetic pleasure in its outward forms.

Perhaps the truth is that Rioja possesses to an extraordinary degree the capacity for both emotional and artistic self-expression. While keenly alert to the sensuous appeal of his surroundings, he also reacts continually to emotional stimuli. His attention, for example, is never completely occupied by the beauty of a flower—its colour and its scent : he must always search for the link that unites the flower and himself in a common bond of feeling.

In Rioja, then, we shall not find the same clear-cut division between sentiment and artistry that we have seen in Medrano. We shall also miss in him one of Medrano's chief sources of feeling, for in his love-poetry emotion has been transformed into pure artistry. The most persistent notes in his verse are melancholy and sensibility to Nature.

Rioja reveals his melancholy both in the peculiar twist which he gives to such literary influences as Horatian philosophy and the current vogue for poems on ruins and also in his personal reactions to events in his own life and of his day. Either temperamentally or because of disillusionment, he believes that the whole of life is sorrow :

> No es más el luengo curso de los años
> que un espacioso número de daños. [1]

Little happiness falls to the lot of man ; human ills are inevitable and inescapable, not to be cured by riches, to be ended only by death. [2] Man, like the *arrebolera* that lives but for a single night, should rejoice at the swift passage of time :

> ¿ Cuál mayor dicha tuya
> que el tiempo de tu edad tan veloz huya ? [3]

Yet, although time's passage makes earthly griefs more tolerable, it also carries away all that is beautiful. In Rioja's sensitive verse we find echoes of most of the possible reactions to the facts of death and decay. Sometimes, as in Sonnet 15, he moralizes upon them ; more often he indulges in the wistful melancholy found in Medrano :

> que todo es humo y sombra y desparece ; [4]

in Pacheco :

> ¡ Cuán frágil eres, hermosura humana !
> Tu gloria en esplendor es cuanto dura
> breve sueño, vil humo, sombra vana ; [5]

in Salcedo Coronel :

> ¿ Qué es la vida sino sombra,
> caduca flor, humo y viento? [6]

" Todo huye como viento airado," [7] he tells us.

> Pasa, Tirsis, cual sombra incierta y vana
> este nuestro vivir. [8]

[1] *Poesías*, ed. Barrera. Sociedad de Bibliófilos Españoles : Madrid, 1867. Silva 7, pp. 238–40. (Unless the contrary is stated, all further references to Rioja are from this edition. The orthography has been modernized).
[2] Soneto 33. [3] Silva 7.
[4] Medrano, Oda 2 : B.A.E., XXXII, 345.
[5] B.A.E., XXXII, 370.
[6] Cit. Pfandl, *Historia de la Literatura nacional española en la Edad de Oro*, Barcelona, 1933, p. 247.
[7] Soneto 29. [8] Soneto 15.

Like so many other poets of the Golden Age, he uses ruins
as an illustration of human transience. Compare one
of his sonnets on the remains of Itálica, in its almost volup-
tuous insistence on the decay of greatness :

> ¡ O a cuán mísero fin, tiempo, destinas
> obras que nos parecen inmortales ! [1]

with the classical Spanish example of the poem of ruins—
the " Canción a las ruinas de Itálica " of Rodrigo Caro.
Sometimes Rioja passes beyond the conventional treatment
and makes a personal application [2] or draws an unusual moral.
But in all these varying approaches to the theme one element
remains constant—the poet's tone of resigned melancholy.
He seems to extend to inanimate stones the sympathy so
typical of his treatment of trees and flowers, and he lingers
sadly over the transformation of the " pompa lisonjera " of
some great city to

> yerba, y silencio y horror vano. [3]

But, on balance, he is more deeply afflicted by the passing
of happiness and beauty than by the decay of greatness.
The swift flight of happy days is an obsession with him.   Man
builds hopes on the prospect of summer—and summer slips
away, leaving only disillusion.   He calls on it to stay ;
but joyful days fly faster than dark ones. [4]   The beauty of
flowers [5] and the beauty of woman [6] are subject to the same
fatal laws.   In poems where amatory themes are allied with
the motif of fleeting time, the tone, though light, has always a
suggestion of melancholy.   The conflict between youth and
love on the one hand, and old age and death on the other,
must produce a restless desire for enjoyment while this is
possible :   an attitude of " carpe diem " is always a confession
of despair.   The lover knows the destined end of corporal
beauty, and yet he appeals against fate :

> Nunca, O tiempo, permitas que los graves
> hielos de edad la púrpura ardïente
> amortigüen, y llama en que me ardieron. [7]

---

[1] *Adiciones a las poesías de Rioja*, ed. Barrera. Seville, 1872.   (This edition will
be referred to henceforth as *Adiciones*).   Soneto 5.
[2] Soneto 29.   [3] *Adiciones*, Soneto 5.   [4] Silva 6.
[5] Silvas 7, 11.   [6] Sonetos 14, 37.   [7] Soneto 5.

Rioja's attitude is sensitive and modern, more akin to Lamartine's " Le Lac " than to Ronsard's " Cueillez dès aujourd'hui les roses de la vie."

Rioja also reveals a more subjective feeling of melancholy based upon his own experiences. In several symbolic sonnets we may sense personal disillusionment. He represents himself as repeatedly falling victim to the deceitfully calm appearance of the sea—the lure of pleasure, the prospect of high office, the hope of self-aggrandisement.[1] Yet, though aware of this, he cannot take warning from his former misfortunes. The memory of past shipwrecks fades from his mind and he embarks once more upon the treacherous ocean.[2] His own fickleness irks him and he seems to think that the bitterest thing about disillusion is the fact that it teaches us nothing, for the human race appears constitutionally incapable of profiting by past errors.[3]

A similar note appears in his love poetry. His passion is always unrequited : he is constantly mourning his loved one's absence, harshness or disdain. These traits, common in Herrera, may clearly be traced back to Petrarch. What is significant, however, is that, though Rioja describes the pains of love, he says so little about the compensating glories. The few occasions when he urges his friend Manlio to love, and sings the praises of a " hermoso incendio " and " tan ilustre fuego,"[4] offer a poor and conventional comparison with the ecstatic, almost religious attitude of a Herrera. Rioja admits the power of love, but before all else it is " engañoso."[5]

The clearest indication of his feelings is to be found in three sonnets which apparently refer to a particular incident. In these poems he imputes some misfortune, presumably an imprisonment, to the machinations of a woman.[6] To judge from the realistic detail of the

> horrendo metal que noche y día
> en torno al pie molestamente suena,[7]

this imprisonment is not merely metaphorical. From his

---

[1] Sonetos 17, 18, 31.   [2] Sonetos 17, 34.   [3] Soneto 31.
[4] *E.g.*, Sonetos 30, 36, and end of Silva 6.   [5] Soneto 23.
[6] Sonetos, pp. 254, 257, 258.   [7] Soneto, p. 258.

3

complaints and insinuations of betrayal one deduces that Rioja had little cause to extol the passion of love and had been led by unhappy experience to believe that disillusion follows in its train.

But the personal note in his *desengaño* sounds most clearly when he writes of riches and position. Himself born in poverty, he had risen to become the favourite of Olivares and had then been thrown into prison by the orders of this very protector. He had, therefore, reason to know how capricious was the favour of the great, and he must often have regretted that peaceful seclusion in Seville which he had left for the turmoil of court intrigue.

These experiences have left a mark on his verse : it can never be serene and objective. He continues in the Horatian tradition by condemning riches, but his lines have an urgency far removed from the Classical spirit. He paints the crimes committed for gold with a bitter realism : even after death man is not safe from greed. [1] The poor must always be scorned and down-trodden, compelled to starve in obscurity or to accept the hazardous patronage of the strong. Only those without experience of poverty praise it : those who have known it realize the trials it brings in an age when wealth alone counts. [2] The *silva* which develops these ideas contains a typical commentary on the society of the day and concludes on a note of utter despair. Let the poor beware of trying to rise above their unhappy state :

> ¿ Qué vale, O pobres, levantaros tanto ?
> Mirad que es necio error, necia costumbre,
> soltar a la soberbia así la rienda. [3]

And let those who read take warning from himself :

> que yo apenas, humilde y sin contienda,
> puedo contar en paz algunas horas
> de las que paso en el silencio obscuro,
> olvidado en pobreza, y no seguro. [4]

Both here and in the symbolic sonnets already discussed, his

---

[1] Silva 2.   [2] Silva 3.   [3] *Ibid.*
[4] *Ibid.* Cf. Soneto, p. 262.

profoundest melancholy proceeds from the realization of his own inability to profit from disillusion and past error.

On religion Rioja writes little even of the " occasional " verse which one would expect from a poet who was also a highly-placed churchman. He is uninterested in religion either from a decorative or from a ritualistic standpoint. Only once—in Sonnet 3—does he manifest some religious feeling, and then it is of a personal kind. It is difficult, however, to agree with Montoliu[1] that this sonnet is in any way mystical : it merely describes in apparently sincere language feelings of unworthiness, weakness and dependence upon God.

The priest in Rioja is always subordinated to the poet and the philosopher ; and in his disillusion he turns to philosophy rather than to the Church. Soneto 15 alone presents a Christian solution to the problem of life, and even this sonnet, in spite of the " celestial tesoro " it offers as consolation for the swift passage of human glory, contains no ring of conviction—merely a pagan resignation in Christian dress : the final note is the " triste fin " which awaits all humanity.

The principal elements of Rioja's philosophy are Classical. The virtues he extols are the Roman virtues of steadfastness and equanimity ; he has the Roman conception of the dignity of the philosopher. To these ideals he adds a lofty pride in personal worth, and an appreciation of the intrinsic value of suffering and pain, which is perhaps peculiarly Spanish. It is difficult to estimate the degree to which his thought is conditioned by orthodox Christianity, but much of it seems typical of the Castilian spirit in its proud austerity.

In Rioja we find an unusually disinterested appreciation of Nature. Earlier poets had either made Nature a decorative adjunct to heighten the emotional colour or the formal effect of their amatory verses, or else, subordinating it to moral considerations, had used it to provide illustrations and lessons. This is not to say that no feeling for Nature existed

[1] Montoliu, p. 281.

in Spanish poetry before Rioja : San Juan de la Cruz and
Lope de Vega would alone prove the contrary. But one of
these called Nature into the service of religion, and the other
regarded it as a background for the human interests which
were his chief concern. Rioja is one of the first poets to
present it without apology and to devote a large part of his
verse to a description of its operations. He has sonnets
which concentrate entirely on some insignificant aspect of
Nature : the naked poplar and the vine which he urges to
cover it with its foliage :[1] a river of his native Andalusia
prevented from drying up by the friendly forest.[2] No moral
is suggested in these ; the Nature-interest is regarded as
sufficient. Much longer poems are addressed to various
flowers, and even where some application is made to human
life, this is never allowed to spoil the graceful description of
the flower.

Rioja does not break completely away from the traditional
association between Nature and love-poetry. But a com-
parison with Herrera shows interesting developments in the
treatment of love-and-nature motifs. Herrera is so
supremely interested in the analysis of his emotions that he
sees the outside world as coloured by his own imaginative,
intensely subjective vision, and his poetry reflects this
distorted view. To Rioja, on the other hand, Nature retains
a separate identity. He sees it as a world apart from him-
self ; and, though he is sufficiently influenced by convention
to introduce it as a background for his love-poetry, he
succeeds in making it the centre of interest.

In Soneto 3, for example, he tells how the wind and the
snow have ceased and winter has given place to the " divino
ardor templado," and, on the banks of the " claro Guadia-
mar ondoso," the sun is melting the ice from the poplars, and
restoring their greenness. This exact description is then
paralleled in a mechanical way in the poet's experience :

> Mas triste yo que de importuno y grave
> hielo siento oprimir la frente mía,
> lejos de ver mi altiva luz ardiente.

[1] Soneto 2. [2] Soneto 4.

The application is perfunctory : and it is obvious that Rioja was more interested in an aspect of Nature than in his lady's disdain.

Again, in Soneto 8, the memorable part is the careful and beautiful description of the rose, which, hidden " en triste sombra y tenebrosa," languishes because its leaves and thorns obscure the sun's rays, and rob it of life ; not the facile and trite comparison :

> A mí en profunda oscuridad y frío
> hielo también de muerte me colora
> y ausencia de mi luz resplandeciente.

This shift of emphasis leads inevitably to a much wider interest in natural phenomena. The poet who loves Nature for her own sake can discover much that will escape one who is concerned only with human values. Rioja has an eye for the smallest details—the weeds lodged in the crevices of rocks overhanging the Betis and the " cercos transparentes " formed by the raindrops as they fall into a pool. And not only does he view the details of Nature in isolation : he has also a clear perception of the entire scheme of things. Rivers are seen in their natural setting of trees, and with grass and flowers form part of the whole panorama of summer. More than most Spanish poets, Rioja dwells upon the interdependence and interaction of the vast hierarchy of Nature, before which he is far from remaining cold and objective. Deeply sensitive to the drama of the seasons, and to the eternal conflict of heat and cold, he cannot but ascribe an emotional response to the world of Nature. On one occasion he asks the carnation :

> ¿ Dióte naturaleza sentimiento ? [1]

and to that question the whole of his work is an answer. He sees the natural world subject to the same relentless laws that rule men, and imagines it reacting with the same sensitiveness. He interprets it through his own melancholy : even the sun, to most poets and thinkers the symbol of changeless power, is shown in decline—one illustration more of the mutability of all things.

[1] Silva 8.

Rioja postulates a certain sympathy between the different components of Nature. Just as the vine, out of gratitude, must cover the bare poplar,[1] so, as the forest has protected the river from the heat of the sun, the river in flood must spare it in its headlong course.[2] Flowers, with their inherent fragility, are obvious themes for this humanized conception of Nature. So he describes the delicate, short-lived rose—languishing, even during its brief life, for lack of sunlight, from which it is obscured by its own leaves.[3] Though in his well-known *silva*, " A la Rosa," he moralizes in the conventional way, it is the rose itself, with its curling inner petals and golden centre, that interests him.

> Para las hojas de tu crespo seno
> te dió Amor de sus alas blandas plumas,
> y oro de su cabello dió a tu frente.[4]

This realism and his melancholy insistence upon the death of the flower give the poem a far greater emotional value than that of Calderón's sonnet upon the rose fantastically described as

> iris listado de oro, nieve y grana.

With this poem should be compared two others not unlike it : Silvas 7 and 11, on the *arrebolera* and the yellow rose.

Trees, again, are to Rioja always living creatures. Soneto 16 may call the ash a " mudo tronco," but no tree is ever that to him. Note, for example, his feeling for the happiness of the poplars in spring (Soneto 3) ; the care with which he portrays the " vasto pino " (Soneto 19) born in the " selva frondosa " and ending as the derelict hulk of a ship ; and the pity lavished in Soneto 13 on the forest as it lies frost-bound in winter :

> ¡ Ay amarilla selva, què desnuda
> yaces, y en cano y yerto humor cubierta. . . . !

The same pity is felt for rivers, now dried up by the summer heat, now covered with ice. Even the divine Betis

---

[1] Soneto 2. Cf. p. 28, above.

[2] Soneto 4.

[3] Soneto 8.

[4] Silva 11.

is subject to these ravages ; its tributary, the Guadiamar, is reduced in summer to a " ceñido humor " and can scarcely flow.[1]

One aspect of Nature in Rioja's work requires separate treatment, for here emotional reactions are complicated by preoccupations with artistry. The sea has played a great part in the work of many writers, and it is difficult to say how far Rioja imitates the emotional attitude and artistic technique of others. In several sonnets which have the sea for theme he employs a procedure which he appears to have borrowed from Herrera.[2] It is well known that Herrera employs a natural setting, usually fantastically exaggerated, to prepare the reader's mind to receive a forceful impression of the poet's emotional state. Though he usually chooses landscapes for this purpose there are examples of his using the sea.[3] Sometimes, however, a simple illustration becomes a moral ; a vivid metaphorical picture of the lover's pains is used to exhort others to take warning.[4] And it is in this form that Rioja adopts Herrera's technique. Rioja constantly uses the image of the sea as an illustration of danger or of life's uncertainty. He trusts himself to the calm sea, and finds himself caught up in a storm. Saved at last, he makes a vow never again to trust its deceptive calm.[5] In Sonnet 17 he gives additional vividness to this type of reference by imagining himself on the point of drowning. In other places he treats the sea on more conventional lines—[6] notably in Sonnets 31 and 35, which liken the inconstant sea to human character. In him, too, is seen the curious dread of the sea which is typical of some Golden Age writers. He seems to have an exaggerated conception of its ruthless power over human life, and this he expresses mainly by the use of epithets and realistic detail. It is significant that three out of his five poems on ruins concern cities that have

[1] Sonetos 7, 4.
[2] Coster (*Fernando de Herrera*, Paris, 1908, pp. 293–4) believes that this literary convention originated with Dante and was developed by later Italian sonneteers.
[3] *E.g.*, Soneto 6 (Herrera, *Poesías*, Madrid, 1914, pp. 50–1).
[4] *E.g.*, Soneto 48, *ed. cit.*, p. 150.   [5] Soneto 11.
[6] *E.g.*, Silva 4 ; *Adiciones*, Soneto 8.

been swallowed up by the sea, and in these three the emphasis is on the power of the sea rather than on the usual moral of the transience of human greatness. [1]

Emotionally, then, the sea is for Rioja, as for Medrano, an element of eternal hostility. Any relaxation of its ruthlessness is matter for astonishment and any pity it may have is reserved for non-human objects. [2] But when he regards it aesthetically he presents it, stormy or calm, with evident pleasure. Despite the excellence of the picture of the tranquil sea in Silva 6, " Al Verano," his storm-scenes are the best. None could deny the sombre energy of

> Crespos montes de humor al cielo vía
> subir, y el mar de oscura sombra lleno
> cambiar varias semblantes, y el terreno
> asiento entre las olas parecía. [3]

In other poems he concentrates on particular aspects of the sea. Silva 10, on the jasmine, compares that flower with the feathery whiteness of foam.

> Naciste entre la espuma
> de las ondas sonantes
> que blandas rompe y tiende el Ponto en Chío.

In these lines sound, rhythm and language evoke the impression of foam breaking along an endless series of waves. The movement of waves, especially as they reach the shore, fascinates him. He describes both their lazy approach in a calm sea and the rude shock of the stormy sea battering the strand ; the waves lapping the sand which once they shook in fury ; and the murmur which arises as they are sucked back along the shore :

> Solo, ofendiendo, el ponto entre sus iras
> suspira en el silencio del arena,
> como si alguna vez fuera ofendido. [4]

In artistry, Rioja shows a great advance on Medrano. His technical effects are more skilfully employed and are developed for their own sake rather than subordinated to

---

[1] Sonetos 22, 29, 39.

[2] Soneto 34.

[3] Soneto 1.

[4] *Adiciones*, Soneto 4.

the illustration of ideas. Sensuous effects are consciously sought after and the poet's language increases in complication to serve these ends.

At first sight Rioja's images seem less considerable than they really are : so closely interwoven are his figures into the texture of his work that they fail to stand out as they would against a plain background. Many of his love-poems are only extended images : so closely has he clung to the material symbol that its emotional significance has become lost. Again, having taken over the whole of Neoplatonic love-symbolism, with its appropriate language, he uses a great mass of imagery as though unconscious of its character. In speaking of love as a flame or a fire, he creates none of the heightening effect of an apt image : the " amoroso fuego," the " soberbia llama," the " hermoso incendio " are mere colourless, lifeless phrases, the commonplaces of amatory verse. Sometimes the plastic possibilities of these images are explored ; Rioja develops the Petrarchan paradox of ice and fire : the whiteness of his lady's brow (" transparente tersa y pura nieve ")[1], concealing the " no vencida hacha abrasadora " of the god of love, which kindles the lover's breast : or the ice of jealousy, which should freeze his " peregrino fuego," yet has the opposite effect :

> más me abraso cuanto más me hielo.[2]

Rioja's poetry, then, is basically a poetry of imagery, consciously or unconsciously employed. His concrete and definite images are sometimes brief similes and metaphors, usually conventional, and sometimes more effective extended comparisons.

The former, found everywhere, add little to the poetic effect. Only occasionally does one find slight touches of originality : the lady's complexion is compared, not merely with snow, but with the snow on Moncayo ;[3] the colour of the carnation is likened to the glow of the sun on that same snow-capped range.[4]

It is in his longer images that he shows most originality and

[1] Soneto 24.
[2] Soneto, p. 264.
[3] Soneto, p. 263.
[4] Silva 8.

beauty. Though not always artistically introduced, they are for the most part apt. Rioja's typical method, chiefly employed in his sonnets on moral themes, is to state the general argument of the poem in the first eight lines and support this by comparisons in the tercets. Sometimes single illustrations are given, but more commonly they go in pairs. Nature is their usual source, the sea preponderating. Sun-images are not infrequent, notably the sun lighting up clouds in its path.[1] The flower-images are generally conventional. Two figures which effectively turn the results of observing Nature to the service of poetry are used to illustrate the swift passing of all that is lovely. The " dulce flor " of Cloris' charms vanishes like the summer meteors which the poet sees

> . . . . en el aire discurrir lucientes
> . . . .
> y morir cuando más resplandecientes,[2]

or like the raindrops which he watches

> formarse en la agua cercos transparentes
> sin dejar de su pompa aun las señales.[3]

Figures illustrating Rioja's favourite theme of the uses of adversity include several of fire acting on clay[4] or on the sterile countryside.[5] The image of clay and the potter's wheel is a familiar one, but much less so is one taken from the making of glass. Indeed, it is difficult to know exactly what the poet means when he compares his unexpected distress in some small trial to glass which

> a luenga edad nunca rendido,
> ni del agua y la llama sojuzgado,
> lo vence y lo consume un blando aliento.[6]

Apart from rare lapses, Rioja's use of imagery shows a distinct advance on earlier poets. It is more varied, less conventional, and on the whole more artistically employed than in most of the Golden Age poets, with the exception of the very greatest.

---

[1] Sonetos, pp. 259, 261.   [2] *Adiciones*, Soneto 6.
[3] *Ibid*.   [4] Soneto 32.   [5] Silva 5.   [6] Soneto 27.

Rioja's technique is perhaps most original as regards choice and use of colour. No longer does the decorative harmony of what Sr. Cossío calls the " cuadriga de luces " [1]—gold of hair, green of eyes, pink and white of complexion—occupy the most important part of the poet's colour-scheme. Of this Petrarchan-Renaissance tradition he merely perpetuates the most obvious commonplaces, in many cases without any pictorial effect or intention. He marks the end of a phase which had begun with Garcilaso de la Vega. As we have seen, Garcilaso seldom uses colour otherwise than to fix the object he is describing in the reader's mind. The process of intensification of colour which he barely begins continues under the stimulus of Renaissance idealization of beauty, until the simple names of colours cease to have any poetic value. Rioja represents its last stage, in which what had once been an attempt to heighten colour-effect by consciously felt metaphor becomes no more than a current statement of fact. Poets then found themselves faced with the choice between further exaggerations—the course followed by Góngora—or a deliberate restriction of the use of colour. This limitation Rioja practises, applying it only to objects of which it is a distinguishing characteristic : to him it is not a decorative adjunct but an integral part of reality.

Rather than use one colour as foil for another, he tends to reinforce single colours—red, white, green—to their highest pitch of intensity. The subtle interweaving of colours in Sestina 1 :

> Crespas, dulces, ardientes hebras de oro
> que ondas formáis por la caliente nieve, etc.

must be considered an isolated feat of virtuosity in the Herreran manner.

His lyrical technique, in contrast to that of Herrera, Góngora or even Medrano, is to present the gradations of a single colour. An example from the Silva " Al Clavel " will illustrate this feeling for the tone-values of colours :

> Cuando a la excelsa cumbre de Moncayo
> rompe luciente sol las canas nieves
> con más caliente rayo,
> tiendes igual las hojas abrasadas. [2]

[1] *Poesía española*, Madrid, 1936, p. 113. [2] Silva 8.

Here the suggestion of colour begins with a mere pink flush seen against a white background (" rompe luciente sol las canas nieves "), then becomes more definite (" más caliente rayo ") and finally resolves itself into the deep crimson (" las hojas abrasadas ") of the carnation.

He is very conscious of the effect of one colour upon another : white is either tinged by red, as in his picture of sun on snow,[1] or completely overwhelmed by it, as in the roses set on a white cloth in Silva 6. When he intends white to dominate, he tones down the red ; so the jasmine of " cándida pureza " has only the slightest touch of pink upon its brilliant whiteness :

> A tu excelsa blancura
> admiración se debe
> por imitar de su color la nieve,
> y a tus perfiles rojos
> por emular los cercos de sus ojos.[2]

Although Rioja may not use white as freely as Herrera and his followers, for whom it was indispensable as a foil to set off their reds and golds, he has a truer feeling of its value, both in a directly pictorial image, such as :

> bañado en cana espuma como cisne,[3]

and in his less plastic, more suggestive evocation of the jasmine. Like Herrera, however, he tends to combine white with light to produce a crystalline transparency, the " vagas luces de alba frente."[4]

Rioja's tendency to break with an earlier tradition is seen in his progressive reaction against gold. Traces of its use, in the Renaissance tradition, to idealize and formalize feminine beauty remain in the first Sestina, the typical first line of which has already been quoted. But on the whole Rioja prefers the natural shade of yellow to its counterpart, gold. For him it is an absence of colour rather than a positive shade : it is the colour of fading vegetation and of the leafless forest ;[5] it is placed against the green of budding leaf as a symbol of decay.

---

[1] Soneto, p. 263.   [2] Silva 10.   [3] Sestina 1.
[4] *Adiciones*, Soneto 1.   [5] Soneto 13.

> Ya la hoja que verde ornó la frente
> desta selva, Don Juan, en el verano,
> tiende amarilla por el suelo cano.[1]

Even the yellow rose is the pallid ghost of some more brilliant beauty that now remains :

> sólo eterna amarilla entre las flores.[2]

But it is to green and red, the colours of exuberant life, that Rioja chiefly devotes his descriptive power. His treatment of the two is different : green is sometimes placed in tiny points against a background which increases its intensity ; green leaf set against sere,[3] " frondosa vid " against bare poplar.[4] Combined with vivid red, green becomes a foil, as in that line which expresses so exactly the effect of a red rose half-hidden among its leaves :

> del verdor que descubre ardiente rosa.[5]

But it is as a single colour, the brilliant shade of new leaves, that Rioja most often uses green, and for him it takes on the quality of flame. The discolouration of leaves in winter is not so much a gradual process of decay as a sudden extinction of a blaze of light. It is like the going down of the sun :

> que fallece a par del día
> si un hermoso verdor un fuego inmenso,[6]

and the ash's red-tipped bud is a " purpúreo verdor."[7]

There is no doubt that Rioja takes a very great aesthetic delight in red. Not only does he introduce this colour with great frequency and develop his effects with extreme care, but he allows it to influence others. This conception of red as the intensest of colours—as a sort of primal or basic colour —makes him prefer to describe it alone ; it needs no intensification, and so he concentrates his efforts on rendering its natural vividness as best he can.

The red which pleases him above all is that of flowers, and his most striking images are used to convey the glowing brilliance of the rose and the carnation. Nothing could be more intense than the effect of this accumulation of bright

---

[1] Soneto 9.   [2] Silva 9.   [3] Soneto 9.   [4] Soneto 2.
[5] Soneto 8.   [6] Soneto 9.   [7] Soneto 16.

reds, the most consistently used being blood and flame.   To
Rioja this colour always seems to glow : he speaks of the
" ardiente rosa," of the " encendida rosa," and, more
vividly, of its " encendidas alas."   The *arrebolera* is
bathed in flame :

> ¿ . . . . en llama, diré, o púrpura bañada ?[1]

and this image is developed in the Silva " Al Clavel " :

> Amor, Amor sin duda dulcemente
> te bañó de su llama refulgente. . . . [2]

where there is to be found the finest of all the evocations of
red.   The images of flame and blood are combined with
the redness of lips to intensify to the last degree the crimson
colour of the carnation :

> Si al dulce labio llegas, que provoca
> a suave deleite al más helado
> luego que tu encendido seno toca
> a su color sangriento,
> vuelves ¡ ay, o dolor ! más abrasado.[3]

It would seem impossible to compress a higher degree of
colour-value into so few lines.

It may be noted that Rioja gains his finest effects without
recourse to words directly expressing colour.   Indeed, his
use of red is the best proof of his interest in what is essential,
rather than in what is formal or pictorial.

In his love-poems, generally speaking, Rioja is not a
poet of light : never does he compose those blinding Herreran
rhapsodies of light in which hair, eyes and brow burn in one
celestial flame.   Occasionally only, he achieves a spark in his
earlier imitative manner :

> o asombren sueltos la purpúrea nieve
> que esparce rayos de invisible fuego
> o recojan en aurea red sus luces.[4]

Yet he is interested in light in the sphere of Nature.   He has
a preoccupation with the varying phases of the sun ; though,
just as he never seems to wish to create an impression of
unclouded splendour in his love-poems, so he seems to lack

---

[1] Silva 7.   [2] Silva 8.   [3] *Ibid.*   [4] Sestina 1.

interest in the blazing sun.   His references to it are com-
pletely conventional, and full of Classical personifications.
His feeling for light expresses itself in subtle gradations of the
sun's intensity, and in the interplay of cloud and shadow ;
he realizes clearly that light has no true existence save in
relation to darkness ; and the impression becomes increas-
ingly more vivid as he introduces the element of darkness.
He envisages sunrise and sunset as conflicts between dark-
ness and light.   Sometimes darkness triumphs, and the sun
pursues an inexorable course towards the " escura noche
fría."   But more often light conquers, as in this description
of the ever-renewed light of day :

> Almo, divino Sol, que en refulgente
> carro, sacas y ascondes siempre el día,
> y otro y el mismo naces tras la fría
> sombra, que huye l'alba luz ardiente.[1]

At sunset he pictures the sun fleeing " con color medroso "
from the " espantable sombra " : and dawn is for him the
gradual infiltration of light :

> Lloro y crece mi llanto cuanto crece
> más la lumbre, y la sombra se desvía.[2]

Clouds lit up by the sun's rays attract him, and the vapour
which is

> encendida en mil colores [3]

as the sun glows through.

Unlike Herrera, Rioja does not give darkness and night
a definite, almost subjectively emotional, value.   He has
nothing of interest here save one perfect evocation :

> Tú las divinas sienes
> ciñes de la callada noche oscura,[4]

and a rather over-personified description.[5]

Light-effects other than sun and stars are rarer, and, on
the whole, less effective.   Exception must be made, however,
for what is probably the finest light-effect in Rioja, if, in fact,

---

[1] Soneto 20. [2] Soneto 12. [3] Soneto, p. 259.
[4] Silva 7. [5] Soneto 6.

the Silva in which it occurs was written by him. The whole poem is an elaborate description of a forest fire, serving as an extended image of the flame of love felt by the poet. Most of the impressions are of the shape of the flames as they leap up and lick the trees, but there is one unforgettable picture, which employs the familiar technique of chiaroscuro. It is a description of the devouring flame :

> esplende y arde en el silencio obscuro,
> émula de los astros :
> arde y esplende al rutilante y puro
> cándido aparecer de la mañana,
> y sobra y vence al sol siempre segura.
> Abrasadora del verdor del pino,
> levanta entre sus ramas
> globos de fuego y máquinas de llamas ;
> y en el sólido tronco y más secreto
> del laurel y el abeto,
> estalla y gime y luce,
> nunca del Euro o Noto escurecida,
> ni de la inmensa lluvia destruída. [1]

Marred though it is by such conventional epithets as " rutilante," " cándido " and the proper names " Euro " and " Noto," and by occasional redundancies, one cannot deny the vigour and effect of the repetition " esplende y arde," " arde y esplende," of the triple verb-forms " estalla y gime y luce," or miss the striking contrast between the " silencio obscuro " and the flaming, crackling fire and the well-managed change from light and darkness to the colour effects of the " verdor del pino" and the magnificent, if slightly Gongoristic, "globos de fuego y máquinas de llamas."

(iii) PEDRO ESPINOSA [2]

It is more accurate to discuss the " themes " of Espinosa's verse than its " sentiments " or " sources of inspiration," for these latter terms imply emotional qualities which he does not always reveal. His perception of reality is not passionate,

[1] Silva, p. 252.
[2] For details of Espinosa's life the student is indebted to the researches of Rodríguez Marín and may be referred to that scholar's *Pedro Espinosa*, Madrid, 1907. All footnote references to Espinosa's works are from *Obras*, ed. Rodríguez Marín, Madrid, 1909.

but contemplative and detached, and he apprehends purely sensuous qualities without relation to their immediate dramatic or emotional value : his " Fábula de Genil " has no human interest ; his " Bautismo de Jesús," little religious feeling. In all his poetry formal aesthetic elements predominate and emotion is transferred to the artistic plane.

Only with this in mind can we, in examining the themes of Espinosa's verse, legitimately enquire into their relation to the ideological background of the age. Since the process of exteriorization has not gone as far in him as in Góngora, however, we may occasionally find a passage which reveals real emotion hidden beneath the elaborate superstructure of artistry. From time to time, such alien elements disturb the smoothly decorative harmony of his verses on both Nature and religion.

In his amorous verse, Espinosa is very much the child of his age. Its atmosphere is that of Petrarchan convention, from which emotion has disappeared, leaving nothing but artificiality. Its characteristic technique is the use of a personified Nature, highly ornate and unreal, to act as a foil to the idealized mistress. The line of love-poetry is continuous from Garcilaso, through Herrera, to Espinosa, but much ground had been covered since those first intimate elegiac verses had been written to the divine Elisa, and Espinosa has more in common with the curious crystallized emotion of Herrera than with the ingenuous sincerity of Garcilaso. Yet he has not Herrera's fervent Neoplatonism, nor those subtle analyses interpreting the most elusive phases of love with a curious dream-like intensity. In his triviality of matter and manner his affinities are with the Italian sonneteers of the *cinquecento :* Bembo, Tasso, Molza, Domenichi and Tansillo.

In his sonnets and madrigals, the elaborate stylization produces a rigid, almost mathematical effect, and inspiration is reduced to a mere play of fancy. In the longer compositions the demands of the poetic medium are less exacting and there is more scope for personal feeling. The influences in " A Crisalda " and the " Boscarecha "[1] are less Italian than

[1] Pp. 7-14.

Spanish. With Garcilaso's eclogues, odes and *canciones* these poems have in common the general theme, the long stanza form and the pastoral setting : individual passages, too, show similarities. Yet equally evident are the differences between Garcilaso and Espinosa as poets of emotion. When he attempts to express his feelings Espinosa becomes clumsy or violent, or approaches the prosaic, or at best achieves a certain passionate sensuality—all attitudes foreign to the ideal, spiritualized love of Garcilaso.

Nature, in Espinosa's verse, is at once the most important and all-pervading element and the most negligible and conventional ; the most artificially distorted theme, and the most sincerely felt reality. It is the raw material of his best work, and the trimming of some of his worst.

Throughout, he accepts the conventional pseudo-pastoral language of the period and uses Nature as a decorative background both to love and to religion. He seems to have attempted to follow Garcilaso's method, but, as we have already seen, he is quite incapable of achieving Garcilaso's characteristic fusion of Nature with personal emotion. Only when he ceases to simulate feeling does he have moments of genuine vision and achieve effects of any subtlety. What could be at once more accurate and more imaginative than his description of the " olivares pálidos " ?[1] And, enlightening contrast between his attitude to Nature as an unfelt background and as a vital presence, we have the insipidity of

> la blanca luna, ornato de los bosques,[2]

side by side with the poetic sublimation of observed Nature to be seen in such a passage as :

> Mientras que las estrellas
> parezcan desde el suelo
> tembladoras centellas ;
> mientras, parados del redondo cielo
> los dos quiciales de oro,
> lleven los navegantes
> por el camino donde no hay camino.[3]

---

[1] P. 11. Al Licenciado Antonio Moreno.
[2] *Ibid.*   [3] *Op. cit.*, p. 14.

Although Espinosa, like Medrano, uses Nature as a store-house of symbols and lessons, the majority of his religious poems ignore it completely. But splendid exceptions are two " Soledades " and the first two of his " Psalmos," in which the Nature-content is far more than the usual decorative border round the theme. Here a pervasive atmosphere of the country, a scent of blossom, show that, in spite of so much artificiality, Nature could be for him a living reality. With Nature, indeed, are connected all the memorable moments of his work, for he reaches his highest point of artistry when building imaginatively upon tree, flower, or river.

With ecstatic intensity he evokes the colours and scents of the Andalusian hillsides : their orchards and orange-blossom, roses and vines.[1]   No less striking is the almost scientific accuracy with which he catalogues wild flowers.[2] And this devotion to the concrete reality of a Nature he has known characterizes even those poems which are most objective and artistically elaborate. His description of the vegetation of the Genil does not include verbena and acanthus, but the humble reeds and cresses, the vines, elms and ivy of the real river as it flows, " clara como el ámbar."[3]

Paradoxically enough, the most perfect expression of his feeling for Nature is to be found in those very poems which seem most remote, artificial and stylized. It is the fantastic world of the " Fábula de Genil " which corresponds most closely to his original experience. Here Nature is being viewed against a background of kaleidoscopically changing decorative forms, and exaggerated or distorted into manifestations yet more luxuriant and complicated, and adorned with yet more brilliant colours. Though the starting-point is again a familiar scene, metaphors and images from diverse aspects of life are introduced to create an effect of rich strangeness.

The progression of Espinosa's technique may be traced

[1] P. 124.   Soledad del Gran Duque.
[2] P. 75.   Soledad de Pedro de Jesús.
[3] P. 26.   Fábula de Genil.

from a mere re-arrangement of pre-existing and recognizable natural forms to a stage where the starting point is a vision of the poet's own fancy. For example, in the " Bautismo de Jesús ", he is describing the Jordan in terms of rivers he knew well, and sufficient particularized detail remains to make the picture perfectly clear. But, though each of the elements of the description is drawn from Nature, each is treated with the rhythmical regularity of a pattern. The natural forms of lush vegetation become rigidly ornamental :

> bellos festones, arcos ambiciosos

and :

> ensortijados lazos y follajes.[1]

Natural objects are described in metaphors derived from other spheres : dawn is a team of horses, or a carpet studded with diamonds ; the sea, blue and silver brocade.[2] These comparisons add an exotic background to Nature, so that the poet's invocation of associations come to be more important than the objects themselves. The early poems " Al Bautismo de Jesús " and the " Navegación de San Raimundo " show this tendency to a marked degree, but the supreme example of this artistic re-creation is the " Fábula de Genil,"[3] which is far more than the re-telling of one of the pseudo-mythological fables so popular among Golden Age lyric poets. Espinosa does not openly abandon the narrative element so highly prized by Golden Age poets and theorists, but his artistic instinct leads him towards a conception of pure poetry. The value of the poem lies in the series of tableaux evoking aspects of Nature, some real or at least based on reality, others pure poetic creations. The narrative links may, and should, be ignored in any consideration of the artistic value of the " Fábula." The real " subject " of the poem is a synthesis of the host of vivid impressions of colour, light, perfume and sound which the poet has received from Nature ; around,

[1] P. 18. Al Bautismo de Jesús.

[2] P. 22. A la Navegación de San Raimundo.

[3] Since this book went to press, the author has had the opportunity of seeing an article on the " Fábula de Genil," by J. M. de Cossío (*Siglo XVII*, Madrid, 1939, pp. 13-33), in which the critic insists on precisely this quality of imaginative invention.

behind and through the nominal theme is seen the brightness of a supernatural universe.

That Espinosa wrote much on religious themes should cause no surprise. It was an age in which even the most worldly poets composed devotional verses and Espinosa was a cleric whose life and doctrine reveal a rare consistency. But the relation of his faith to his poetic experience is difficult to assess.

The bulk of his religious verse is distinguished chiefly by technical virtuosity. Until he became a hermit, it is, as it were, religious by accident. The early poem " Al Bautismo de Jesús,"[1] for example, belongs essentially to the class of the " Fábula de Genil " : the protagonist is not Jesus, but the paganly pastoral Jordan flowing through a poetic Arcadia. Even at the sacred moment when Christ stands in the water, Espinosa is less interested in His baptism than in plastic values ; and the final impression is not of the Holy Spirit, but of birds singing praises and of the " mudos peces " raising aloft their silvery scales.

No devotional fervour is to be found either here or in similar Baroque poems which Espinosa wrote after his conversion, such as the sonnets to the Virgin belonging to the period 1605-1615. His didactic and narrative poems written for specific purposes are overlaid with artistry : St. Francis becomes the Phoenix ; St. Ignatius of Loyola is symbolized by fire and gold ; and the poem to St. Peter significantly entitled " A las lágrimas de San Pedro "[2] is a symphony in lachrymosity. Most of these poems show the same blend of a rhetorical Baroque with colourless conceptism of the Ledesma type. Such an approach must necessarily exclude direct emotion.

To this Espinosa is brought nearest through the medium of Nature. His two long poems termed " Soledades " are paeans of praise to Nature's God. Though he was strongly influenced by the theological conception of a universe stored

---

[1] Pp. 17-19. The same may be said of the early sonnet " A la Asunción de la Virgen María " (p. 20) and the " Navegación de San Raimundo " (pp. 22-5).
[2] P. 70.

with symbols interpreting God's love to man, his approach is essentially individualistic. For him the vast harmonies of the nineteenth Psalm must be tuned to the compass of a pastoral flute[1] ; and the emphasis is shifted from the " tabernacle of the sun " to the " venas de los lirios."

Occasionally, however, we sense that personal feeling of devotion to God which is the soil most propitious to the mystical spirit[2]—in the short " Plegaria," for example, in the sonnet on the Ascension, in the " Soledad de Pedro de Jesús " and in parts of the " Psalmos." The second " Psalmo " shows more than incipient mysticism : Nature takes her rightful place in the background ; and in the foreground is love. The poet's aim is the absorption of Union :

> Anégame y escóndeme en tus llamas ;
> hazme, Señor, contigo un mismo espíritu,[3]

and there are reminiscences of St. Augustine and of the " Cántico Espiritual " of San Juan de la Cruz. But in spite of these moments Espinosa is not a mystical poet : there is no steady progress along the Mystic Way—only a poignant longing for the vision splendid once glimpsed but never recaptured.

Espinosa, indeed, shares with Lope de Vega something of that uncertainty that quivers between bitter self-questionings and fervent love. Had he pondered more deeply and more constantly on this problem he might have become a great religious poet. As it is, his sensitive perception of the dark background of sin, suffering and death throws into brilliant relief his wistful evocations of perfect Love and unclouded Glory.

In artistry, Espinosa is very markedly a poet of his age. Manner is more to him than matter ; emotions and ideas he tends to transpose into symbols or images : the essential aspect of his verse is thus aesthetic. He exemplifies exactly the qualities of display, sensuous exuberance, decoration, formalism, exaggeration of means without reference to end,

---

[1] Pp. 60–1.

[2] On this aspect of Espinosa's verse, see E. Allison Peers : " Mysticism in the religious verse of the Golden Age—III," in *B.S.S.*, 1944, XXI, 139–45.

[3] P. 63.

which are found in those aspects of life and art known collectively as the Baroque. The sections of this study which follow discuss in turn his use of decorative motifs, his love of the rich and exotic, the large part played in his work by colour, and such characteristic devices as repetition, accumulation and parallelism. In a fuller treatment it would be necessary to analyse his language, to survey his imagery and to examine his metrical resources.

Not least clearly does Espinosa reflect the insistence of the Baroque on decorative values. His poetry resembles a highly ornate structure, built of the richest materials imagination can conceive, carved and chased, burnished and refined into fantastic convolutions. Coherent design is lost beneath the weight of fretted and inlaid richness ; decorative motifs are repeated so that no inch of space is free of its garlands, hanging fruits, naked cupids or cherubim ; the capricious lines of the design are for ever branching off and forming new shapes ; a wayward vitality pervades every element so that it cannot find repose, but must contort itself into twisting curves, or spin itself out into endless chains of arabesque. Everywhere dazzling richness, intricacy of detail, complication of line : the complete triumph of means over end.

Whether Espinosa writes of love or religion or Nature he can never resist the impulse to convert emotion into decorative patterns, and work out every possibility of ornamental arrangement, irrespective of the claims of the poem as a whole. The sober impressiveness of emotion transposed to an artistic medium is unknown to him : the medium becomes all-important. His art is accumulative and repetitive, based on the appeal of certain decorative motifs arranged in a thousand different patterns which simulate variety but remain fundamentally the same.

The " lazos y follajes," which are as typical of his art as of a Baroque altar, appear in early and late poems, religious and secular. He loads all indiscriminately with festoons and garlands—lover and martyr, pagan temple and Christian shrine.[1]

[1] P. 13, Boscarecha ; p. 68, A San Acacio ; p. 12, Al Licenciado Antonio Moreno ; p. 78, Soledad de Pedro de Jesús.

This florid materialism, as we have already hinted, is very evident in the religious poems. His Virgin, for example, resembles a typical Baroque image : surrounded by seraphs whose snowy temples are wreathed in gold and " armados de jazmines," and who bear flowery helmets and wield spears of laurel, she accepts the gifts of the faithful,[1] the rich Chinese damask, and Moorish carpets,[2] while clouds of " sacro incienso " float to Heaven.[3]

As the head of each saint has its " cerco de luz "[4] and each martyr his wreath of laurel, so Espinosa develops to the limits of their decorative possibilities the sacred insignia of Christ : the nails, wounds and, above all, his favourite symbol, the crown. It may be that " amor no se paga sólo en rosas,"[5] but the poet's homage to Christ is expressed by preference in flowery garlands.

> Deste sidonio acanto
> y estas del prado estrellas
> coronaré las aras de mi amado.[6]

But it is in his treatment of Nature that Espinosa indulges most freely the rich pattern-making propensities of the Baroque. From the highly conventionalized " cintas de azándar y verbena " and garlands of lilies of the earliest amatory sonnets to the wayward exuberance of vegetation of the two " Soledades," there is a constant interweaving of rich colours into complicated patterns. Nature is miraculously formalized into " coronas y festones," " arcos," " hilos," " sartas," and " arabescos " ; and, especially in certain poems,[7] flowers and plants are crystallized into jewel-like brilliancy and filigree intricacy by means of terms significantly borrowed from the embroiderer, the painter, the gilder, the silversmith and the Baroque architect.[8]

---

[1] P. 76. Soledad de Pedro de Jesús.
[2] P. 60. A Nuestra Señora de Archidona.
[3] P. 45. A Nuestra Señora de Monteagudo.
[4] P. 48. Al Beato Ignacio Loyola.
[5] P. 81. Soledad de Pedro de Jesús.
[6] *Op. cit.*, p. 80.   [7] See p. 44.
[8] P. 61 : Psalmos, I ; Pp. 124, 128 : Soledad del Gran Duque ; Pp. 73-4 : Soledad de Pedro de Jesús.

Espinosa has exquisite feeling for dynamic curves, whether to express the limpid beauty of a pure line such as this :

> Arrojan los delfines
> por las narices blanca espuma en arco
> sobre el profundo charco.[1]

or the tortuous windings of the " mil pasos entre calles de azahares " described in the " Soledades." Here the imagery reflects the strange complication of line :

> Con pie curioso, por los verdes valles,
> construyendo períodos de parras,
> el guarnecido arroyo de entretalles
> verás, en trenzas de cristal, bizarras
> varas trepando inexplicables calles
> volcar su arena lo que el indio en barras,
> y seguirás la margen de sus yerros,
> ciñendo en breve anillo muchos berros.[2]

and the effect is of an intricacy at once delicate and yet grandiose in its sweep.

In these examples Espinosa has been forcing definite themes and motifs, either from Nature or from religion, into Baroque channels. He has nearly succeeded in stripping them of all but decorative elements, but even the supreme art of a Góngora could not entirely remove the emotive associations from Nature or reduce religion to a play of symbols. More purely Baroque, then, because entirely free from human emotional elements, are the pure creations of Espinosa's fancy in the realm of form and colour. An example of these is the fabulous world of sea-gods, nereids and tritons evoked in the " Fábula de Genil." The variety of figures, their strange aspect, seen through the glimmering of the green ocean-depths, some bright with jewels, some with the vague glint of the gold that covers their shoulders, and others, wraith-like :

> con ropas blancas de cuajada espuma :[3]

all this is truly Baroque in its juxtaposition of textural

---

[1] P. 23. A la Navegación de San Raimundo.
[2] P. 75. Soledad de Pedro de Jesús.
[3] P. 30. Fábula de Genil.

effects. Even more so is the description of the palace of
Betis. Here is the essence of the typical style : richness of
materials—silver, gold, diamond, coral, pearl, crystal ;
formlessness of structure, with details standing out as though
lit up by flashes ; the massive gold hinges and the columns
which, like many an architectural counterpart, are " más
hermosas que valientes." [1]   Picked out in high lights are the
decorative motifs : the " follajes de carámbano " hanging
from the ceiling and culminating in " racimos de aljófares
helados " [2] which are monochrome versions of the festoons
and vine-wreaths decorating pilasters of church or sacristy.
Nor could there be lacking the most typical decorative
emblem of the age, the cornucopia, with its curving lines and
overflowing wealth of flowers :

> Brotando olor los cristalinos cuernos,
> de tiernas flores y de tallos tiernos. [3]

The pompous ostentation of the Baroque found one of its
most characteristic expressions in funereal ritual. It de-
lighted in the contrast of ceremonial magnificence with the
grim lesson of " memento mori," and of splendid monuments
with mortal decay. Of this trait the description of the
funereal honours of the Duke of Medina-Sidonia is a signifi-
cant expression ; the solemn dignity of the files of black-
robed Orders set against the sombre richness of the lords and
dignitaries ; the grandiloquent roll of the dead Duke's
titles. Decoration, ornament all the time : even the grave
has its garlands, though they be of ashes :

> no de verde lauro
> coronado veréis mi monumento ;
> mas de cenizas débiles : [4]

Innumerable funereal sonnets of the Golden Age celebrate
the magnificent tombs erected to the dead. The Baroque
poets never tired of lauding the splendour and rich ornament,
the symbolic urns and columns of these monuments ;
all this is glimpsed in Espinosa's unparticularized reference to

---

[1] P. 28.   [2] P. 29.   [3] P. 30.
[4] P. 8.   A Crisalda.

the tomb of the Duke, built " con arte nueva," whose " arti-
ficiosa traza " and " valiente arquitectura " have brought
fame to its designer. The ducal standard floats above,
" gravemente," touching the gilded roof, and the tomb shines
through the darkness with the brilliant glow of the torches,
that favourite decorative symbol, so that the poet sees it as a
pattern of light.[1]

So, while one Duke is welcomed at birth with baskets of
lilies and garlands[2] surrounding his cradle, another is laden
with funereal pomp at his death. The occasion changes, but
the ornamental emphasis remains—one of the most constant
characteristics of Espinosa's verse.

The preceding section will have given some hint of the
stress which Espinosa lays upon colour. He did not imme-
diately achieve the daring flexibility in its use that charac-
terizes his best poems, but the progress of his evolution in the
art is constant and easy to trace.

At first he seldom escapes from the colour-effects of con-
temporary Neoplatonic love-poetry. Conventional back-
grounds —" claveles," " aljófar," " purpúreas rosas," " per-
las," " cristal," " tapetes de esmeralda "—set off the beauty
of the mistress whose lips are " grana " and cheeks " púr-
pura y jazmines." These verses show few, if any, hints of his
later colour-technique. The transition stage appears in the
" boscarecha " addressed to Moreno. Here, he feels, the
stock description of Dawn as roses and pearls lacks vitality,
so he begins to reach after something more dynamic and
violent. First he produces the rather crude and inartistic :

> cuando, en los palacios del Oriente,
> sobre alcatifas blancas
> encarnados cojines
> puso el pardo crepúsculo al Aurora.[3]

But soon afterwards he achieves a superb effect—dramatic,

---

[1] P. 88. Relación de la forma que se tuvo en el entierro de Don Alonso
Pérez de Guzmán . . .

[2] Pp. 114–115. En su nacimiento, que fué Pascua de Reyes.

[3] P. 13.

majestic and yet subtle.   He pictures dawn as a team of
horses snorting light from their nostrils :[1]

> cuando los caballos
> que están apacentados de rocío
> bordaron de matices,
> con la lumbre que arrojan sus narices,
> el monte verde, el cristalino río. . . .[2]

Here is a new and vivid world, one in which is set the best
of Espinosa's verse.

The next step forward in the poet's technique is seen
in the sonnet " A la Asunción de la Virgen María,"[3] where
Espinosa realizes at last the magnificent richness of colour
used for its own sake. He describes the whiteness of " blancas
hachas " and " blancos cirios " against a background of
" turquesadas nubes y celajes " ; and evokes impressions of
heraldic pomp with his " amaranto y plateados lirios."[4]
The sensuous impressions in this poem are extraordinarily
delicate and complex, but colour plays an important, if not
a preponderating, *rôle*.

But none of these poems is a preparation for the burst
of splendour in the " Navegación de San Raimundo."[5]
Here the poet's technique has suddenly become mature
and self-conscious, and he boldly essays the possibilities of
pure and vivid colour. His real subject is the Mediterranean.
The colour-values are intense, almost violent.   Dawn is
described in terms of white horses drawing a silver chariot :
the sky is a rich carpet " sembrada de diamantes " and
turned to shades of " génuli, carmín y azul ceniza "[6] with
the growing light.   All this is unnatural, and suggests the
brilliantly crude colours of certain crystals rather than the
kaleidoscope of merging shades that make up the dawn.
But this raw intensity was exactly the effect desired by

---

[1] The idea, of course, is not original. With a little less pictorial effect and
a shade more personification this would be a mere Classical allusion. It is
the insistence on plastic values which makes it interesting.

[2] P. 13.

[3] For a fuller treatment of this sonnet, see the author's " New
Interpretations of Spanish poetry—III," in *B.S.S.*, 1942, XIX, 101–3.

[4] P. 20.   [5] Pp. 22–5.   [6] P. 22.

Espinosa, and he attains results of daring beauty. The
symphony of the sea is represented in brilliant tones of green
and blue ; and against this is placed the pageant of the
sea-folk who inhabit the fantastic submarine caverns : its
red and greens (" entre esmeraldas y sanguinos corales ") ;
the blues and whites of dolphins, green nereids :

> destilando de las verdes crines
> aljófar. . . . ;

and the sirens :

> sobre pintadas conchas de ballenas.[1]

Typical, too, among the poems of the first group, in its
use of colour, is the " Fábula de Genil." Here the effects
are more varied and less intense. From the variegated
hues of the flowers on the river's banks, Espinosa passes to
its dim tree-shadowed course, suggesting rather than
painting. Brilliant in the extreme, on the other hand, is
the picture of the submarine palace of the personified
Guadalquivir. First, the effect is of gleaming metallic
richness : the palace is of " plata lisa " ; its golden-hinged
doors of " claros diamantes " are

> ricas de clavazones de corales
> y de pequeños nácares cubiertas.[2]

Then, into the transparent brilliance of the " gran techo
cristalino," of the translucent jewelled walls and of the
clear springs gushing from the ground, Espinosa introduces
the shadows of a submarine twilight. This atmosphere of
dim green, bare of specified colours, gives way to a picture
of defiantly sensuous brilliance :

> Vido entrando Genil un virgen coro
> de bellas ninfas de desnudos pechos,
> sobre cristal cerniendo granos de oro
> con verdes cribos de esmeraldas hechos ;
> vido, ricos de lustre y de tesoro,
> follajes de carámbano en los techos,
> que estaban por las puntas adornados
> de racimos de aljófares helados.[3]

[1] P. 23.   [2] P. 28.   [3] P. 29.

Then follows a tableau of almost impressionistic technique : the procession of sea-gods, a succession of bright points of colour, actual or implied.

In this, the last poem of his first period, Espinosa's colour-technique may be said to have reached its full development. Realizing at length the possibilities of colour, he has achieved a boldly individual technique. Thereafter his preoccupation with colour as an isolated element ceases, and he concentrates on combining the various sense impressions in order to produce a complete evocation of the material universe. Never again does he employ colour as lavishly as here ; indeed, the verses written during the decade 1605-1615 show what seems an ascetic revulsion from it. Gold, silver and fire—all used with a symbolic function— are typical of this period, and they are never used either vividly or extensively. Contrast the sonnet on the Assumption of the Blessed Virgin, replete with decorative colour, and that on the Ascension of Christ, with its stress on the emotional and intellectual, where no concession is made to the eye save in the opening line, in which Christ is described as ascending in a " nube de oro."[1]

In such of these poems as have colour-values, Espinosa seems to be evolving a new technique. Instead of juxta-posing vivid hues, as before 1605, he now works in groups of shades, each group possessing a unity of tone. The first method is that of the stained-glass window, in which brilliant colours are separated by a hard line of division ; the second, that of an oil-painting in chiaroscuro, in which the areas of colour and high light are made more impressive by the background of darkness from which they emerge.

This homogeneity of colour-grouping is seen even in a poem with as little colour, quantitatively speaking, as the *canción*, " A Nuestra Señora de Archidona."[2] Here the scheme is a transposition into a celestial key of the typical colours of the Herreran love-sonnet : white, gold and red. The red, softened to pink, serves to bring out the idealistic beauty and heraldic pomp of the white and gold. So in the

[1] P. 39. [2] Pp. 58–60.

opening stanzas the Virgin is compared first to a " blanca paloma " and then to the " rosada Aurora." These comparisons are perfectly conventional ; their only significance is their colour-value. Later on in the poem the two colours are again combined to describe the souls in bliss, and finally, the harmonizing gold is introduced in the mention of " rubias aristas."

This is an example in which the technique is not fully worked out : probably Espinosa himself was unconscious of his effects. A more finished instance of the same type is found in the " Soledad de Pedro de Jesús."[1] The seraphim who wait upon Our Lady—" colmadas de oro las nevadas sienes "—are " armados de jazmines " and wear " yelmos de rosa " like the souls in bliss. Green, too, the fourth constituent of the Herreran " cuadriga de luces,"[2] is introduced here, both for realistic effects and also decoratively.

This combination of colours owes much of its effect to its position in the poem. It forms a delicate yet glowing interlude between colour-schemes of very different types. It recalls the delicate precision of a primitive Italian painting, and forms a subtle contrast in textural effects between white of snow and jasmine, red of rose, green of bay and metallic gold, suggestive of rich brocade. To be paralleled with this effect, but with the emphasis now on the richness of material and artifice, is the passage in the *canción* " A San Acacio,"[3] in which is evoked this splendid vision of blue and red, white and gold :

> Mirad de azules y encarnados jaspes
> arcos soberbios de gentil tesoro.
> . . . .
> Ved, sobre bordaduras de giraspes,
> ir blanqueando entre celajes de oro
> los cortesanos de la Corte Santa.

Here the vigour of the one pair of colours balances the ethereality of the other.

The general impression that certain colours—such as

pink, white, gold, and, to a lesser degree, green—are stylized combinations expressing spirituality is not true without exception, and some colours seem to have several functions. Green is found everywhere ; blue, intense and opaque in the early poems, now clear and translucent, can be used idealistically, as when the Virgin's eyes are compared to sapphires.[1] In startling contrast to this type of colour-effect is the range of harmonies used to describe natural scenes : a flower symphony in white, green and red[2] continues with a change of key from white to yellow. But by far the most interesting development during this period is the treatment of single colours—notably green. The " Soledad de Pedro de Jesús " contains whole stretches of poetry which play on green in its various shades and textures. Only the faintest note of silver or crystal is introduced to intensify these subtle harmonies ; Espinosa groups together the smooth green turf, a rippling fountain, silvery leaves of creepers, and laurel trees shading the traveller from the sun. Fern and moss grow in a dim grot whose

> pavimento es jaspe, el tapiz hiedra.[3]

The whole effect is one of cool, dim shade, with suggestions of lush vegetation. It is an amazingly delicate composite sense-impression in which colour is sublimated and refined.

Another colour singled out for this intense treatment is red, or rather the red and gold of a rose.[4] The gold is no longer the foil of pure white, but the rich bright yellow of the rose's heart. Here every image reinforces the vivid intensity of the crimson flower, with its golden centre, its yellow pollen, and the " oro líquido " of its nectar :

> Reina coronada de oro,
> te guardan picas de bronce.
>
> Del botón desabrochada,
> desfluecas en arreboles.

[1] P. 79.

[2] P. 81. ("Tú, suma de claveles . . . ")

[3] P. 74.

[4] P. 102, A la Rosa. Cf. Rioja, " A la Rosa," for the same image : *Poesías*, ed. Barrera, Madrid, 1867, pp. 248–9.

> Copa en que bebe el olfato
> el sacro néctar de Jove,
> donde en púrpura no estás,
> estás en ámbares nobles. [1]

By this insistence on particular aspects the familiar rose takes on a sumptuous exotic quality.

Reviewing the later period as a whole, we shall perhaps decide that, in a man of such gifts, the use made of colour is over-restrained ; but the closer our examination of it, the stronger is the relief into which the artistic value of the colour is thrown. Working with a stylized palette of white and pink and rich gold, and also with a natural set of bright reds, blues, greens and whites, Espinosa achieves wonderfully unified combinations ; but perhaps he will be remembered chiefly for the delicate gradations of dim green that make parts of the " Soledad de Pedro de Jesús " a true poetic evocation of the woodland.

Being essentially decorative, Espinosa's verse is naturally repetitive, symmetrical and patterned. His technique is a necessary consequence of his poetic approach : an art that begins by substituting the plastic symbol for the pure idea ends by ordering these symbols without reference to any logic outside itself.

Repetition is as much an essential of his art as it was of the Arab craftsman who made a few simple elements into a hundred patterns. Running through his work are constant echoes of theme, idea, image and phrase. The two " Soledades " are similar in theme and have identical stanzas. This is also true of the " Canción a Crisalda " and the " Boscarecha." The series of poems on St. Ignatius describe the same incidents, employ the same imagery and even introduce the same puns—those on " compañía " and " Ignatius—ignis." Ideas and phrases found in early poems can be rediscovered, in a more highly developed form, in later ones. A striking phrase from the " Boscarecha " (p. 14) :

> . . . . por el camino donde no hay camino,

[1] Pp. 102-3.

5

resounds in " A San Acacio " (p. 68) and finally dies away
in a half-line of the " Soledad de Pedro de Jesús " (p. 72).
An epithet that described the Virgin (p. 79)—

> Fuente de la luz de las estrellas—

is taken up much later, with the difference of a word (p. 109),
to eulogize the Duke of Medina-Sidonia. An unusual
image from the early " Al Bautismo de Jesús " (p. 18) :

> No donde el agua frágil bullidora
> del mal acogimiento de las piedras
> murmuraba con labios espumosos . . . .

is recalled (p. 126) in the " Soledad " written after 1615 :

> De las piedras el mal acogimiento
> no murmure con labios espumantes. . . .

Within individual poems, repetition is often used for
effect. Sometimes this is the natural reiteration of intense
emotion ; more usually it is purely stylistic—to produce a
definite plastic impression, to indulge a puerile word-play,
or to combine sound and sense in onomatopoeic harmony.

If repetition is a pervading influence in Espinosa, other
devices are used more consciously and are therefore more
easily isolated. The decorative elements which so often
take the place of emotions and ideas lend themselves to
artificial and complicated arrangements. Once love poetry
has turned from essentials to the interplay of " bellos ojos,"
" claro sol," " oloroso aliento," " frescas rosas," the whole
emphasis falls on the cunning and unexpected combinations
that can be made of these stereotyped elements. So, too,
religious verse that has lost its vital inspiration comes to
depend on the successful interweaving of symbols fixed by
convention.

The result is the evolution of the most elaborate and
complicated artifice in construction. Most characteristic of
Espinosa's earlier poetry, but appearing sporadically later,
is the parallelistic technique : this mannerism of developing
two or more ideas with corresponding nouns, adjectives and
verbs appears in the early work of Lope de Vega, and is also
characteristic of the style of Calderón, especially coupled

with the device of accumulation. In its purest form—that is, involving whole poems—Espinosa uses it in amatory verse written before 1605 and in one or two religious poems at the beginning of the 1605-15 group. Throughout this later period it appears in the modified form of more limited verbal juxtapositions and antitheses, and is completely absent from verse written after 1615. There seems little doubt that this is a mannerism especially suited to his earliest poetic style, but that increasing complication and irregularity of syntax made him drop it later.

The most extreme examples of this formalized construction are the early love sonnets and one or two sonnets to Our Lady on the same model. They are built up on an almost mathematical formula, and two, or sometimes even three, themes are kept in balanced motion like the balls in a dexterous conjuring trick. Though this type of construction is found only in a few sonnets, the principle influences many other poems. Nor is parallelism of idea a necessary condition of formal symmetry : in fact, the absence of comparison or contrast of idea often brings out the decorative aspect of this device the more clearly.

With the device of symmetry may be combined that accumulation of substantives so characteristic of Espinosa, especially after 1605. He particularly favours the attachment of a string of nouns to a governing verb, generally *dar*. The nouns are indiscriminately abstract and concrete, and their combination with *dar* sometimes produces a sort of word-play :

> . . . . dando a los hombres Dios ejemplo,
> lumbre a su Iglesia, a Francia la victoria,
> nuevo mundo a su fe, a su nombre templo,
> fin a las armas y a su intento gloria.[1]

These accumulations are usually found in poems which have little plastic appeal, in contrast to the parallelistic arrangements, which were always found in combination with richness of imagery and colour effects. In fact, the enumeration or catalogue often has an inartistic formlessness which separates it clearly from the symmetrical devices.

[1] P. 46. Al Beato Ignacio de Loyola.

These two technical tricks which dominate Espinosa's poetic style are among the chief causes of the impression of artificiality produced by his verse. They are both studied self-conscious mannerisms, the poet's effort to bring all his work into line with a decorative conception. Each represents a different phase of this effort ; the parallelisms belong to the rigidly ordered ornamental world of love-poetry, dominated by the sonnet-form, which is revealed in the poems written before 1605. The middle period (1605-15) is transitional, and both types of technique are found, while the latest verses are a full expression of that more capricious artificiality towards which the poet has been long tending. Here the smoothly flowing lines demanded by the exclusive use of a symmetrical technique are out of place ; the lines are broken, distorted, varied, not to be bound by one type of structure ; and the accumulative device takes its place among the other exaggerated mannerisms that make up the tangled pattern of this last period.

From the aspects of Espinosa's verse studied in the preceding sections it is possible to draw certain conclusions. A gradation can be noted in his response to the three lyric themes : Love, Religion, Nature. His love-poems show clearly that he neither felt emotion nor tried to produce it in the reader ; his religious verse, though for the most part coldly elaborate, contains an occasional expression of direct emotion,[1] while his reactions to the natural world reveal a most interesting paradox. Though Espinosa nowhere expresses a direct love of Nature, certain passages of objective description[2] possess a genuine emotion engendered by the poetic form itself. The undeniable excitement felt in his best Nature passages is, like that of Góngora's *Soledades*, induced by the translation of carefully selected details of external phenomena into an artistic medium, and constitutes the emergence of an emotion of aesthetic, as opposed to human, origin.

---

[1] *E.g.* : " No quiero más que soledad y Cristo." (P. 73. Soledad de Pedro de Jesús).

[2] *E.g.*, p. 27. Fábula de Genil. " Allí del olmo . . . trinando."

Spanish poetry had long taken human emotion for its starting-point, and Garcilaso, Herrera, Luis de León, San Juan de la Cruz and Lope de Vega reveal in varying degrees a preoccupation with human values as the basis of their poetry. Espinosa shows a different approach, and leads up to a new type of lyricism reaching its fullest development in Góngora : he is a poet of transition, but it is important to realize that the transition was not merely from simple to *culto* diction, but from emotion to image, from sentiment to symbol.

If this essentially artistic, rather than emotional, standpoint is kept in mind, even Espinosa's untypical and imitative verse will not appear incongruous. He adopts the amorous sonnet of the current type because, in its stylization, it offers rich opportunities for decoration and colour : he writes in the florid style of contemporary religious poetry because emotion can thereby be turned into objective symbols.

Throughout one is prepared for the quintessence of his style to be found in a handful of poems which show he has at last discovered an adequate medium in which to express himself. These include the best and most typical of his early poems : " Al Bautismo de Jesús," the sonnet " A la Asunción de la Virgen María," the " Navegación de San Raimundo," and the " Fábula de Genil " ; and, of the later groups, the " Soledad de Pedro de Jesús," the " Soledad del Gran Duque," and the verses " A la Rosa."

These compositions represent to an intense degree his qualities as a poet. They reveal his peculiar artistic method, which is the reception and imaginative transformation of sense-impressions into creations of pure beauty, and the view of the universe this involves. Here Espinosa is typically objective : no breath of extraneous emotion ruffles these fairy creations ; he has the disinterested creative instinct of a pagan god, and, using the pastoral convention as a new mythology, he creates his own hierarchy.

Human interest has no place in the elaborate world of his imagination ; his nymphs, deities, even his sacred personages, are no more alive, and no less decorative, than the wreaths and garlands, emblems and decorative motifs that adorn his verse. Nor is there any movement in his universe : it is a petrified world ; action is seen as its plastic result ; for him the tempestuous waves of a storm resolve themselves into an ornate froth of foam :

> Tórnase cana espuma el mar cerúleo.[1]

In contrast to the absence of movement, there is a hyper-sensitiveness to delicate impressions ; he evokes with loving care the

> blandas sillas de mojados céspedes[2]

and delights to trace the sinuous, semi-human movements of water :

> con pie blando, en líquido camino.[3]

The essential quality of Espinosa's poetry, as of Góngora's, is the evocation of pure matter in its colour and brightness. In contrast to the interior flame of the subjective lyric, which, culminating in San Juan de la Cruz, burned up material things in its consuming fire, Espinosa's verse opens up worlds of exterior light and colour ; his poetry is a vast tonal symphony ranging from huge glittering harmonies to subtle half-lights, and in these pure creations of light and colour lies his distinctive contribution to the Spanish lyric.

---

[1] P. 24.   A la Navegación de San Raimundo.
[2] P. 30.   Fábula de Genil.
[3] P. 28.   *Op. cit.*

II

THREE STUDIES IN GOLDEN AGE DRAMA

(i) THE SPANISH PEASANT IN THE DRAMA OF
LOPE DE VEGA

It is impossible to estimate at all accurately the propor-
tion of Lope de Vega's plays dealing with humble people,
for he rarely confines himself to a single aspect of society.
Frequently the high-born personages of the courtly plays,
either hunting or fleeing in disguise, come into contact with
peasants, while the quiet life of the domestic comedies is
often interrupted by the appearance of courtiers. Investiga-
tion, however, shows that the number of plays dealing with
peasants and peasant life increases considerably in Lope's
later years. This growing preoccupation with rural customs
becomes interesting if we attribute it to the five or six years
(*c.* 1590-5) spent by Lope in Alba de Tormes during his
exile from Court. These years were undoubtedly among the
happiest of his life and inspired much of his love for Nature
and rustic scenes, a love to which he often gave expression
long after his return to Madrid. *El Aldehuela*, written in
1612-4, is the direct result of the period spent in Alba de
Tormes, for, besides being a rural idyll, it is a token of
respect and gratitude to the house of Alba.[1]

Most of the domestic plays are to be found in the largest
group, " Comedias de asuntos de la historia patria."[2]
These naturally lend themselves to the portrayal of national
life and customs. Often the story of fictitious peasants is
woven round the life of a historic personage, but sometimes
the peasant himself existed in history and has been vividly
resuscitated by Lope's imagination, as, for instance, Sancho

[1] See Vossler, pp. 38–41 ; Morley and Bruerton, *The Chronology of Lope
de Vega's " comedias,"* New York, 1940, p. 252.

[2] The classification is that of Menéndez y Pelayo.

in *El Mejor Alcalde, el Rey*. There are also several domestic plays among the " Crónicas y leyendas dramáticas de España " and the " Comedias novelescas." Surprisingly few of the " Vidas de santos " contain pictures of humble life, and those which do are not of great value from this point of view, because the saint is of course idealized, while the other characters are of very secondary importance. The shepherds of the " Comedias pastoriles " are traditional and in no way mirror normal country life. Similarly, the humble characters of the Biblical and Classical plays are bound to lack the freshness of Spanish peasants drawn from life, while the *autos* and the mythological plays scarcely provide an opportunity for the introduction of domestic scenes.

It is interesting to note that all the " Comedias de historia extranjera " deal with kings and courtiers. Lope is essentially a national dramatist, and consequently his intimate plays, which treat of the lives of common people, are very Spanish. The scenes of practically all of them are set in the Peninsula, and practically the whole Peninsula is represented in Lope's plays, from the Guipuzcoan port of Pasajes to the far South. Sometimes, however, the scene is laid elsewhere. *El Villano en su rincón*, one of the most charming rural compositions, is for some reason located in the surroundings of Paris, though it might just as well, and indeed more appropriately, have been placed in Spain, for the scenes are those of Spanish peasant life. The characters also are typically Spanish : the king is the " tipo de monarca donjuanesco y justiciero "[1] so common in Spanish history and literature, while Juan Labrador belongs to that interesting class of stern old patriarchs like Tello el Viejo of *Los Tellos de Meneses*. Save for the stage directions and some occasional name, there is not the slightest reason to suppose that the action does not occur in Spain.

The " Comedias aldeanas " are the most national because country life is least subject to the fluctuations of fashion and

[1] Joaquín de Entrambasaguas, in the prologue to his edition of *El Villano en su rincón*. (Madrid, C.I.A.P., 1930, p. 17).

foreign influence. To a large extent the Court reflects phases in international thought and outlook, but, in the Middle Ages and for several centuries later, these reactions and counter-reactions scarcely penetrated to the country. Lope draws for inspiration on the whole of Spanish history, reproducing it accurately and with a wonderful intuition, but the spirit of the country people is always the same— contented and loyal, but protesting and, if necessary, revolting against tyranny and injustice. *Los Prados de León* belongs to the reign of Alfonso el Casto in the ninth century and *Peribáñez* to that of Enrique el Doliente in the fifteenth ; yet, though the historical background and atmosphere of each of these periods are faithfully reproduced, the spirit of the peasants is unaltered.

For his material and inspiration Lope draws from the rich sources of national folklore. Nothing is beneath his notice : even some of the heroic plays introduce local legends.

The origin of a great number of his plays lies in some ballad fragment or popular song. Sometimes the story is to be found there in embryo, while on other occasions there are only one or two suggestive words which have fired his imagination. Often these words are incorporated in the play, or, to be more precise, the play has been built round them. Although they are key-words, they are scarcely noticeable, so well does Lope recapture the atmosphere of the old popular verse. Thus the key to *El Galán de la Membrilla* lies in two insignificant lines of an old song sung by musicians at the instigation of Ramiro :

> Que de Manzanares era la niña,
> y el galán que la lleva, de la Membrilla. . . .

Menéndez y Pelayo asserts without hesitation that these lines form part of some traditional song which Lope must have heard in his youth when he travelled through the district of Manzanares, and that he has woven the plot around them. It is true that they do not suggest one half of the story of Don Félix and Leonor, but Lope's fertile imagination could easily develop these bare outlines into the intense and real existence of individuals of flesh and blood.[1]

He also found material in popular fables and sayings. The main theme of *Los Novios de Hornachuelos* develops an old saying : " Los novios de Hornachuelos, que él lloró por no llevarla, y ella por no ir con él." This saying refers to a bride and bridegroom who had never seen each other until their wedding, and were both so extremely ugly that when they met face to face neither could see any good in the other. This unpromising anecdote provided material for a witty and amusing interlude of village life, which contrasts with the grand and tragic element of the other theme.

As might be expected, a large number of plays derive from popular tradition or legend. In his classification of Lope's work, Menéndez y Pelayo devotes a whole section to " Crónicas y leyendas dramáticas de España." *La Serrana de la Vera* is merely a dramatization of a well-known legend of Extremadura, while *La Mayor Desgracia de Carlos V* develops the popular belief that Charles' unexpected defeat was due to supernatural intervention. This same play introduces the well-known legend of the bell at Velilla del Ebro, which was said to ring of its own accord to foretell war or a death in the Royal Family. To a lesser author such readily accessible material might be a pitfall, but Lope's dramatic instinct enables him to adapt these legends. He increases our interest in the *serrana* by making her of noble birth, omitting her traditional violence and causing her, though vindictive, to remain faithful ; eventually the story is rounded off with a happy ending. This is an early play, and far from one of Lope's best, but it illustrates his process of dealing with ready-made plots.

The spirit of the peasants remains fundamentally the same throughout Lope's plays, and, although individual characters vary greatly, it is possible to generalize to some extent, and to distinguish certain very common traits. Nevertheless it must be remembered that there is no fixed type ; each

---

[1] *Cf.* the sources of *El Caballero de Olmedo*, *Peribáñez*, *Las Almenas de Toro*, *El Vaquero de Moraña* and many other plays.

character is drawn directly from life, and endowed with a personality essentially his own.

The peasant's life is uneventful ; and he tends to sink into a kind of lethargy, from which only a complete upheaval can rouse him.   In many cases his intellect is as simple as are his customs, for, though he may not be obtuse, he has not acquired the habit of involved reasoning. We do, however, often find a shrewdness and rapidity of comprehension amounting almost to intuition, since the intervening steps of reasoning are omitted.   Thus the portrait is sufficient to tell Peribáñez of the Comendador's love, and when he is put at the head of the peasant army he immediately understands the motive. Nuño, in *El Mejor Alcalde, el Rey*, guesses at once what has happened to Elvira : it seems as if his intuition had warned him from the beginning that Tello's desire to postpone the wedding was dangerous.

On the other hand, there is the extremely simple kind of peasant, whose intelligence and intuition are equally dormant.   Such a figure is Fileno in *El Labrador venturoso*, with his childish simplicity before the King and his insistence on the fifty geese and the Moorish tunic which Zulema had promised him.   Peasants of this kind are either very minor characters, or else serve the purpose of the *gracioso*, thus forming a complete contrast with the superior *labrador*, as in *El Mejor Alcalde, el Rey* and *Fuente Ovejuna*. Even the *gracioso* is an individual capable of making himself liked ; he is not wholly comic.   For this reason we are sorry for Fileno when Elvira buoys up his hopes by pretending to love him.   It is a common illusion of the simple peasant that he can win his master's lady. Pelayo imagines himself as Sancho's rival, and, in *Los Tellos de Meneses*, Mendo makes very determined efforts to win Laura, apparently with complete confidence in his power to do so.   This illusion is caused by his incapacity to grasp a situation ; his dull wits make him an easy prey to deception.

The average peasant is helpless in crises, not only because of the slow working of his mind, but because he lacks initiative.   He needs a leader before the true worth of his character

can be displayed. A typical example is to be found in
Los Jueces de Castilla, where, although both right and might
are on their side, the peasants are crushed by an act of
blatant tyranny ; only when Nuño and Laín arrive and lead
them do they rise in opposition. Once having rallied, how-
ever (as in *Fuente Ovejuna*), they are brave and steadfast
against all odds.

Humility is one of the peasant's most usual qualities : he is
awed if he chances to meet a nobleman. The young Isidro,
who is so sensible about the true value of most things, has a
great respect for the children of Don Juan and Don Alonso,
and, on account of their birth, does not consider himself
worthy to play with them. Mendo, in *El Cuerdo en su casa*,
is a model of humility, and, although he has risen so high in
the world as to possess his own flocks and to employ his own
men, he does not forget, or allow his men to forget, his lowly
origin as a charcoal-burner.

Connected with this humility is the peasant's reverence
for religion. He is very sensitive to all kinds of superstition,
but there are also indications of a deeper reverence underlying
this superstitious fear. Before the birth of San Isidro his
parents receive visions of his greatness, which they describe
to their neighbours ; it is not surprising that the parents are
awe-stricken, but the neighbours, too, readily accept the
marvellous interpretation of the dreams. Later they all
show the greatest respect for Isidro's religious tendencies.
Similarly San Diego de Alcalá is highly respected by his own
father, who falls on his knees before him. San Diego, while
still an ordinary peasant, shows such reverence that he can-
not bring himself to dust the faces of the images in the church.
Contrast this humble simplicity with the arrogance of the
Queen, who tries to cut off San Isidro's little finger as a relic,
or of the priest who steals some of the saint's hair. It must,
however, be admitted that all these outward signs point
rather to a superstitious credulity than to any understanding
of the meaning of religion.

The peasant is unwaveringly loyal, and, once his support
has been gained, its continuance can be taken for granted.

In the first place he is loyal to his fellows : Nuño and Nise, in *Los Prados de León*, do not desert each other when the entire range of the social scale seems to separate them, and they even come to Court and brave the King's wrath.   The situation may take a less personal form than this, for any peasant can expect the support of his fellow-villagers.   When Belardo, in *Los Embustes de Celauro*, has been robbed of the dress, all the peasants band together to punish the thief, despite their fear of more robbers lurking in the vicinity. In *Fuente Ovejuna* we have a splendid example of the loyalty of every individual to the entire community ;   all personal differences, and safety itself, are laid aside for the common cause.   Peasants are also loyal to their master, whether he be villager, noble or king.   Pelayo, in *El Mejor Alcalde, el Rey*, accompanies and helps his peasant-master, Sancho, in his difficult campaign against Tello.   In *El Mayordomo de la Duquesa de Amalfi* Doristo and Bartola willingly receive and rear the Duchess' children in secret, and even stand by Antonio when the truth is known.   Lastly, the loyalty of the peasant towards his king is a theme often used by Lope ; Juan Labrador is only acting in a normal way when he gives up his wealth and even his sons for the king whom he has never seen.

His loyalty to his master makes the peasant a conscientious servant.   In *La Niñez de San Isidro*, Bato complains that their overseer, Pedro, grumbles more about their work than does their master, " sin ser suyo el interés."   There is a suggestion that Casilda is equally conscientious when Peribáñez is away and his responsibilities lie on her shoulders.[1]   Pedro Crespo represents a sense of duty dependent on his loyalty to the community.   He is unwilling to accept the office of *alcalde*, but, having once done so, he immediately sends for the *vara* in order to be ready for any emergency.   His judgments are entirely impartial.

The peasant always appears as a man of sound common sense. In some ways he has a sensitive soul and is moved by natural beauty, but he has no time for extravagant pleasures

[1] *Peribáñez*, II., vii.

or conventional forms of politeness. In *El Aldehuela*, Antón, who is a peasant to the core, is disgusted by Fernando's high ideas and delight in courtly pleasures, which to him appear nonsense. Mendo in *El Cuerdo en su casa* is the practical man *par excellence*. He objects to refined forms of courtesy for very definite reasons : the will to pay compliments, he says, is soon subordinated to habit, and what began with friendship ends with deceit.[1] A game fails to interest him if its chief recommendation is that it is fashionable ; placing money in a pool, therefore, and successively winning and losing it holds no attraction for him, even though it may absorb nobles for hours on end.[2] He shows the same *llaneza* when he refuses to alter the ways of his house at the instigation of Don Leonardo.[3] Leonardo says that he ought to have a chair in case any great lady should visit his home ; Mendo replies that if great ladies choose to visit him they must be satisfied with what they find. Then Leonardo says that he must at least buy a silver jug and goblet, but Mendo answers that glass is both cheaper and cleaner. All his protests show a similar interest in practical utility. It is the same spirit which so frequently causes peasants to praise their nourishing country fare, as opposed to the piquant dishes of the Court, which end by ruining the digestion.

This simple, practical way of seeing things sometimes leads to impressive images, such as that of Tello in *El Galán de la Membrilla* :

> Sabe muy bien Vuestra Alteza
> que le aposento en el alma.
> Y cabrá, porque en la iglesia
> oí decir que cabía
> Dios, siendo infinito, en ella.[4]

Like practically all Lope's characters, both high and low, the peasant woman likes to be admired, and the man to indulge in harmless flirting. Nevertheless they are just as

[1] III, ix.

[2] A juego de ganapierde
nunca tuve buena gana ;
que el que pierde entonces gana,
y el que gana, después pierde.   (II, xii.)

[3] I, xv, xvi, xvii.

[4] Ac. Ed., IX, 123.

particular about their honour as any nobleman.   María, the miller's daughter, in *El Aldehuela*, exclaims :

> Yo soy honrada, y estimo
> más mi honor que las riquezas.[1]

Here is the same sentiment as that which causes Pedro Crespo and Peribáñez to avenge the stain on their family honour with relentless thoroughness ; Peribáñez acts as though he were the social equal of the Comendador, as indeed he is justified in doing, since the Comendador has girt on his sword and he is therefore nominally a *caballero*.   His determination to take his revenge at all costs is proved by his care in preparing for any emergency ; it was actually at his own request that the Comendador girt on his sword.   To all rules, however, there are certain exceptions, and we find a few peasants to whom honour matters little.   Such, for instance, is Filena in *El Sol parado*, who needs no encouragement from the Maestre to be disloyal to her absent husband.

The peasant's anxiety for his honour arises from his pride, which is a very characteristic trait in him.   Though he may be humble in the presence of nobles, he is proud of his own lineage and family traditions.   Often, however, his pride is more in the nature of independence of spirit.   It is this pride which prevents Tello in *El Galán de la Membrilla* from letting Félix marry his daughter, for he fears that people will think that he is using his wealth to buy good blood into the family.[2]   The same spirit appears in *El Aldehuela ;* Antón is not sure whether he wants to marry María when she accepts him rather reluctantly, even though this acceptance is the culmination of months of anxious desire and courting.[3]   We

---

[1] *Cf.* Tello in *El Galán de la Membrilla*, who is actually more grieved about the loss of his honour than of his daughter.

> ¡ Muerto soy ; mi honor es muerto !

he says, and

> ¡ Oh hacienda vil !   ¿ qué vales sin la honra ?

See Ac. Ed., IX, 109–11.

[2] Ac. Ed., IX, 92.

[3]   .   .   .   no hay estado peor
que el de esposo aborrecido.
Ver que es mía me consuela,
aunque siento este desdén,
mas si no me quiere bien,
más mal hay en el Aldehuela.

> Ac. Ed., XII, 246.

see the same independent spirit on a larger scale when the villagers of Fuente Ovejuna protest against the tyranny to which they are subjected.

Some of Lope's finest characters belong to the type of the village patriarch. Two of the most striking examples are Tello el Viejo (*Los Tellos de Meneses*) and Juan Labrador (*El Villano en su rincón*). The country landowner is always highly conscious of his own importance and responsibility, and expects absolute obedience from everyone on his land. " Rey soy en mi monte yo," says Laurencio in *La Carbonera*, and this is the attitude of many others. Juan Labrador is so much a king that he orders the real King about, even while believing him to be a very prominent nobleman.[1] Nobody thinks of trifling with such people as Tello el Viejo and Juan Labrador ; Tello exacts the last halfpenny from the men who work for him, and woe betide Silvio when he loses one piglet's trotter ! Yet nobody is more generous than Tello when it comes to giving donations to the local church ; we are also told that Juan Labrador gives the greater part of his income to the poor. Respected by his own servants and neighbours, the " labrador " is perfectly content to live just as his ancestors did. Celio, in *Con su pan se lo coma*, declares that, if the King were to give him his whole realm, he would not change for it a single hour in the mountain.[2] Tello el Viejo is an extreme traditionalist, and objects to the slightest change in the workings of his household. Mendo, in *El Cuerdo en su casa*, also belongs to this patriarchal group because of his independence and, above all, his conservative ideas. It is this complete contentment which so tantalizes the King in *El Villano en su rincón ;* though comparatively devoid of material pleasures, Juan Labrador is infinitely happier than the King himself.

Confined as he is in most ways to the village, there is one institution outside it which does interest the farmer, and that is the Throne. His loyalty comes before anything else, and

---

[1] Ya advertid que habéis de hacer
mientras en mi casa estáis
lo que os mandaré,
he says. *El Villano en su rincón*, II, xi.

[2] Ac. Ed. (nueva ed.), IV, 330.

he willingly places all his valued possessions at the King's disposal. Juan Labrador's outlook is remarkable. He is extremely devoted to the King, though more as an abstract idea representing the monarchy and Divine right than as a man ; yet, in spite of this devotion, he fully intends to die without ever seeing the King, lest he should be dazzled. This sense of obligation to the Throne, however, does not make the countryman at all servile.

Though there are so many characters who belong to this type, they are all clearly individualized. In Mengo of *El Sol parado* we have an extreme case, where husbandry and traditionalism have drowned all better instincts and feelings. He is a mean, jealous old man. Not only does he entertain malicious suspicions of his wife's intentions in sheltering a pilgrim, but he also begrudges the pilgrim his very bread and wine. Mengo, however, is a very rare example and an unimportant character ; as a rule, the village patriarch is a fine figure whom we both love and admire. According to Professor Schevill, Lope's purpose in creating such characters was to " embody the uncorrupted ancient Spanish virtues," thus " making the contrast between the manners and morals of his own day and those of an idealized Old Spain very clear to his audience." [1] Even more obvious is the contrast between these idylls and the artificial life of the Court, both existing in contemporary life side by side.

A number of Lope's finest heroines are to be found among the peasant folk, for greatness of character does not necessarily imply greatness of birth. Take, for example, Elvira, the staunch heroine of *El Mejor Alcalde, el Rey*, whose powers of moral endurance are infinite, for it is only through physical weakness that she finally succumbs ; Casilda, the equally loyal and strong-willed heroine of *Peribáñez y el Comendador de Ocaña ;* or Laurencia of *Fuente Ovejuna*, who alone possesses the power of decision and leadership lacking in the men of the village. These humble women all have a high degree of moral courage, loyalty and devotion, and are unsurpassed by

[1] Rudolph   Schevill :   *The   Dramatic   Art   of   Lope   de   Vega*,   University   of California, 1918 p. 102.

6

any of Lope's nobler heroines ; it might even be argued that their temptations are greater, and therefore their resistance is finer.

Although Lope draws his peasants from the life, he does not deny himself a little artistic touching-up at times ; though in the character of each *villano*, therefore, there will be good points and bad, many of his actions may be somewhat idealized. Lope's rustic amusements are often quite intellectual ; thus the reapers of *El Labrador venturoso*, when tired with the heat of the sun, prefer singing *coplas* to lying peacefully in the shade ; even their choice of song is made very deliberately and leads to a discussion as to whether it should deal with love or with Mars.[1] Much more elaborate is the ceremony portrayed in *El Vaquero de Moraña* after the harvest has been gathered in. The peasants come to their master wearing ears of corn in their caps, and carrying a cross made of corn. Musicians accompany them. They praise the crop, and pay their master lavish compliments in carefully constructed verse, requesting that the cross should be left on the threshold to give delight to all who pass.[2] Farm labourers whose love of their work and of their master is so great as to inspire such delicate homage surely never existed outside Lope's fertile imagination.

Calderón's humble characters often seem unnatural because they discourse on learned subjects. Lope has too real an understanding of his peasants to commit this fault, though they do at times utter poetical speeches when his artistic nature apparently asserts itself at the expense of his realism. Bras, the simple peasant of *La Carbonera*, is exceedingly eloquent in describing the royal procession which he saw while at Court. Every detail of the pageant is described, and also the beauty of the dawn which preceded it.[3] Far from reflecting the crudeness of an illiterate peasant, this speech shows a strong instinct for picking out the essential elements of a description, and also a certain sensibility to beauty. The first scene of *El Mejor Alcalde, el Rey*, when

[1] Ac. Ed., VIII, 27.   [2] Ac. Ed., VII, 569.
[3] Ac. Ed., IX, 544.

Sancho meets Elvira by the river, is full of poetry and of images delicately portrayed. In their context these and similar passages do not seem inappropriate, as they usually have some emotional significance. Bras himself declares " Amor me ha enseñado," and the same explanation is even more applicable to Sancho. Even if there were no explanation, the charm of the poetry would probably blind us to its unsuitability.

Many scenes are neither more nor less than rural idylls. In *El Sol parado*, for example, the scene in which the Maestre loses his way and meets the peasant resembles one of Santillana's *serranillas* translated into action. It would be foolish to try to establish its relation with real life ; it is to be enjoyed for its poetry, and nothing more. Similarly, the whole of *Los Prados de León* is a poetic fantasy ; if it were regarded more seriously, the play would crumble to pieces, for the plot is extremely flimsy.

A great many of the plays representing country life contain scenes which are clearly idyllic, though they undoubtedly have their origin in reality. Nobody would deny that villagers sometimes gathered on the village green to dance, but they certainly did not do so as frequently as Lope would have us believe. *El Aldehuela* opens with a scene of this kind. The peasants are all singing the praises of María, who is soon to be the bride of Antón. The general theme of their songs is her beauty, which makes her the light of all their lives. Although she is only a local peasant, there is no suggestion in their attitude of malice or jealousy. One fine April morning, in the first act of *Los Prados de León*, the peasants come down to the fountain to dance, to the accompaniment of musicians who play and sing. Often on such occasions the song is topical and concerns the people in the play, but here this is not so. Although similar scenes are common in Lope's plays, they usually have some distinguishing feature ; here, for instance, it is the light-hearted quarrelling which preceded the dancing, and the jealousy of Nuño and Silverio. In *El Villano en su rincón* we are told that there is an elm tree where the young people of Miraflor dance at night to the music of *tamboril* and guitar. Soon afterwards, we see them doing so. The unusual feature of this scene is the arbitrary pairing of the peasants for marriage. This is apparently done in all earnestness : Feliciano and Constanza, when paired, make arrangements for their wedding festivities. To anyone reading the plays these idyllic scenes tend to become a little monotonous, though they certainly add charm to the story. However, Lope wrote his plays, not for reading, but for representation, and therefore was concerned mainly with dramatic effect.

This idealization of rustic life is not merely a literary pose ; it springs from a genuine love of the country. There are numerous eulogies of the country which to a large extent express the views of the author. Fabio, in the second act of *Con su pan se lo coma*, enumerates month by month the simple, homely pleasures with which he is familiar : the blazing pine-logs in January and February, olives in March, fresh cheese in April, growing fruits in May and June, threshing in July, the harvest and nut-gathering in August and September, grapes in October, wine-pressing in November, all leading up to the wonderful climax in December, the feast of the Nativity. This sequence of events, repeated year after year, constitutes the peasant's life, yet it is by no means monotonous. Fabio derives a conscious and active delight from looking at the fields of green and gold, from watching his companions gathering in their flocks and tackling fierce bullocks, or even from the village festivities. Juan Labrador of *El Villano en su rincón* is equally appreciative of the blessings with which he is surrounded. He thanks God fervently for his crops and his flocks, for his olives, his beehives, his grapes and all his other possessions, but most especially for his contentment with God's gifts. Lope always represents contentment as being the chief blessing of country life, worth more than crowns and riches :

> Quien de gusto es rico
> no puede ser pobre,

says Antona in *El Cuerdo en su casa* (I, iv).

Nature itself is often highly praised. In *La Madre de la mejor*, for example, the peasants try to dissuade Joaquín from burying himself in the wilderness by reminding him of the

beauty of the country—mountains, meadows, stubble, pas-
tures, springs, orchards, vineyards, trees, wild flowers, fruits,
corn and the song of the birds.   Liseno especially shows an
imaginative appreciation of what he describes.   He likens
the healthy, lively flock to snow on a plantation of black
poplars, and he speaks of cows ruminating in sweet-smelling
pastures, and goats climbing among the trees, so that they
appear to be hanging from the leafy branches.   In a few
suggestive words he summons up a picture as clear as any
detailed description.

Many of the most vivid touches could come only from the
pen of one who was preoccupied with Nature, even though
his knowledge of Nature were rather general.   The second
part of *Los Tellos de Meneses* contains a striking simile com-
paring the social aspirant to a sunflower : the great sun-
flower is fascinated by the sun, which it strives to reach ; it
opens wide its golden sphere and grows taller and brighter,
until the very sun which drew it up shrivels it.

Contrast with Court life is naturally a theme which pro-
vides plenty of scope for praise of the country.   Juan Labra-
dor is far happier in his rustic isolation than the King in the
midst of his luxury.   For pure enjoyment rustic life cannot
be excelled : such is the belief of Bamba.   He prefers his
solitude to the company of envious courtiers, and he would
rather witness the sunrise than the King's levee.[1]   Tello el
Viejo takes considerable pains to prove that all the pleasures
of Court life exist also in the country.   The cities are amply
represented by green fields, and the vassals by flocks of sheep ;
the noble may wash in a silver dish, but it is no more silver
than the fresh spring, while the constant flatterers at Court
are like nothing so much as twittering birds.[2]

The bustle of Court compares unfavourably with the peace
of the countryside. Court life, says Bamba, is too complicated
and fraught with worries ; he has no time to interest himself
in what the King wears ;   the peasant's honour is far safer
than the noble's ;   and the flattery, the pride of ancestry, and
the humility necessary in the King's presence fill him with

[1] *Comedia de Bamba.* Ac. Ed., VII, 43.
[2] *Los Tellos de Meneses,* Part II, I, v.

horror. [1]   The countryside is free from the pitfalls of the Court.   Gerardo, in *Los Embustes de Celauro*, recognizes this, and regrets that he ever brought his son out of the country, where he would have met fewer dangers. [2]

The very subject of *Con su pan se lo coma* is a contrast between Court and country.   Two twins, Celio and Fabio, are very much devoted to each other, and to all that surrounds them.   Then Celio goes to Court and is carried away by the splendour of his new life, only, in the end, to be disillusioned, and to recognize that his old connections were, after all, far better.   In the town he goes to bed in the early morning and rises when most people are just taking the siesta ; his meals are at correspondingly strange times.   This is completely different from the simple, natural life which he led at home, making the distinction between day and night which Nature intended.   Perhaps the most striking contrast —and certainly a deliberate one—is that between the two weddings.   Celio's is very elaborate, but somehow, with its formal array of knights bearing different devices, lacks vitality.   Fabio's is simple, and is celebrated with sincere gaiety.   The cowherds all come down from the mountains to make merry, and fires are lit about the countryside.   There are plenty of bulls to fight, and the peasants dance and sing with genuine happiness.

Lope's love of the country is not confined to its purely idyllic aspects.   As an artist he often adapts his material to conform with poetic illusion, but he is sufficiently a realist to insert scenes and details which form a strong link with real life.   Thus his pictures are by no means one-sided. His idealism consists more in the over-emphasis of a single aspect than in the deliberate misrepresentation of facts.

Occasionally we find little domestic scenes which, though not perhaps of great value for the study of customs, are

[1] Ac. Ed., VII, 51.

[2] . . . . . . en la villa fué
adonde yo le embarqué
para perderle en la mar.
Que si aquí en aquesta sierra,
adonde yo lo he criado,
le hubiera siempre guardado,
menos peligros encierra.   (III, vi.)

impressive by their intimacy and show Lope as a great realist. At the beginning of the second act of the *Comedia de Bamba*, for instance, Bamba is ploughing his little piece of land, when his wife calls that his meal is ready and is growing cold. Bamba calls back " Ya voy " and continues with what he is doing. It is at this moment that the courtiers find him. There is a similar scene in *La Niñez de San Isidro*,[1] when Bato returns from the fields earlier than is his custom. He immediately calls for the stew, but Inés replies that it is not yet ready. When Bato protests there arises an argument as to when the peasant should have his supper. Inés declares that nightfall is the proper time, but Bato says that if he finishes work early he must sup early.

Many speeches and scenes remind us that, even outside the story of the play, these people live their own lives, of which the adventures related in the play are only the outstanding incidents. Casilda tells her companions of the pleasure she has every evening when Peribáñez comes home after the day's work ; how he jumps from his mule to kiss her, and feeds the animals before he sits down to his supper of stew and olives ; with supper the day ends and they retire to bed.[2] This simple occurrence represents the daily round, and to Casilda it is more real than the fatal infatuation of the Comendador. By means of such passages, though in themselves they may not be notable, Lope is able to produce a genuinely rustic atmosphere.

At the end of the second act of *El Galán de la Membrilla* there is an equally homely scene. It is not yet dawn, but Tello is already shouting to arouse the household. If they are so slow, he declares, the night will be over before they are up. Everybody, including Leonor, must arise at this hour. At the merest suggestion that Leonor should not be awakened yet, Tello replies :

> ¿ Qué queréis, que al sol aguarde ?
> Mucho la cama os envicia.

While he is rousing the household he is actually at the same time giving orders for the day's work : " Ensilla tú

[1] Ac. Ed., IV, 518.
[2] *Peribáñez*, I, xiii.

la Rosilla "—" Echa aquellos gansos fuera "—" Saca esos puercos de ahí "—" Calienta ese horno "—" Pon ese carro "—" Saca esas mulas."

In *La Carbonera*[1] the King asks all the peasants what their occupations are. Menga bakes bread ; Flora spins ; Inés carries food to the workmen ; Benito takes the pigs to the field, keeps an eye on the shepherds, mows the hay for the oxen, and sometimes goes to the *carbonería* ; Parrado, a swineherd, also loads the charcoal which goes to Seville.

El Cuerdo en su casa opens with a realistic account of shepherd-life. The shepherds are grumbling about the cold winds and the snow and hail, though it is nearly summer. Bitterly they contrast their life with that described in pastoral novels,

> donde todo es primavera,
> flores, árboles y fuentes.

Despite his pride in his own pastorals, Lope could see the unreality of the *genre*. When their master arrives, their grumbles turn to praise as they describe the fleeces and cloaks which form their bed and the winds that send them to sleep. Their supper, too, is of the simplest kind—kid, butter, milk and wine—but they declare that for inducing sound sleep it is unsurpassable.

Lope is intimately acquainted with the life of all types of peasant, and likes to sketch them in their natural element or to describe their daily occupations. One of the most pleasing descriptions is provided by Juan Labrador in *El Villano en su rincón* (II, xi). Juan Labrador is a prosperous farmer, and therefore his standard of living is naturally higher than that of the average peasant. Nevertheless, he allows himself no unnecessary luxuries, and even in the winter rises at dawn to attend Mass. On his return he breakfasts from two rashers of bacon, a young pigeon, and perhaps a capon. If either his son or his daughter is up by then—he is apparently less strict than Tello in *El Galán de la Membrilla*—he discusses the farm work until eleven, when the three have lunch together. This meal, though rich and

---

[1] Ac. Ed., III, 362.

nourishing, consists entirely of home produce: turkey; stew containing beef, mutton, a fowl and parsley; and finally, fruit, cheese and olives. After the siesta Juan Labrador takes his mare, two dogs and a crossbow, and, making the round of his land, shoots a couple of hares and possibly a partridge or two; or he may fish in the river. On his return he has a light supper, and retires, thanking God for this life of simple pleasures. This is a typical day in the life of a man in his position.

Several plays offer glimpses of popular administration. *San Diego de Alcalá* opens with a meeting to discuss various matters of public interest, such as the distribution of charity. The meeting proceeds with perfect order and harmony, except for the selfish arguments of the hidalgo. Similar scenes exist in *La Comedia de Bamba*, with the election of the new *alcalde*,[1] and in *Los Jueces de Castilla*.[2]

There are numerous illustrations in Lope of how news was passed from place to place in song. In *El Labrador venturoso*, Fileno asks what was the whole cause of the war then in progress, and Riselo replies:

> En las copras, a la he
> se dice todo,

and proceeds to sing them.[3] Song took the place of the modern newspaper: if we can judge by the importance attached by Peribáñez to a snatch of song heard at a most critical time, it seems to have been regarded as absolutely reliable. When he is gravely suspicious of his wife's fidelity, he hears a peasant singing of how the Comendador made love to her and was rejected. His mind is immediately set at ease, and he says:

> Notable aliento he cobrado
> con oír esta canción,
> porque lo que éste ha cantado
> las mismas verdades son
> que en mi ausencia habrán pasado.[4]

The speed with which news travelled in this way is remarkable. In *Los Jueces de Castilla* the tidings of Don Alfonso's

---

[1] Ac. Ed., VII, 47.
[2] Ac Ed., VII, 388 *ff.*
[3] Ac Ed., VIII, 28.
[4] *Peribáñez*, II, xxi.

exile precede him, so that when he arrives in Castile he hears a peasant singing of his misfortune, although it has only just occurred.[1] The *labrador's* song in *El Caballero de Olmedo*[2] even foretells an event which has not yet taken place, describing it as though it has already happened.[3]

Among the more picturesque customs is the festival of the Virgin described in *La Niñez de San Isidro*.[4] With great rejoicings the peasants bring their crop of wheat to the hermitage, in a cart adorned with ears of corn and a cross. A similar custom is practised, but with more ceremony and music, in *San Isidro de Madrid*.[5] In the play *San Diego de Alcalá*[6] there is a religious procession in which the image of the Virgin is borne among many flowers, and accompanied by sacred music.

When the Feast of the Assumption is drawing near, Casilda begs of her husband that they should go to Toledo to see the procession, " not merely for pleasure, but as an act of devotion."[7] This involves many preparations. For one thing, they must hire a cart in order to keep up their social status. We are told that in summer the thirty odd miles from Ocaña to Toledo can be done in ten hours or even less. Moreover, new " gala " clothes are essential for the ladies, and Casilda and her friends discuss them with great interest.[8]

Los Tellos de Meneses, Part II,[9] contains a detailed account of a baptismal ceremony. The church itself is resplendent with decorations. The first of the party to arrive are thirty of the foremost young men of the mountain, on horseback. Then Pelayo appears with a rich ewer, and is soon followed by two more peasants bearing brightly polished dishes. A silver veil covers the priest's fee, a candle and a salt-cellar. *Mazapán*, made in the form of Tello's ancestral arms,

---

[1] Ac. Ed., VII, 391.   [2] III, xviii.

[3] *Cf.* R. Menéndez Pidal : " En España la historia versificada tuvo más arraigo que en los otros países de epopeya, como lo muestra el hecho de conservarse en los siglos XV, XVI, y XVII muy viva la costumbre de noticiar al público los sucesos en el viejo metro épico de romance ; en romances se divulgaban las noticias de la guerra de Granada, de la victoria de Lepanto o de los sucesos de Flandes." (*La España del Cid*, Madrid, 1929, I, 56). From this it would appear that the custom still remained, even in Lope's day.

[4] Ac. Ed., IV, 528.   [5] Ac. Ed., IV, 587.   [6] Ac. Ed., V, 39.

[7] *Peribáñez*, I, ix.   [8] *Op. cit.*, I, xiii.   [9] I, xii.

is carried in on a scarlet cloth, and is the centre of interest
of all the young people in the district. Last of all comes
the coach with the parents, the godparents and the child.
The child is first named, then immersed in the font, and
finally anointed with oil. The godparents are reminded of
their sacred responsibility, and the crowd then disperses,
the priest taking charge of the *mazapán*. In the first act of
La Comedia de Bamba[1] a baptismal party makes a brief
appearance, with the conventional " plato, jarro y vela,"
and an interesting point is raised when the mother of the
child says :

> la ley
> que el padre no esté le avisa,
> cuando el hijo se bautiza.

This was not the case in *Los Tellos de Meneses*, nor does it
seem to be in *El Cuerdo en su casa*. The main concern of the
latter play is the profane celebrations, which took the
form of a great feast with abundance of fruit and
sparkling wine.

Descriptions of wedding festivities are numerous. Usually
there is a great feast, with village dancing and song in the
open air, and sometimes fires are lit at night all over the
countryside.[2] One of the most detailed descriptions is that
of the wedding of San Isidro.[3] All the peasants come in
and sit at the table—the ladies on cushions—while at the
same time the musicians are playing. A silver dish is placed
on the table. Two couples dance, but not the bridal pair ;
the stage direction says, " pónganse juntos y bailen con los
pies, haciendo que trillan." The most curious feature of the
ceremony is an orange, placed on a stick and containing
two *reales*. Lorenzo takes this when he dances, and then
gives it to Teresa, who dances alone. At the end of her
dance she places it on the silver dish and offers it to the bride.
Finally, all the peasants approach Isidro, and present him
with a wreath of flowers.

If the wedding is that of a rich *labrador*, or is patronized by
such, there is usually amateur bull-fighting in the square.

---

[1] Ac. Ed., VII, 49.   [2] *Con su pan se lo coma.*

[3] *San Isidro, Labrador de Madrid*, Ac. Ed., IV, 563.

Juan Labrador[1] undertakes to make Feliciano's wedding a memorable occasion and promises to provide two bulls ; they must, of course, be two of the most spirited. " Busca dos toros fieros como leones " is his order. It is actually this custom which sets in motion the sequence of circumstances leading to the tragedy of *Peribáñez,* for the Comendador is injured when attacking a bull. Bull-fighting is not limited to weddings ; there is no reason to suppose that a wedding was the motive for this sport in the second act of *El Aldehuela.* A more formal and spectacular bull-fight forms an important part of the festivities to welcome the King at Medina del Campo in *El Caballero de Olmedo.*

In *El Labrador venturoso*[2] reference is made to an interesting sport, called " correr sortija," practised apparently by the higher-class *labrador.* We are told that these are " fiestas públicas," not apparently to celebrate any particular occasion or event. The pomp and splendour of courtly tournaments are imitated as far as possible, as the following stage direction shows :

Sale Lauro con baquero y máscara, lanza pintada, y por padrinos dos damas con máscaras, y dos tarjetas, en una pintada la luna, y en la otra el sol.

Fileno, the *gracioso*, must of course try to rival Lauro :

Sale Fileno, vestido de papel, como los muchachos que van a los gallos, con su rehilero, y por padrinos todas las tres damas que han salido.

The actual sport is described in the text :

ZULEMA : ¿ Qué fiesta es ésta que hacéis ?

LAURO : Correr lanzas a caballo ;
que lo que habéis de juzgar
es quién da mejor el blanco
de aquella sortija puesta
entre aquellos olmos altos,
cuál va más firme y derecho,
cuál más galán y bizarro,
la invención y mejor letra.

[1] *El Villano en su rincón*, II, vii.
[2] Ac. Ed., VIII, 20.

This is interesting because of its relation with the old English sport, " riding at the ring," which, however, was confined to knights and was rather more complicated.[1]

Lope's interest in country life can be attributed to three main causes. First, there is his love of a simple, innocent existence, very different from his own turbulent career in Madrid. Equally real, though perhaps less obvious, is his love of Nature itself ; towards the end of his life, when so many of his human ties had been broken, he derived his sole enjoyment from his garden. Lastly, as a poet, he recognized the artistic value of rural idylls, not merely following the pastoral convention of Theocritus, but based directly upon his own observation of the actual life of peasants. Though art and poetry at times demand a certain amount of idealization, Lope never loses sight of his original model, and his most idyllic scenes are not entirely remote from real life. In this consists his perennial freshness.

That Lope was intensely interested in the lower classes is clear from the large proportion of his plays which deal with humble people, and from the fact that even such of these as are of very secondary importance in the play are still individuals, and not mere tools of the plot. His interest is further proved by his dependence for plots on popular legend. It speaks well for his knowledge of country people and customs that he can build up such vivid pictures from very scanty material. The source of *El Mejor Alcalde, el Rey*, for example, is a dull matter-of-fact account of a land robbery, but Lope transforms it into a moving drama of individuals stirred by passions : both the people and the incidental scenes of Galician manners come to life before us.

To Lope, the peasant is too real a being to become a mere literary type or a pastoral puppet. He may occasionally be idealized beyond the bounds of probability, but never beyond the bounds of possibility ; usually, in both his merits and his failings, he is natural and human. This refusal to

---

[1] A ring and a sandbag were hung at either end of a horizontal rod, pivoting on a pole. The knight had to gallop forwards and send his lance through the ring. If his aim were not absolutely true and he touched the ring, the rod would swing round and the sandbag knock him off his horse.

exalt the peasant to great heights does not indicate that Lope considered him unworthy of such an honour, but that he so fully understood the joys and sorrows of the *pueblo* that he could not present a false picture of them.

There is no hint of patronage in Lope's portrayal of humble people : indeed, he associates himself with them. It is significant that, when he wishes to introduce himself into a play, he does so, not as a dazzling hero, but as a simple, unassuming shepherd. Belardo has a diversity of *rôles*, but his character is consistently that of the naif and kindly peasant, often overlooked by fortune. *Belardo el furioso* is a rough draft of the *Dorotea*, and the mad shepherd symbolizes Lope himself, deserted by Elena Osorio. But Belardo does not usually represent any particular event in Lope's life ; he is merely a much simplified sketch of what Lope believed his own character to be. Again, in *Los Embustes de Celauro*, he appears to us passionately, and even madly, in love. Often we see him inconveniencing himself to help someone who is in trouble, as in *Don Juan de Castro* (Part II) and in *La Inocente Laura*. More frequently still his *rôle* is entirely unimportant. In *Con su pan se lo coma* he only appears in two brief scenes, as a simple and humble old peasant, greatly absorbed in his sheep. In *Peribáñez*, despite his age, his loyalty obliges him to go to war, but he is not attracted by its glamour, for he says he understands more of donkeys and pack saddles than of the knights of Castile.[1] There is always something very likeable about this naif peasant. He may at times suggest the *gracioso*, as when he insists that the feminine of *potro* must be *potra*,[2] but he always preserves a simple dignity which the *gracioso* lacks.

Lope paid yet another compliment to the importance of the people by catering exclusively for their tastes. To please them he deserted the Classical and Italian schools and looked for inspiration in primitive drama, in popular songs, and, above all, in the thoughts and feelings of the people themselves. He picked out what was essentially national. " Ningún poeta dramático anterior a Lope," says Montoliu,

[1] III, ii.

[2] *Con su pan se lo coma.* Ac. Ed. (nueva ed.), IV, 300.

" fué tan consecuente como él en su fidelidad a la máxima
de que el pueblo es, en último resultado, el único juez
competente en el arte dramático." [1] While this is quite true,
the question of motive arises and of how far this system con-
forms with his own tastes. In the *Arte nuevo de hacer comedias*
he praises Classical precepts, but at the same time he
admits his own neglect of them, and proceeds to establish
new and practical rules of art with infinitely more evidence
of sympathy than he showed for the Classical drama.
Vossler asserts that his culture was as much popular as
academic ; that on the solid dogmatic bases provided by
masters in his youth he himself built up, rather spasmodically,
an extensive knowledge and wide interests by much reading
and by observation of the material and intellectual ten-
dencies of the day. [2] All that is essentially national in his
work is consistent with his own tastes ; but he also goes
farther than this in his desire to please the people. Just as
some authors feed the public with horrors, Lope panders
to common taste in his religious plays by a rather cheap
superfluity of miracles and other supernatural occurrences,
not always justified dramatically. [3] Montoliu is inclined to
overstress, or rather to misinterpret, the significance of this
desire to please the people. Lope's aim may have been
partly complimentary to the lower classes, but it was chiefly
commercial. Play-writing being to him less a poetic mission
than a means of livelihood, his first principle was naturally
to please his public. In the *Arte nuevo* he himself declares :

> Escribo por el arte que inventaron
> los que el vulgar aplauso pretendieron,
> porque como las paga el vulgo es justo
> hablarle en necio para darle gusto. [4]

[1] Montoliu, p. 572.   [2] Vossler, Chap. XIV.

[3] Ghosts commonly make their appearance on the slightest pretext, though
certainly such scenes are often among the most impressive. The tradition of the
Morality play is continued in the frequent introduction of allegorical figures,
of which the most common are the Devil, la Envidia and la Mentira. Biblical
miracles are adapted to wholly unworthy circumstances : Isidro, for example,
strikes a rock and produces water to satisfy Don Iván's thirst ; María, Isidro's
wife, walks across the river to him ; San Diego feeds many of the poor with his
own small supper ; the Master of Santiago commands the sun to stand still,
so that he may win his battle before nightfall, etc.

[4] *Arte nuevo de hacer comedias*, ll. 45-8.

Yet, whatever his aim, he had an extraordinary power of interpreting the feelings and ideas of the people, and this fact alone illustrates the sympathy which he felt for them.

Lope continually shows us that there can be as much to admire or to love in peasants as in nobles, for some of his most successful characters are to be found among the villagers. He does not, however, concentrate only on the heroes and heroines, for the secondary characters are also painted kindly, as is Belardo himself. Even the peasant *gracioso* is something more than a *gracioso*. Villains of peasant caste are rare ; it is usually a noble who upsets the domestic tranquillity and gives rise to the events of the play. The few villains who do exist among peasants are usually only rivals in love, driven to malicious actions by jealousy : such, for instance, are Ramiro in *El Galán de la Membrilla* and Menga in *La Carbonera*. Never are they as despicable as political villains can be.

Lope frequently draws contrasts between high and low, to the advantage of the latter. Perhaps the most obvious example is in *El Cuerdo en su casa*. Leonardo, the noble, is so anxious to settle someone else's affairs that he neglects his own, and in the end he is forced to admit that it is the poor uneducated man who has been " el cuerdo en su casa." Again, in *El Villano en su rincón*, the villager is able to find a peace of mind which eludes the King, simply because he has moulded his life according to his principles. The contrast is at its most vivid in *Fuente Ovejuna*, where the terrible outrages of the Comendador stand out clearly against the background of rustic tranquillity. To some extent the peasant is exalted whenever a nobleman dishonours a peasant, as in *Peribáñez* and *El Mejor Alcalde, el Rey*. The *labrador* himself is perfectly satisfied and would not change his lot for that of a noble ; sometimes a young peasant is attracted by the glamour of society, but our sympathy always remains with his conservative old father.[1] *San Diego de Alcalá* is a eulogy of the simple life, but it opens with a very unflattering picture of a country hidalgo ; here, again, the contrast with the other members of the village

[1] E.g., *Los Tellos de Meneses* (Part I).

council is obvious.   How can a rusty javelin and six tarnished lances over the door compare with ten flitches of bacon ? This scornful remark of the *regidor* symbolizes the empty traditionalism of the one class and the practical common sense of the other.

Frequently, then, Lope took up the cudgels for the peasantry against the nobility.   Although he had a high conception of the full abstract significance of nobility, he recognized that social inferiority need not imply inferiority of other kinds.   Above all, he insisted on the full rights of every man, whatever his station.   Oppression of the poor he utterly condemned, man of his age though he was.   He himself did not belong to the nobility and at the same time was unwilling to be counted a man of the people, but he extended the same feeling of brotherly goodwill towards both high and low.

(ii) RELIGION AND SUPERSTITION IN THE PLAYS OF ROJAS ZORRILLA

THE seventeenth century in Spain was an age of reflected glory and idealism.   Although the visionary fervour of the *conquistadores* and inquisitors had degenerated into mere greed and jealousy, this was not always apparent to the superficial observer.   The outward forms of religion with which people still occupied themselves were now little more than a social duty.   Traditionally, therefore, religion continued to be a prominent factor in Spanish life, and as such finds its way into the drama of the period.

Since Rojas essayed all the current forms of drama, he naturally did not neglect this important branch : indeed, it occupies roughly one-third of his work.   He is believed to have written a considerable number of *autos sacramentales*, but very few of these are extant to-day.   We have, however, some dozen or more plays in which the whole action depends on the religious views of the characters ; necessarily these involve a special dramatic technique, for supernatural intervention may at any moment disturb the natural

7

sequence of cause and effect. Since the construction can therefore afford to be loose, Rojas wisely chose religious subjects for most of those plays which he wrote in collaboration with other authors. From the dramatic standpoint such plays are usually valueless, but they are interesting for the views which they express.

The *autos sacramentales* are symbolical expositions of ecclesiastical dogma. Since their original purpose was to celebrate the festival of Corpus Christi much stress is laid on the importance of the Eucharist ; this theme is treated with greatest emphasis in *Los Obreros del Señor* and *Los Árboles*, in which the whole action, even the Crucifixion, leads up to the supreme moment of the giving of the Host. All *autos*, however, could not deal with one and the same subject, and therefore other aspects of Church teaching are also represented through allegory. Most *autos* include the Crucifixion, stressing man's subsequent freedom from sin and death. This is rarely portrayed as in history, for the use of symbolism permits a free presentation of facts ; frequently there is a dramatic struggle between the two allegorical figures representing Christ and death.[1] *Los Árboles* further stresses the doctrine of the Trinity and exalts the virtue of humility. The *autos*, therefore, are mainly cold theological expositions, based upon an accepted plan. They are not intended to possess the warmth of feeling of an ordinary drama, for their twofold purpose is to instruct and to uplift. Even the characters are significant as types rather than as individuals. Adam represents the whole of mankind ; all who oppose the teaching of Christ are grouped under collective heads such as Judaism and Heresy ; many other characters are mere personifications of abstract ideas, as for example, la Culpa, la Malicia and el Sueño. Even Christ appears as an idea rather than as a person. *La Viña de Nabot* is perhaps the *auto* which most nearly resembles an ordinary drama, for it closely follows the Bible story, with its adventures and passions. Yet even here the vineyard is symbolical, and the characters are either personifications or representations of some trend of mankind.

[1] E.g., *El Galán, discreto y valiente, El Caballero del Febo.*

So far, then, Rojas follows the usual tradition ; the more personal touch is found only in minor details. Possibly a little bitterness can be traced in the lines :

> Porque en el mundo,
> aunque goce de tu gracia,
> ha de perder la cabeza
> quien dice verdades claras.[1]

It may be that Rojas had experienced the necessity of suppressing his own higher aspirations for fear of the scorn of others. When Culpa taunts Adam with the everlasting effect of his original fall, Adam prefers to look to the source of his strength instead of to his weakness, and replies in the metaphor of the old Japanese proverb, " Turn your face to the sun, and the shadows will fall behind."[2]

The most striking manner of expression is perhaps found in the *auto, El Gran Patio de palacio,* in which man wants to claim the Elder Brother's riches and yet remain independent and without obligation. Rojas portrays Christ's infinitely patient pleading with man and man's rough rejection of Him. Inspiration gives warning of the danger of procrastination, but in vain. Finally, when man admits that he has no legitimate claim on his Brother's riches and asks for grace, all is given to him freely and liberally. *El Auto Sacramental del Galán* also shows the human heart in a position to choose between the world and Christ, influenced on the one side by Flattery, Vanity and Malice, and on the other side by Inspiration, or the Holy Spirit. The need for this definite choice is constantly stressed.

Several of Rojas' *comedias* portray sudden and striking conversions. The method in which these conversions take place varies, but the result is always the same. *El Pródigo de Arabia* shows three entirely different calls to Christianity : Raquel has a vision of the Crucified One, in which the Virgin Mary tells her that Christ has died for her ; Efrón believes through an inner conviction ; and Mahomet, as the result

---

[1] *El Caballero del Febo*, Madrid, 1664, p. 176*b*.

[2] Cuando en las espaldas da
el sol, la sombra a la cara
trae uno, mas cuando en ella
da el sol, viene a las espaldas.

Los Obreros del Señor, Madrid, 1675, p. 163*b*.

of the personal witness of other Christians. In *La Baltasara* we have a complete study of the process of enlightenment of one who has lived an extremely worldly life ; gradually, as the conflict deepens in her mind, material things grow dim and the spiritual world becomes the only reality to her. Sometimes, as in *La Loca del cielo*, the devil moves the first pawn in the game, for it is when he oversteps the mark in planning someone's downfall that that person becomes aware of the spiritual battle and seeks the grace of God. Whatever the cause of conversion, its effect is invariably entire separation from the world, in the form of a hermit's life of penitence and adoration. Catalina, in *El Pleito que tuvo el diablo*, testifies to the real difference that conversion can make to life : she now sees God in everything, and all Nature seems to be praising Him. [1] So joyful is she that she proposes to take the veil.

Saints play a prominent part in the religion of these plays. The worship of some of the most devout characters very nearly approaches the adoration of an effigy in the place of God. Magdalena is one who errs in this direction, which may perhaps explain her weakness in the face of temptation, and her submission to her father's wishes despite her own vocation to be a nun. When she withdraws for her devotions, it is not with God, but with the image, that she wishes to commune. [2] Similarly, in *Nuestra Señora de Atocha*, all spiritual

[1] Cuanto miro es un retrato
de los cielos, todo es dicha,
todo es bien, todo es descanso.
Hasta ahora no nací,
ya sí, que a la vida nazco.
. . . .
No hay cosa que no derrame
alegría ; en todos hallo
una consonancia, y orden,
que a Dios están alabando.
Flor de las mejores comedias, Madrid, 1652. End of Act III.

[2] MAGDALENA : Ausente el que debo amar,
irme quiero a consolar
con mi Santa Magdalena.

JUSTINA : Con la mucha devoción
que a esta Santa Imagen tiene
mal apenas se detiene
en otra conversación.
La Segunda Magdalena, Act II.

power is centred in one particular wooden effigy of the Virgin. The purpose and plan of *Los Tres Blasones de España* is to show how God can work not only through His living and His departed saints, but also through those who are as yet unborn. The deliberate intervention of the dead in the affairs of the living is again emphasized in *El Mejor Amigo, el muerto*, when Lidoro constantly acts as a kind of guardian angel to the man who had befriended him during his life. The strong influence of the supernatural mars the dramatic technique, though it provides Lidoro with an opportunity to sing God's praises.

If Rojas highly honours the departed Saints, he praises living Christians no less. Santa Isabel is a typical example of one who is so entirely faultless as to be quite devoid of personality. It is striking to note that in *La Vida en el ataúd* both Aglaes and Milene are strangely attracted to the servant Bonifacio ; it appears that Christianity has some curious irresistible power.

The devil occupies an important position in Rojas' theology. Whenever Divine power is manifested, he is always busy working in the opposite direction. His power is great, but not unlimited : we see its limitations in *La Loca del cielo*, where he confesses that he is allowed to mislead but not to kill,[1] to persuade but not to compel.[2]   It is because he is unable to kill that he has to urge Pelagia to take her own vengeance. However much the devil may tempt, he cannot violate man's free will ; and when, as invariably happens, God grants enlightenment, he is impotent. His

[1] Si Dios me diera licencia,
    aquí los matara a todos,
    sin que ellos se acometieran ;
    mas como el poder me quita,
    siendo yo quien en su inmensa
    Deidad atreví mi intento,
    pondré lazos en la tierra,
    para que los hombres caigan,
    y entre los delitos mueran.
        La Loca del cielo, Act I.

[2] Tu piedad me desvela
    que no tenga más fuerza ni cautela,
    que sólo persuasiones,
    sin que puedan lograr ejecuciones,
    mis ardientes desvelos.
        Op. cit., Act. III.

power is further restricted by the possession by every Christian (as in *Los Trabajos de Tobías*) of a guardian angel. So desperate is the struggle between spiritual forces that it is lifted almost beyond the human sphere.

> Hoy la batalla se han dado
> cielo y tierra por Pelagia,

says César at her death.

Throughout these plays both miracles and visions abound. The Divine providence which watches over all Christians often works in a spectacular way : thus Santa Isabel is protected from her husband's wrath when the alms that she is carrying are transformed into flowers. When Christians are involved in a battle against heathen the angels themselves come down to fight for them.[1] Even the blunders made by over-rash believers may be rectified in this way, for when Gracián has slain his daughters for fear they should fall into Moorish hands the Virgin Mary resuscitates them after the battle is over.[2] Miracles are also wrought by the powers of evil, and anyone who has sold his soul to the devil has power to appear and disappear at will, to be caught up by clouds, and even to invoke the dead.[3]

Similarly visions may be either from God or from the devil. Saints are frequently granted visions for their encouragement,[4] and by this means the Christians in *Nuestra Señora de Atocha* are assured of victory in answer to prayer.[5] Unbelievers, too, may be visited in this way, for Aglaes, in *La Vida en el ataúd*, has a dream in which she sees Bonifacio in glory. Usually there is some definite purpose in such a vision : the Roman consul, Datián, in *Los Tres Blasones de España*, has a vision of Christ crucified, and is told to abandon the siege of Calahorra ; although he disobeys the voice, it has served as a warning to him, and his ultimate fate will be his own responsibility. A similar vision in *El Pródigo de Arabia* is the means of Raquel's conversion.

The conception of God shown in all these plays is on the whole consistent. First, He is omnipotent. All so-called natural laws can be overruled by His power, for the fulfilling

---

[1] *Nuestra Señora de Atocha.* [2] *Ibid.*
[3] *Vida y muerte del falso profeta Mahoma.*
[4] *E.g., Santa Isabel*, B.A.E., LIV, 264a. [5] Act II.

of His will.   Consequently anyone trusting in His protection
is safe from all assailing forces.   *La Viña de Nabot* illustrates
the power of Jehovah, and shows that He is a jealous God
who will not share His throne with idols.   He is also omni-
present :

> Adonde quiera que vos
> le busquéis, le habéis de hallar,

says Lidoro.[1]   God is the Author and Giver of all good
things ; every blessing that we possess is evidence of His love
to us.[2]   He is merciful and ever ready to forgive ; however
great man's sin, God's mercy is correspondingly great.[3]
He is, moreover, a God who answers prayer.   In *El Desafío de
Carlos V*, Carlos lays the needs of his hungry soldiers before
the Lord, and immediately his prayer is answered by the
arrival of money from the Pope.   The fact that the answer
was on the way even before the prayer was uttered is far
more indicative of God's power and surveillance than any
miraculous bread from Heaven could have been.   He
always shows the same care for Christians ; it is for this
reason that Lidoro is allowed to return to earth to help the
man who had befriended him,

> pues lo que por ti se ha hecho
> también lo ha hecho por mí.[4]

Consequently He supports His own people in battle. When the
conflict is between Christians His support is not arbitrary,
but must necessarily be partial.   In the first two acts of

[1] *El Mejor Amigo, el muerto.* B.A.E., XIV, 478.
[2] . . .   amor es dar.
> Dador de la vida es Dios ;
> siempre está dando y haciendo
> bien a los hombres que ama ;
> da el verano, da el invierno,
> da las flores, da los frutos,
> da las aguas, da los tiempos.

El Desdén vengado (ascribed to Rojas Zorrilla by Cotarelo y Mori and others),
Lope de Vega, Ac. Ed., XV, 410*b*.

[3] EFRÓN :   Es Dios misericordioso,
> siempre perdona los yerros.
> MAHOMA : ¿ Y si es mayor el delito ?
> RAQUEL :   Cuanto es mayor el exceso,
>   es más la misericordia.
> MAHOMA : Luego si humilde y sujeto
>   yo le pidiera perdón . . .
>   RAQUEL : Él te perdonará.

El Pródigo de Arabia, Act III.   In this, as in many other passages, the direct
influence of Scripture is evident.

[4] *El Mejor Amigo, el muerto.* B.A.E., XIV, 478.

Los Tres Blasones de España the situation is clear, as the struggle is between pagans and Christians ; in the third act, however, both sides are nominally Christian, but God's support is no less definite. He can read below the surface and knows which side deserves the victory.

Rojas' theology is on the whole orthodox, sometimes to an almost exaggerated extent. His complete loyalty to the Church is shown by his intolerant attitude, in the *autos*, towards Judaism, and also towards Mahomet.[1] Sometimes his adherence to tradition becomes little more than blind superstition. Miracles performed for unworthy ends are frequent. People tend to rely upon the power of an image as such, rather than on the greater power which it symbolizes, and Rojas portrays this reliance as being well justified. Often they are too materially minded to appreciate symbolism ; they therefore regard religious rites and ceremonies as having a supernatural power of their own. In *El Pleito que tuvo el diablo*, Catalina is demon-possessed because she was baptized only in the name of the Father and the Son ; until she is re-baptized in the name of the Holy Trinity she is, despite her own will, her faith and her prayers, in the power of the devil.

Even more noticeable in Rojas' work is its fatalism. He appears to believe very strongly that every individual has a fixed destiny, determined by the influence of his own particular star. One's destiny is ordained prenatally.[2] Every incident in one's life is therefore to be accepted with resignation ; whether it be falling in love,[3] or receiving an

---

[1] In *El Pródigo de Arabia* and in *Vida y muerte del falso profeta Mahoma*, Mahomet is represented as a reprobate, deliberately scheming to deceive the people.

[2] Naciste para casada
    como yo para soltera,
says Andrea in *Entre bobos anda el juego*. *Clásicos castellanos*, XXXV, 149.

[3] Pues ya que fué mi estrella,
    Leonardo, quererla así . . .
El Desdén vengado, Lope de Vega, Ac. Ed., XV, 402*b*.

    Que no es belleza recelo,
    sino influencia del cielo,
    yo amar y ella aborrecer.
    Op. cit., XV, 406*b*.

    En fin, ¿ que os queréis casar ?
    . . .   Es influencia de mi estrella.
La Traición busca el castigo, B.A.E., LIV, 238*a*.

affront,[1] or killing a man in self-defence,[2] all is the appointment of destiny.

> ¡ Por cuán extraño camino
> trae un hombre su destino
> como a mí me trajo ahora !

exclaims Don Diego.[3]   No effort, however strong, can alter the predestined plan, nor can any conjectures foresee it.

Such a belief is bound to have a marked effect on conduct. Men are eager to obey what they believe to be their " star," rather than follow what may appear to be the obvious line of action. Julia, in *Los Bandos de Verona*, is torn between obedience to her father and what she thinks to be her destiny :

> Obedecer a mi padre
> no es obedecer a mi estrella. [4]

Fatalistic belief exempts one from moral responsibility, for all blame can be attached to " la estrella " ; this is the chief excuse which Julia makes for her obstinate refusal to marry either the Conde or Andrés.[5]   Fate may also free one from the need to exert oneself in any way since circumstances will inevitably arrange themselves without our intervention ; self-control is a needless art to acquire : it is much easier to let things take their course. [6]

---

[1] ¿ Qué es vuestro mal ?—Un agravio.
  ¿ Quién lo ha causado ?—Mi estrella.
Donde hay agravios, B.A.E., LIV, 151c.

[2] .   .   .   cuando a mis pies desangrado,
    por mi suerte o su destino,
    cae mortal.

  Op. cit., LIV, 153a.

[3] *Don Diego de Noche*, B.A.E., LIV, 218b.

[4] *Los Bandos de Verona*, B.A.E., LIV, 368c.

[5] JULIA :   Padre mío,
        ¿ los astros no influyen todos ?
  ANTONIO : Todos influyen precisos.
  JULIA :   Pues ¿ qué culpa tengo yo
        de lo que un astro ha influído ?

      B.A.E., LIV, 377c.

[6] Si me quiero refrenar,
    no he de poder moderar
    los impulsos de mi estrella.

  Peligrar en los remedios, B.A.E. LIV, 355b.

However strange may appear the workings of destiny, the righteous man is usually recompensed in the end, while retribution overtakes the hypocrite. In *La Traición busca el castigo* Juan believes García to be guilty and is incited by Andrés to kill him by treachery ; Nemesis, however, selects the traitor, Andrés, and it is he who, in the dark, receives the blow intended for García.[1] Mortal men may make mistakes, and try to punish the innocent or free the guilty, but a just Heaven intervenes. After signing Berenguel's death-warrant, the Count makes a last desperate effort to save his life by handing him the keys of the prison, but, even as he is escaping, Berenguel is seen and shot. The Count acknowledges the overruling of God in this act, for Divine justice must be carried out, even in this world.[2]

Dreams may have a prophetic significance ; and their foreshadowing of tragedy often stimulates interest. Numerous examples could be cited : Progne dreams of Tereo's foul deed ;[3] Alejandro, in *El Más Impropio Verdugo*, is shown his own death at his father's hand ;[4] Alejandro, in *No hay ser padre*, sees himself mortally wounded by his brother ;[5] and Constanza dreams that Berenguel murders Ramón.[6] In *La Hermosura y la desdicha* Pedro has a symbolical dream of a white dove wounded by a hawk, which later proves to have been a supernatural warning of the danger ahead.[7] The significance of dreams and visions is not always prophetic ; it is a vision, for example, which informs Rugero of the true identity of his victim.[8] Berenguel sees his dead brother's shade, but, far from repenting or fearing, wishes only that

---

[1] B.A.E., LIV, 254. Cf. *Santa Isabel*. Through his own officiousness the scheming Carlos suffers the terrible fate intended for his rival. (B.A.E., LIV, 269).

[2] Yo le vine a dar la vida,
no quiso el cielo, y así
al que dió la muerte a Abel
ha muerto como Caín.
El Caín de Cataluña, B.A.E., LIV, 293c.

[3] *Progne y Filomena*, B.A.E., LIV, 41.   [4] B.A.E., LIV, 174.

[5] B.A.E., LIV, 393.   [6] *El Caín de Cataluña*, B.A.E., LIV, 279.

[7] B.A.E., LIV, 454c.   [8] *No hay ser padre*, B.A.E., LIV, 401.

Ramón were still alive in order that he might be murdered over again.[1]

The significance of omens is also studied, for they too may give warning of an approaching tragedy.   As Colatino takes leave of his beloved wife a dove pierced by an arrow falls at his feet, and he knows that this bodes ill.[2]   A similar foreboding seizes the Queen in *La Prudencia en el castigo*, when the glass falls out of the mirror which she is using.[3]   Even an Arab calling his wares in the street may have a sinister meaning,[4] while the omens which accompany Persiles' and Segismunda's attempt to flee are numerous.[5]

> Preñada está la noche
> de sombras y de portentos,

exclaims Jarimón in dread.   One omen consists in Segismunda's pistol discharging, and another in her stumbling. " ¡ Qué de agüeros ! " she cries.   In situations involving great nervous strain the interpretation of small incidents as omens might be explained psychologically ; however, sinister portents are by no means confined to such occasions, for when Colatino sees the wounded dove there is not the slightest suspicion that any misfortune could occur.   Omens are always taken with the utmost seriousness ;   they are sufficient to cause Solimán to strike camp and abandon the battle when victory seems within his grasp.[6]

In *La Hermosura y la desdicha* the prevalence of superstition is lightly satirized.[7]   When Pedro tells Monzón of his dream, adding :

> y aunque el sueño es cosa incierta,
> esto a mi desdicha aplico,

---

[1] *El Caín de Cataluña*, B.A.E., LIV, 291c.

[2] *Lucrecia y Tarquino*, Act I.

[3] *Parte 44 de comedias nuevas*, Madrid, 1678, p. 368.

[4] . . . y no es bien que un pregonero
(que parece mal agüero)
me esté gritando al oído.

El Más Impropio Verdugo por la más justa venganza, B.A.E., LIV, 173a.

[5] *Parte 30 de comedias nuevas*, Seville, 1638, pp. 407–8.

[6] *El Desafío de Carlos V*, B.A.E., LIV, 420.

[7] B.A.E., LIV, 454c.

Monzón scornfully replies :

> Pues yo no lo aplico tal,
> que a un caballero cristiano
> creer en un sueño vano
> ni en agüeros le está mal.

He then pours scorn on those who stay in bed all day if they spill a little salt, and relates the story of a page-boy who upset the salt-cellar and whom his master stabbed to death on the spot. This speech is striking because Monzón speaks with obvious feeling ; the story of the unfortunate page is told in such a way as to bring out the pettiness of the motive for which so cruel an act was committed. It is interesting that he condemns superstition as being unworthy, not of a brave or of a sensible knight, but of a Christian knight ; discrepancies of that kind usually passed unnoticed. It is the cultured man who toys with superstition, while the servant scoffs : this is not the only time that Rojas puts wise words into the mouths of babes and sucklings. Nevertheless on this occasion Pedro is justified in taking his dream symbolically, though the servant is too materially minded to appreciate such subtleties.

Those plays in which diabolical influence is over-emphasized degenerate into little more than *comedias de magia*. *El Pleito que tuvo el diablo* is a typical example of this tendency, for the way in which people are constantly flying about destroys all logical development.[1] Men's minds and wills are of very secondary importance. There is little difference between the supernatural in plays of this kind and in such definitely pagan ones as *Los Encantos de Medea*. In both cases it is magic rather than religion.

Lo que quería ver el Marqués de Villena is interesting because it is primarily a study of what is called white magic.[2] No apology is made for the introduction of this subject ; indeed, magic is accepted even as a suitable study for students at the university. In the Middle Ages this had been the current attitude, but with the Revival of Learning and the coming of

---

[1] Cf. *Vida y muerte del falso profeta Mahoma* and *Los Trabajos de Tobías*.

[2] For the literary significance of this play, see S. M. Waxman : " Chapters on Magic in Spanish Literature," in *Revue Hispanique*, 1916, XXXVIII, 325, 409–17.

the Inquisition magic became a forbidden art. Rojas is therefore careful to distinguish between black and white magic, and, by condemning the former, to avoid trouble with the authorities. Villena dabbles only in white magic, and so is able to overcome Fileno's black magic. Reference is made to some of the common legends of magic, such as the bottled devil, and the leaving behind of a shadow in order to evade capture. It is interesting to find, during the decline of the Golden Age, so much that is completely mediæval. This is not the diabolical magic of Calderón's *Mágico Prodigioso*, nor of Mira de Amescua's *Esclavo del demonio*, nor even of Rojas' own *Pleito que tuvo el diablo* and *Los Trabajos de Tobías*. In the hey-day of the Golden Age, as represented by Lope de Vega, superstition was confined to ghost scenes and a certain amount of prophecy through omens and dreams. Now, however, the era of the *comedia de magia* is approaching, and the spectacular is sought to conceal lack of literary inspiration. It is therefore not surprising that Rojas should try his hand at this, as he did at most current forms of drama.

It would be difficult to judge how far the superstitions found in his plays were actually credited by Rojas. There is a definite consistency of creed, but this may be the effect rather of a habit of thinking along popular lines than of any deep-rooted conviction. The insistence laid on the immutability of fate and the use of omens may be no more than a very effective and common dramatic device, while miracles and black magic are merely stage machinery, essential to a certain type of play. Moreover, they have the useful function of capturing public interest, and of covering up deficiencies in the construction of the plays. Whether Rojas had any more serious intention than this is doubtful.

(iii) ROJAS ZORRILLA AND SEVENTEENTH-CENTURY SPAIN

Rojas Zorrilla was essentially a man of his age. Since he had never travelled, his ideas were bounded by the frontiers of his own country. Consequently it is to be expected that his plays will portray the Spain of his day ; indeed, even

CARL A. RUDISILL LIBRARY
LENOIR RHYNE COLLEGE

those plays which deal ostensibly with foreign countries or previous centuries are in reality pictures of this same society, for they reflect both its superficial customs and its essential spirit and outlook on life. That this reflection was deliberate Rojas himself admits in *Don Diego de Noche*, where he says:

> Como esto es imitación
> de las costumbres del pueblo,
> tal vez la lengua o la pluma
> dicen lo que no quisieron. [1]

In contrast to an idyllic rural existence, court life appears full of deceit and treachery,[2] and even when no such contrast is drawn the picture is not usually entirely favourable. In *Santa Isabel, Reina de Portugal* we see with what flattery it was customary for courtiers to address the monarch, for not only does the despicable Carlos speak to the King in the most extravagant language,[3] but the terms in which Ramiro, the hero, addresses the Queen are scarcely less exaggerated.[4] This same play reveals other vices of the Court. All the courtiers are dependent on the King, and the opening scene shows us a number of soldiers and public servants reminding him of their services and claiming the promised reward. The King evinces no interest and merely refers their case to his favourite Carlos, who, as he well knows, is not likely to be generous. It is only because one soldier is particularly importunate that he receives a diamond. Even the *gracioso*, Tarabilla, understands the futility of the King's promises, and does not hesitate to protest when the King orders him to be given a thousand *escudos*, preferring to be promised a smaller sum which he would be more likely to receive.[5]

---

[1] B.A.E., LIV, 224c.

[2] Such is the picture in *Del Rey abajo, ninguno*, and *Don Pedro Miago* :

> Hay laberintos en [el palacio]
> que enredan al más sabio
> y perderán al más cuerdo,

says Don Pedro (B.A.E.. LIV, 533c.).

[3] B.A.E., LIV, 259c.   [4] *Op. cit.*, 261b.

[5] B.A.E., LIV, 256.

Several plays reveal the extent of the King's authority over his subjects ; he can not only order them to marry, but even tell them whom to marry and when, the penalty for disobedience being death.

> Será Madama Leonor
> esta noche vuestra esposa . . .
> hoy os casad, o mañana
> os cortarán la cabeza,

says the King of France to one of his Counts.[1]   No doubt in Rojas' day royal power of this kind was not openly exercised, but it existed nevertheless.   On the other hand, even the King is powerless against tradition.   In order to pass unrecognized by García, King Alfonso tells his follower, Mendo, to appear less deferential, and therefore to put on his hat ; Mendo obeys, claiming at the same time that this privilege makes him a grandee.   The King can only reply :

> Pues ya lo dije, no puede
> volver mi palabra atrás.[2]

Whatever the customs and privileges associated with royalty, the monarch is always described with the same respect, and even with awe.   However unworthy he may be as a man, the dignity of his rank never suffers.   This attitude reflects the old belief in the divine right of kings.   What the king is in himself is entirely overshadowed by the sacred charge of being God's minister on earth, chosen by Him to rule in His stead and under His direction.   " Estás en lugar de Dios," says Constanza in *El Caín de Cataluña*.[3]   When one recalls the splendour and majesty of the Spanish court in the sixteenth and seventeenth centuries one is not surprised to find this attitude reflected in the literature of the time.   The peasants think of the king not only as God's representative, but almost as a deity in himself, invested with such an awful majesty that the very sight of him would blind eyes unaccustomed to such brilliance.   Both García del Castañar and Don Pedro Miago liken their monarch to the sun, which, from a distance, imparts life, but burns at close quarters.[4]

---

[1] *No hay duelo entre dos amigos*, Act III.
[2] *Del Rey abajo, ninguno*.   B.A.E., LIV, 5a.
[3] B.A.E., LIV, 290a.   [4] B.A.E., LIV, 2a, 531c.

Nobles are naturally less in awe of the king, since they are accustomed to his presence and share his less admirable secrets, but they nevertheless maintain the greatest respect for the royal office. Although the Condestable in *Casarse por vengarse* and García in *Del Rey abajo, ninguno* both prize their honour almost more highly than anything in the world, the King is the one person on whom they cannot dream of taking vengeance.

> No he de permitir me agravie
> del rey abajo, ninguno, [1]

declares García. Nor is this mere convention or cowardice, for García could easily have slain the intruder in the dark and professed ignorance of his identity. The fact is that the King is exempt from many of the moral laws which bind ordinary people, and, although García's honour suffers no less, the King is not answerable as anyone else acting similarly would have been. [2] Consequently the King may intrude as he will in the private affairs of his subjects.

The stratum of society which Rojas most often portrays, however, is that which he probably knew best—the upper middle class life of Madrid which forms the basis of *comedias de capa y espada*. This is the society portrayed in *Abre el ojo*, a play which shows men and women with no other occupation in life than flirting. The growing sense of personal honour and of the indignity of work resulted in a complete lack of purpose among the young men and women of all but the lower classes. Their only occupation was amusement, and each sex appeared to regard the other as the main form of diversion. Andrés in *La Traición busca el castigo* is notorious for his weakness where women are concerned, but in Rojas' plays this weakness is almost equally prominent among all the men of his position. The libertinage of the age is described by Flora in *Primero es la honra que el gusto* when she

---

[1] B.A.E., LIV, 45c.
[2] Juan to the King :

> Lo que es en el rey hazaña
> es en el vasallo error. . . .
> La ley que me obliga a mí
> no os obliga como ley.
> (*También la afrenta es veneno.* B.A.E., LIV, 601c).

endeavours to explain her mistress' apparent fickleness.[1]
The result of this degradation of love is that none dare be
lovers openly, and in many plays secrecy is the cause of
innumerable complications.   Even where a match would be
perfectly reasonable, as in *Lo que mienten los indicios*, the lovers
prefer to conceal their love, although they thereby run the
risk of losing each other.   Since love is a game, risks, ob-
stacles and rivals are all additional thrills.

> No hay gusto en el amor
> si no hay picante de celos,

we are told.[2]   There are illicit meetings under cover of
night, notes carried by furtive servants, meaning glances
exchanged at church or during the morning stroll.   Were it
an easier game, it would lose much of its fascination.   Even
mutual doubts concerning fidelity add zest.   Therefore if
the man is too vehement he may easily lose the lady, who
prefers to be kept in suspense ;   only uncertainty will hold her
affection.   Aglaes and Milene in *La Vida en el ataúd* admit
this fact to each other, Aglaes adding :

> amor
> aún se enfada en las ternezas
> demasiadas.[3]

> [1] En Madrid no hay
> dama ninguna que pueda
> con solo un galán pasar
> por que son tan redomados
> aún los más finos, que ya
> cualesquiera dellos es
> de su bolsa más galán
> que de su dama ; y así
> mi ama quiere imitar
> el común estilo, haciendo
> como todas las demás :
> que galanes y camisas
> siete se han de remudar
> cada semana.
> (B.A.E., LIV, 446*c*).

Cf. the scene in *Sin honra no hay amistad* (B.A.E., LIV, 306), referred to below,
in which Doña Juana opens letters from no less than six lovers.

[2] *Obligados y ofendidos* (B.A.E., LIV, 62*a*).

[3] *Parte 32 de comedias nuevas.*   Madrid, 1669 :

> AGLAES :   Tienen una falta.
> MILENE :   ¿ Y es ?
> AGLAES :   . . .   querernos tanto :
>   no quisiera yo a los hombres
>   tan ternísimos.

8

The woman may easily repel her suitor in the same way, for Bernardo complains to Inés :

> Si tú me quisieras menos
> yo te quisiera algo más. [1]

Clearly, then, the joy of the game is in the pursuit rather than in the capture.

The artificiality of this conception of love is further proved by the readiness with which it can be set aside for the sake of convenience. [2] Some plays in which the situation has become very much involved end with a re-shuffling and an arbitrary pairing of lovers, when, despite former declarations of love, everyone appears to be satisfied with this new and convenient arrangement. Such is the *dénouement* of *Entre bobos anda el juego* and of *La Hermosura y la desdicha*. For some, whose honour is less precious, daring flirtations with three or four suitors are possible. *Abre el ojo* gives a vivid picture of this side of Madrid life ; like Celia in *El Desdén vengado*, Doña Clara is a typical social parasite who lives on the generosity of her various suitors, playing off one against another. There is an entertaining scene in *Sin honra no hay amistad* where Doña Juana opens letters from six of her many suitors, making scornful remarks about each. [3] She regards marriage purely as a commercial undertaking, and is most impressed by the suitor who, in presenting his credentials, remarks : " Mi madre es muy rica, y está tan vieja que se morirá dentro de un año, mes más o menos."

Typical also of this society is the exaggerated sense of *pundonor*. Although this code is no doubt in its details and its rigidity a purely literary fiction, it has its roots in the spirit of the age, a spirit of pride and personal independence, of deep sensitiveness and fear of the scorn of others. The ideal of individual liberty was a mere chimera, for never was man more of a slave to the social order than when the creed of

---

[1] *Sin honra no hay amistad* (B.A.E., LIV, 298c). *Cf.* Don Clemente to Doña Hipólita in *Abre el ojo* :

> Si tú no fueras cansada
> te quisieras mucho más.

(B.A.E., LIV, 123).

[2] *E.g.*, in *Lo que quería ver el Marqués de Villena.*

[3] B.A.E., LIV, 306-7.

personal honour was at its height ; men strove to satisfy the dictates, not of their conscience, but of public opinion, and the thing which they valued most in life lay entirely in the hands of others.   The close social cohesion of the seventeenth century demanded that any lack of harmony between the individual and society should be considered infamous.   Moreover, respect for personal dignity was in fact egocentric, and each man defended his own rights without caring greatly for those of his neighbour.   While the " honourable " man would not brook the slightest offence against himself, he never hesitated to satisfy his own passions.   Dishonour consisted not in committing, but in receiving, an injury.   Thus a code which owed its origin to such high motives as chastity and the defence of the weak ended in the perversion of all ethical sense whatsoever.

Rojas' characters, like typical Spaniards of the seventeenth century, show an unbalanced sense of values : the slightest insult, whether intended or not, is readily seized upon as the pretext for a duel.   In *Cada cual lo que le toca* the cause of the original quarrel was a mere dispute during a game of *pelota ;* rather than appeal to the judgment of a third party and risk being proved wrong, Don Pedro preferred to kill or be killed in a duel.[1]   The frequency of duels is illustrated by the person of Don Lope in *No hay amigo para amigo*, of whom Luis says :

> Sin que ninguna le importe,
> de Flandes llegó a entender
> que se vino a componer
> las pendencias de la corte,[2]

while his servant remarks :

> Ahora que hay duelo y pendencia
> está mi amo en su centro.[3]

Lope, however, is by no means unusual in this respect, for with the growth of the military spirit human life was held cheaply, and duels were the usual outcome of any serious argument.

---

[1] See *Teatro antiguo*, II, 36.   *Cf. El Catalán Serrallonga*, B.A.E., LIV, 565c.
[2] B.A.E., LIV, 84c.   [3] B.A.E., LIV, 88a.

Though often disapproving, Rojas faithfully portrays the code of honour in all its essentials. He introduces men desperately anxious, above all, to preserve their reputations, even at the expense of life or virtue. Whether guilt be real or not is of little matter ; the important thing is that it should be concealed. This regard for public opinion is carried to such an extent that Antonio, in *Sin honra no hay amistad*, would even kill his sister, whom he knows to be innocent, merely because other suspicious minds demand that he should.[1] Similarly the gravity of an offence is greatly minimized so long as it is kept secret. For this reason Juan in *Donde hay agravios no hay celos* fights Lope inside the house rather than in the open.[2] The problem of taking vengeance without appearing to do so gives rise to many ingenious plans, such as the manner of the death of Blanca in *Casarse por vengarse* when her husband causes a portion of wall to fall upon her as if by accident ; or the reticence and scheming of the King in *La Prudencia en el castigo* who secretly poisons the Queen, and kills his rival in a cave which is said to be enchanted.

Merely to relate an offence, whether or not it be true, is to commit it.[3] If the story must be told to a friend, the barest outlines are given, and all names omitted. In *Obligados y ofendidos* Pedro receives a letter from his father summoning him home to avenge the family honour, but not giving any account of the nature of the affront. " No os digo quién es la causa de mi deshonra hasta que me veáis," the letter runs ; " no firmo hasta que me venguéis, que no es razón que estén juntos el nombre del ofensor y del agraviado, ni es bien que se nombre vuestro padre quien no tiene honra que dejaros."[4] Nor can Federico, in *El Más Impropio Verdugo*

---

[1] B.A.E., LIV, 315*c*.   [2] B.A.E., LIV, 166*b*.

[3] Llegando aquí a decilla
has cometido la ofensa ;
. . . . es deshonra
en la mujer la sospecha.

> (*La Prudencia en el castigo. Parte 44 de comedias nuevas.* Madrid, 1678, p. 346).

[4] B.A.E., LIV, 69.

por la más justa venganza, explain what his *celos* are, even to appease his lady, for the very account would aggravate his dishonour.[1]

The extreme frailty of honour is much stressed. A metaphor commonly employed both by Rojas and by other writers is the likening of honour to glass.[2] It can be shattered by the merest breath of suspicion, and therefore innocence must suffer if there is the slightest rumour against it.[3] Moreover, the mere suggestion of an offence injures not only the person directly concerned but also his family name throughout all generations.[4] Honour, therefore, is not affected by concealed guilt, as it is by questioned innocence. This is further evidence that what men valued as honour was not any real quality, but only reputation, whether true or false.

Since honour is so frail, it must be carefully guarded, and due caution must be observed in the matter of marriage. A careless marriage may so easily be the cause of loss of honour. This is a point which is often overlooked by the characters in the plays, though Don Juan, in *La Traición busca el castigo,* seems to recognize it when he says :

> Mal haya aquel que se case
> de fino o de enamorado
> con mujer que no conoce ;
> en la tratada hay engaños,
> ¿ qué hará en la no conocida ?[5]

---

[1] B.A.E., LIV, 175*c.*

[2] *E.g. :*   ¡ Ay padre don Félix, que es
>   muy vidrioso el honor !
> *La Traición busca el castigo.* (B.A.E., LIV, 248*c*).
>   Mira que es vidrio el honor
>   y que el aliento le quiebra.
>   (*La Prudencia en el castigo,* ed. cit., p. 346).

[3] *Cf.* the case of Antonio, in *Sin honra no hay amistad,* cited above.

[4] *E.g. :*   . . . es deshonra que pasa
>   desde mi hermana al blasón
>   de la sangre antigua y clara
>   de los Medicis.
> (*El Más Impropio Verdugo por la más justa venganza.* B.A.E., LIV, 175*c*).

[5] B.A.E., LIV, 249*c.*
Cf. Juan in *Los Bandos de Verona :*
>   Lo que es para una vida
>   no se elige en sola una hora.
>   (B.A.E., LIV, 376*c*).

Many plays provide concrete examples of the results of hasty marriages,[1] which suggests that Rojas was fully alive to the danger.

Every precaution is taken to preserve this flimsy treasure, but once it is damaged vengeance must immediately follow. Sympathy and regret are of no avail ; the full penalty must be paid.[2] This may be a never-ending process, for if Juan avenges his honour by killing Pedro in a duel, Pedro's brother is then obliged to uphold the family name by killing Juan, and so on.   The paltry causes for which mortal duels were fought illustrate this thirst for danger and adventure at all costs.[3] The fact that, despite the grave issues at stake, duels were engaged in rather as a game is illustrated by the lack of feeling displayed ; seconds are sorted out in order that the two sides may be evenly balanced without anyone's being deprived of the joy of participating ; nobody seems to care which side he supports.[4]

Honour is of supreme importance ; in fact it is the greatest treasure a nobleman can possess.   Loss of life itself is preferable to loss of honour.

> La reputación es antes
> y después será la vida.[5]

Therefore honour must be defended at the risk of one's life, and it is better to kill one's friend than to assail his honour. Fernando, in *La Confusión de la fortuna*, knows that by being a lover of the King's sister he is a worse traitor than the man who tried to take the King's life.[6]

[1] *E.g., Cada cual lo que le toca.*

[2] La ofensa pide el castigo
pero no pide consuelo.
    (*La Traición busca el castigo.*   B.A.E., LIV, 248a).

[3] *E.g.,* the mere squabble on the tennis courts which is the cause in *Cada cual lo que le toca* and *El Catalán Serrallonga.*   B.A.E., LIV, 565c.

[4] See *Abre el ojo,* B.A.E., LIV, 140.

[5] The king in *El Desafío de Carlos Quinto.*   B.A.E., LIV, 419c.

[6] Esta es la afrenta mayor
y así será más sentida
que la suya fué a la vida,
y la mía fué al honor.
                (Act III).

The seventeenth century was an epoch of unrestrained passion, and therefore the conflict often arises between the claims of love and of honour. Rarely does love triumph.[1] *Casarse por vengarse* illustrates the cold, conventional attitude, for after Blanca's death the Condestable remarks with selfish satisfaction : " Así vivirá mi fama."[2] Although to us the end may seem anything but happy, to Rojas' contemporaries the one essential was the preservation of " honour," and therefore Cuatrín can refer to the apparent tragedy as a ' fin dichoso.''

Not only is death preferable to dishonour, but dishonour may itself cause death. This point is illustrated in *También la afrenta es veneno* : no sooner has the King forced Juan to receive back his dishonoured wife than Juan falls dead. Charlemagne believes that he cannot be an honourable man, for, if he were, the knowledge of his wife's infidelity would have killed him.[3] Dishonour, then, is a sword which pierces to the very heart.[4]

In thus portraying the conventional code of honour Rojas reflects the proud spirit of his age. At the same time his picture is more faithful than that of many of his contemporaries, for, instead of confining himself to the falsities of literary tradition, he frequently protests in favour of common sense or true morality. Frequently where the circumstances appear to demand a mortal duel the characters manage to arrive at some more convenient arrangement, because they realize how foolish it would be to fight for convention's sake when no ill-feeling exists between them.[5] *Sin honra no hay amistad* is typical of Rojas' attitude, for, though Melchor

---

[1] Charlemagne, in *Los Carboneros de Francia*, continues to love Sevilla even after he has exiled her.

[2] B.A.E., LIV, 121.

[3]   Mi agravio y deshonor, mi mal es cierto.
          No tengo honor, pues no me caigo muerto.
                    (*Los Carboneros de Francia*. Barcelona, 1757, p.11).

[4]   Penetran todo el pecho
              las heridas de la pena
              si es la deshonra la pena.
                    (*Sin honra no hay amistad*. B.A.E., LIV, 297*a*).
Cf. :   Me han de costar la vida,
                    pues me quitan la honra.
                    (*Obligados y ofendidos*. B.A.E., LIV, 63*b*),

[5] E.g., in *No hay duelo entre dos amigos* and *Obligados y ofendidos*.

and Antonio love the same lady, each is ready to stand aside in favour of his friend and rival. Nor is friendship the only thing which is ever prized more highly than *pundonor*.[1] On other occasions vengeance is withheld because it is argued that forgiveness is a life-long punishment. The pride of the Spaniard makes it difficult for him to accept forgiveness, and he would rather settle the matter with his sword. It is therefore subtler not to gratify his desire but to keep him under a perpetual obligation.[2]

Closely connected with the code of *pundonor* is the question of women's rights. Rojas stresses the completeness of the authority which fathers had over their daughters. Just as the king commanded his courtiers to marry as he wished, so the father was notably tyrannical in his choice of a son-in-law, regardless of his daughter's inclinations.[3] If the father was dead, the brother had a like authority. Women were not considered capable of choosing for themselves, and their supposed weakness gave them the power to claim the protection of any gentleman, who, even though a complete stranger, was obliged by his honour to give this protection, whatever the risks involved.[4] Far from fearing the consequences, the gallant usually relished the possibility of adventure. The woman's fate, therefore, rested entirely with her father or brother, and later with her husband. Her honour was their affair rather than her own. She was kept in almost entire seclusion until a suitable husband was chosen for her, where-upon she merely passed from her father's dominion to that of her husband : at no time could she consider herself her own mistress.

[1] *E.g.*, the brotherly love and patience of Ramón in *El Caín de Cataluña* despite Berenguel's jealousy and treachery.

[2] No siempre tienen los males
  medicina en el acero ;
  remedios hay más suaves.
    (*El Más Impropio Verdugo por la más justa venganza.*
        B.A.E., LIV, 182*b*.)

Cf. No hay amigo para amigo. B.A.E., LIV, 101*b*.

[3] *E.g.*, Liseno in *La Loca del cielo* (Act I) :
  Tu esposo solo ha de ser
  César o habréis de escoger
  su mano, o la sepultura.

[4] *E.g.*, *Primero es la honra que el gusto.* B.A.E., LIV, 443*a*.

While portraying these circumstances, Rojas does not overlook the resentment, and even the rebellion, of these unfortunate daughters.[1] It is to be questioned, however, whether the heroic choice of death rather than marriage, made by so many of his characters, is drawn from real life. In thus protesting, nevertheless, they call attention to the suppression to which they are subjected, which is no doubt what Rojas intended.

The religious fervour which characterized the rise of Spain to glory had faded. Bravo Carbonell[2] points out how in the seventeenth century the cloister was a refuge from the temptations and misfortunes of the world : all disappointments and all lusts were drowned in the convent. In *Lo que son mujeres*, Serafina deems her young sister to be too much interested in men, and consequently plans to put her in a convent,

> Pues en un convento vea
> su humanidad reprimida . . .
> en un convento, es notorio
> que templará este deseo.[3]

The ladies think of church as a place where fine clothes can be sported before the eyes of admiring gallants, and their one interest during the service is to observe who is there.[4]

Abre el ojo is rich in details of Madrid life in Rojas' time. Reference is made to the removal of furniture by *ganapanes*, or porters, in open handcarts through the narrow streets of Madrid,[5] and information is given regarding the exact price

---

[1] *E.g.*, Isabel in *Entre bobos anda el juego* ; Julia in *Los Bandos de Verona* ; Inés in *Donde hay agravios no hay celos* ; Juana in *Cada cual lo que le toca* ; Leonor in *Primero es la honra que el gusto* ; and others.

[2] J. Bravo Carbonell : *El Toledano Rojas*, Toledo, 1908, Chap. IV.

[3] B.A.E., LIV, 191. *Cf. Sin honra no hay amistad*. B.A.E., LIV, 310c. When Doña Juana and Doña Inés are fleeing from Bernardo's wrath, Doña Juana says :

> . . . de los Ángeles vamos
> al convento, cuyo asilo
> procuro ampare dos vidas.

[4] *E.g.*, Laura in *La Hermosura y la desdicha* :

> Gran fiesta, por vida mía,
> hemos tenido este día ;
> Inés, ¡ qué aseo y grandeza,
> qué lucida gentileza,
> en toda la iglesia había !
> (B.A.E., LIV, 453b).

[5] See B.A.E., LIV, 143 and 125c.

of various articles.   Clara has an apartment of five rooms for which she pays a hundred ducats in rent,[1] while Julián buys a carpet and half a dozen walnut chairs for three thousand *reales de plata ;* had the chairs been upholstered in leather they would have cost at least another thousand *reales.*[2]

The stress laid on the prices of these and other articles indicate the importance which money had taken in the minds of the people. Spain might be idealistic in one way, but those who wished to better themselves recognized that the achievement of their ideal depended upon the acquisition of material wealth.

Rojas is especially realistic in his portrayal of social aspirants and the inferior nobility. Since work was to be avoided, there were necessarily many who had to live by their wits and keep up the appearance of wealth, whatever their actual poverty. In *Abre el ojo* we see several representatives of the impecunious gentry who were so common. Clara is a social parasite, and sponges on all her suitors since she has no income of her own ; when she receives gifts she usually sends them to neighbours and other friends in the hope of drawing a bigger gift in return.[3] Don Clemente, at his wits' end for money, is reduced to selling his father's silver salt-cellar.[4] Don Juan, too, is very careful with his wealth, and asks his landlady not to demand rent while he is away from his rooms.[5] We are told how he has bored a hole through to the next compartment, so that he may read by his neighbour's light, and how he often has nothing for supper but dry bread.[6] He is only too glad to accept Don Julián's invitation to a meal, reflecting what a different matter it would have been had he invited Don Julián.[7] Since the common desire was for social advancement, and since this could only be purchased by money, wealth was eagerly sought by all. Laín, the old servant in *La Hermosura y la*

---

[1] B.A.E., LIV, 125*a*, 129*b*.
[2] B.A.E., LIV, 134*a*, 123*c*. The price of many other articles is also stated. *E.g.,* LIV, 130*c*, 131*a*.
[3] B.A.E., LIV, 131.
[4] *Op. cit.,* 130.   [5] *Op. cit.,* 129.
[6] *Op. cit.,* 127.   [7] *Op. cit.,* 135*a*.

desdicha, says that if he becomes rich he will not be the first to rise in the world, for he has seen many who have acquired wealth try to forget their original state and to pass as gentlefolk ; one who now lives as a grand lady under the name of Doña Laurencia was formerly the scullery-maid Lorenza. He also mentions other evils which he bewails as being rife : merchants swindle, wine-merchants water down their wine, gamesters cheat, and women are not recognizable as their real selves. In the quest for wealth and nobility, honesty has become an entirely lost virtue.

> . . . es muy hombre de bien,
> mas hoy engañan también
> los que dello se han preciado.
> Todo es engaño y malicia.
> Ya perdido el mundo está.[1]

Students have an equally precarious existence, and they, too, are obliged to live mainly by their wits. Their roguish tricks are well illustrated in *Lo que quería ver el Marqués de Villena* by the incidents of the stolen turkey and the wine. When they have no money Cetina takes a leather bottle, half-full of water, to the tavern, where he asks for wine ; when the bottle has been filled he pretends to discover that he has lost his money ; the barmaid demands the return of her wine, but of course it is now well mixed with the water, and when she has poured out half the contents of the bottle Cetina goes home with diluted wine.[2] The student's ingenuity is scarcely less than that of the *pícaro.* The money which a student receives from home is inadequate and consequently he has to live in a disreputable district, in a sparsely furnished room well covered with cobwebs.[3]

If their life is in some ways similar to that of the lowest ranks of society, they also have much in common with the fashionable people of Madrid, and all the students are accompanied by their own servants who study " a gorrón," or in exchange for their services. Their conduct is as dissipated

---

[1] B.A.E., LIV, 454.
[2] B.A.E., LIV, 332.
[3] *Obligados y ofendidos.* B.A.E., LIV, 64.

as that of all young men of the time.   Crispinillo, describing student life, says :

> Cada uno tiene . . . una gorrona ;
> y no pienses que es delito
> cometido al pundonor,
> porque su amor no es amor,
> que es meramente apetito.[1]

Dice and cards form part of their amusements, and one of their favourite occupations is duelling.   Their skill in fencing is hard to beat.

Their actual study is of very secondary importance. Crispinillo says that their concentration during lectures is devoted, not to the lecture, but to disturbing each other ; inkpots are frequently upset.   Nevertheless, they often use Latin phrases, and they indulge in such intellectual pursuits as debates to decide which is the most useful science.[2]   Their interest in their studies is sufficient to win them the privilege of electing their own professors, a custom which is illustrated in *Lo que quería ver el Marqués de Villena*.   The " juez del estudio " has authority to interfere in their private lives : he comes to investigate, for example, after having seen a woman entering some students' quarters.[3]   Among so many cunning youths, however, his solitary task is hopeless. *Lo que quería ver el Marqués de Villena* is mainly interesting for its intimate pictures of student life ; we see the students in a body, singing and joking, and we also see them divided into two rival camps, the Manchegan and the Castellano Viejo. There is a realistic scene when Cetina receives a letter from his father, and all his friends excitedly expect it to contain money ; when their hopes are disappointed they express their grumbles in light-hearted song.[4]   They are all completely carefree and live entirely for the present.   In short, their life may be summed up in Crispinillo's words :

> Rezar, aun no sabe tanto,
> reñir, es cosa precisa,
> estudiar, cosa de risa,
> hacer mal, cosa de llanto.[5]

---

[1] *Ibid.*

[2] *Lo que quería ver el Marqués de Villena.* B.A.E., LIV, 324.

[3] B.A.E., LIV, 339.   [4] *Ibid.*   [5] B.A.E., LIV, 64.

Rojas pays comparatively little attention to the lower ranks of society, but *Obligados y ofendidos* contains an illuminating sketch of life in a prison.[1] There is a spirit of gay cama-raderie, and as the tankard is passed round each prisoner relates the misdeed for which he is there. Thus glimpses are afforded of the lawlessness that underlay the brilliant life of the Spanish cities, for the lower classes were mainly obliged to live by their wits. Mellado had been paid fifty doubloons to give a *licenciado* two sword-thrusts one night ; the *licenciado*, however, was not taken unawares ; Mellado was caught, and for his crime he anticipates six years in the galleys. He makes his living by hiring his services for night assaults ; this was a common way of disposing of one's enemies, and the Count of Belflor himself is to be killed by masked men for the price of five hundred ducats. Neverthe-less, Mellado has his good points, and he exhibits the staunch loyalty of which even scoundrels are capable ; for, although he was tortured, he would not tell who had bribed him to stab the *licenciado*, nor will he identify Don Pedro as the man who killed Arnesto. He has nothing to gain by this loyalty, but there is honour among thieves, and all law-breakers are united against the " justicia." Borrego, who tells his story with carefree humour, is in prison for having stolen a doctor's purse. Crispinillo had taken part in a street brawl. Ganchuelo's crime is assault, for he had slashed the face of an old fruit-seller who used foul language to him. However, he adds, he has managed to prove that someone else did it, and so he is to be released. None of the prisoners shows the slightest concern at having been caught ; danger is all in the day's work, and they are probably as used to being in prison as out of it.

Rojas also describes the life of the bandits who infested the highways and were a menace to travel. They not only rob their victims, but often, as a precaution, kill them, even though, like Serrallonga, they may dislike doing so. Poverty and social dishonour drove many to live as outlaws, adding to the unrest of an already restless age.

[1] B.A.E., LIV, 76.

Rojas' plays do, therefore, clearly reflect the Spain of his day : they describe not only the empty life of the rich, and the hypocrisy of the would-be rich, but also the crimes to which the poor were driven by the very conditions under which they lived. While the rich had no other concern than " el solo culto de la mujer como elemento de placer, el juego como distracción, y la espada como oficio,"[1] and while the inferior nobles tried to maintain their rank, " sin comer muchas veces, pero siempre nueva la grande pluma del airoso chambergo, reluciente la espada, bien calzada la alta bota, erguido el bigote y cuidada la capa amplia y corta,"[2] the oppressed of society were driven to the existence of Rinconetes and Cortadillos ; yet, if by this means they achieved wealth and status, they were more than willing to live as nobles, ignoring the poor. In Rojas' plays the first impression is of a brilliant, prosperous Spain, and this too was the superficial appearance of the Golden Age, but underlying this splendour, both in reality and in Rojas' drama, can be discerned the contrasting poverty of the masses.

[1] J. Bravo Carbonell : *El Toledano Rojas, ed. cit.*, p. 57.
[2] *Op. cit.*, p. 70.

III

THE RELIGIOUS DRAMAS OF CALDERÓN

The year 1681 saw the death of Calderón and the birth of Calderonian criticism. Throughout the seventeenth century in Spain, the struggle against *europeización* took the form of a vigorous defence of the national tradition expressed chiefly by Lope de Vega and Calderón through the medium of the *comedia*. Traditionalism engaged Neo-classicism on the dramatic plane and the great figures of the theatre became pawns in the bitter controversies between the rival schools. Calderón lived on in stage and print. The advent of romanticism exalted him to the ranks of the world's premier dramatists. The Schlegels, chief mouthpieces of Teutonic criticism, led the way with their extravagant praise.[1] A few voices, notably those of Grillparzer and Lord Holland, sought to rescue Lope de Vega from the oblivion into which he had fallen, but in vain. Calderón reigned supreme. When the full tide of romanticism had ebbed, and a period of more exact scholarship opened, there began a further revaluation of literary reputations and Lope gained what his great contemporary had lost. The youthful Menéndez y Pelayo, in a work which later he would have greatly modified, definitely gave Lope the palm and belittled the scope and universality of the Calderonian drama. To-day a revival of interest in the Baroque has led to a new swing of the pendulum, and, just as the younger school of scholar-poets has rehabilitated Góngora, so criticism is seeking to bring to the forefront the writer who has been called the greatest of Spanish Baroque artists.

A glance at any one of the current bibliographies will reveal the extent of the contribution made to Calderonian studies by Germany. Critic, littérateur and cleric—all have

[1] H.R.M.S., I, 84-8.

done their part.   Since the days of the Schlegels the succes-
sion of translation, commentary and appreciation has not
ceased.   The names of Fastenrath, Gries, Lorinser, Eichen-
dorff and Schmidt, to mention but a few, bear witness to the
strength of the Calderonian tradition.   By contrast, Great
Britain has little to show save occasional translations and a
few odd pages of criticism.[1]   The slight monographs of
Archbishop Trench and Miss Hasell, the introductions and
renderings of MacCarthy, the " grey veil " of Shelley's
fragments, the free versions of Fitz-Gerald and a well
edited volume of selected plays by Maccoll for long constitu-
ted Britain's sole tribute.

Moreover, the works of our nineteenth-century Calder-
onians, while valuable in their day, suffer from the circum-
stances in which they were written, to say nothing of their
authors' viewpoint.   Their criticism lies wide open to the
charge of that " provinciality " which Arnold thought a blot
on so much of his country's literature.   The atmosphere of
the nineteenth century was hardly propitious to appreciation
of what Donne calls " the three-piled Papistry of Spain " and
of its representative dramatist.   In the main, our criticism
during that period assumes an attitude of patronage which
damns with faint praise.   It attempts to admire the art
while condemning the religion which elicited it and refuses
to recognize an objective historical fact which is fundamental
to an understanding of the " Poet of Romanism."   The
strength of religious feeling in Spain, its pervasion of all aspects
of Spanish life, and its expression in ways which to the stran-
ger might seem impious were fatal to its just appraisal.   The
purely meridional concept of religion is offensive to many
even to-day ; by members of Protestant schools of criticism
it was deemed superstitious, unprogressive and fanatical :
one of them, indeed, Sismondi, unable to comprehend a
creed not his own, went so far as to condemn Calderón out
of hand as " the poet of the Inquisition."   British critics,

---

[1] Although, as is pointed out in the preface, no reference has been possible
to any publication later in date than 1940, it should be added that A. A.
Parker's *The Allegorical Drama of Calderón* (Dolphin Book Co., 1943) is a notable
exception to this statement.

while somewhat more accommodating, have gone for their
inspiration mainly to the same source : hence the unsatis-
factory nature of their judgments.

An actual contemporary phenomenon cannot be dismissed
without invalidating all criticism. To condemn a man's
premises and then to arraign him for producing " inferior "
drama may be excellent partisanship, but it is not detached
judgment. Whether the " limitations " of Calderonian
drama are interpreted as the result of religious views or
otherwise will depend on the critic but they must be accepted
by him willy-nilly.   For the *drama religioso* is an indissoluble
marriage of religion and art.

It is obvious that such criticism in this country has not
fulfilled the requisite conditions of impartiality or possessed
sufficient interest in the plays to examine their content in
detail instead of merely describing their plots.   Moreover,
Calderón's religious dramas have not previously been
treated as an entity but always included in a general study of
his total output. Even foreign criticism has neglected all
but the better known of these plays, concentrating, for the
rest, on that more fascinating *genre*, the *auto sacramental*.
Thus much recent German work has been devoted to the
autos, while Spain itself, apart from occasional investigations
into the sources of the major plays, has produced little of
importance. A notable exception will be found in the
penetrating analyses of Sr. Valbuena Prat, which have
revealed unexpected depths of content extending over the
whole corpus of the dramas.

The *dramas religiosos* seem to have fallen between two
stools : while several of them, even judged by secular
standards, attain the rank of masterpieces, the remainder
hardly rise above the mediocre.   They have found themselves
in a kind of no-man's land of criticism, branded with the
disapproval of previous critics, hostile in faith and animated
by prejudice, and yet, for reasons difficult to fathom, they
have also been neglected by the sympathetic.   They still
labour under the disadvantage of the severe strictures of
Menéndez y Pelayo.   The masterpiece, no matter to what

9

group it belongs, will always attract attention : not so its humbler partner.

No excuse, therefore, need be made for a further study of Calderón. The facts justify the choice of subject. It only remains to define the limits and aims of the present analysis. The presentation does not claim in any of its aspects to be either complete or definitive even as regards my own mind. It is, in fact, an interim study, which I hope later to enlarge and develop by considering the plays under examination as dramatic wholes. It should then be possible to attempt a revalidation of dramatic values and to point to conclusions.

In order that the material to be studied might be presented in its appropriate setting, the analytical pages, which form Sections II to IV of this essay, have been prefaced with a summary account of the poet's age, his philosophical and theological background and his intellectual formation. Against this background has been prepared, as it were, a cross-section of Calderón's work, which will reveal its points of contact with the purely secular and with the later developments of the *autos*. The religious plays are truly representative of the dramatist, for in them can be found not only his beliefs and his whole philosophy of life, but also the predominant social motifs of his drama. Within their framework all the Calderonian trends of thought meet and combine. They are chiefly noteworthy as the most striking expression of Catholicism and its dogma that dramatic literature possesses. Theology is clothed in the robes of art and brought on the stage. Mediaeval doctrines, modified and refurbished by Counter-reformation thought, once again become the content of literature. As the poet of certitude whose ideology is nevertheless tinged with the sweet melancholy of Christianity, Calderón affords to all who approach him in the proper frame of mind, and are prepared to make the necessary concessions, something of the grandeur of the greatest Biblical passages and the content of the mysterious but fascinating dogmas of the Church. God presides over his drama and rules his creations, and he willingly accepted the gentle bondage, for he was convinced that in Him alone was to be found true peace.

It is possible that some may miss in Calderón the poignancy of a Pascal, the apocalyptic thunderings of a Bossuet or the mental torments of a like mind who sought his inspiration at the same source as the Spaniard—the renegade Donne. Calderón, like his fellow-Christians, also features the dualism of the spirit and the flesh which a modern Frenchman, Mauriac, has found at the centre of Christianity, and which underlines the agonized cry of Pascal, the grim warnings of Bossuet to the brilliant court of France, and Donne's morbid interest in the animal aspects of life. But, despite his insistence on the ever-presentness of Death and the fundamental antagonism in man, he avoids the asperities and bitterness of over-emphasis. The harshness of Christianity has been toned down so that Death holds no terrors and life no psychological agony. Despair is replaced by a sweet pessimism akin to melancholy. For Calderón, Bossuet's unbending "Dieu veut *tout*" does not imply a heart-rending divorce from the pleasures of this life but simply a gentle separation. In essence the conflict is the same, but the Spaniard sees it in a more subdued light. The practical problems of life may have pressed hard but the counsels of an à Kempis or an Augustine to shun the world and its miseries were easy to a mind prepared by nature to fulfil them. In his plays the dramatist mirrors his own mild acceptance of the choice. For the dramatist of the Faith the "Quid prodest?" held only one answer. In his contrasts of the Real, the Eternal and the Absolute with the Apparent, the Transitory and the Relative the antagonism is clear-cut but never crude. He points the way, but not harshly. Nor does he seem to have experienced the spiritual aridity of the mystic or the unbearable mental questionings of the great apologists of Christianity. Religion came to him in the guise of a consoler—not as an irritant, but as a balm. He saw events naturally *sub specie aeternitatis* but experienced none of his contemporary Catholics' regrets. The mind receives Christianity and can make of it a relief or a torment, according as one reads its lessons. For Calderón, the " quia fecisti nos ad te et inquietum est cor nostrum donec requiescat in te " lost the terrible significance it held for others. Certitude for him implied peace throughout and was not, as for Pascal, a miraculous sign that mental torment had ended. Calderón's faith, unlike that of the great French apologists, lacked certain intellectual qualities, that questing and restless enquiring spirit which is the Gallic heritage, and endows even the believer with something of scepticism. The Frenchman wishes to make his faith " reasonable " : the Spaniard prefers it devotional and pietistic. The difference is national rather than personal. It is useless to pursue the comparison further. Within the Church also there are many mansions.

Little attempt has been made in these pages to assess values or apportion blame. Ideological analysis was the aim rather than pure criticism. Only where the argument so demanded has a defence been made. In no way is it suggested that the religious *genre* constitutes the major production of Calderón. It quite obviously does not. A mere chronicle of the Virgin written in honour of his cherished city of Toledo, a religious play which has nothing religious in it but the name, another which is a mere re-handling of an *auto* are obviously small fry. But nevertheless the presence within the group of an excellently contrived, well constructed and vigorously managed plot, of a drama of martyrdom which epitomizes the poet's favourite teachings, and of another which, though vigorously attacked for its artistic defects, yet reaches heights of religious feeling rarely matched contribute to its value. For the purpose of rounding off the analysis I have departed from precedent by including material from *La Vida es sueño,* usually classified as a *drama filosófico.* The lessons it teaches are complementary to those of the religious plays proper.[1]

---

[1] Most of this essay was written at a time when war made study in Spain impossible, a disadvantage which has sometimes compelled excessive reliance on second-hand sources and impaired both fulness and balance.

I[1]

THE AGE OF CALDERÓN

Many years have passed since Taine first formulated his theory of the three agencies that go towards the production of the work of art and thus minimized the personal *rôle* of the artist. The debate still continues. Quite recently Professor R. W. Chambers has brilliantly championed the individual personality against that nebulous entity the *Zeitgeist*, which, according to his thesis, has vitiated so much criticism, both past and present.[2] While every sympathy can be entertained for a reaction against a mechanistic conception of literature which completely subjects the human factor to external influences, it seems that truth lies rather in the middle way ; that even man's unconquerable mind is conditioned by its social environment and that criticism must of necessity make allowance for contemporary influences of every sort—social, historical and theological. A writer cannot be isolated from his age but must be judged with reference to his contemporary background.

In few literary figures is the *milieu* (taking the word in its widest sense) so important as in Calderón. He wrote for his contemporaries, his fellow-countrymen and co-religionists, with no concern for either the outside world or posterity. He wrote as a Spaniard, a Catholic and a theologian. Without taking into account the intensity of religious feeling

---

[1] The plays referred to are indicated by the following abbreviations : *La Aurora en Copacavana* : A.C. (*IV*, 235) ; *Los Cabellos de Absalón* : C.A. (*II*, 421) ; *Las Cadenas del demonio* : C.D. (*III*, 531) ; *Los Dos Amantes del Cielo* : D.A.C. (*III*, 235) ; *La Devoción de la Cruz* : D.C. (*I*, 54) ; *La Exaltación de la Cruz* : E.C. (*II*, 355) ; *El Gran Príncipe de Fez* : G.P.F. (*II*, 329) ; *El José de las mujeres* : J.M. (*III*, 357) ; *Judás Macabeo* : J. Mc. (*I*, 311) ; *El Mágico prodigioso* : M.P. (*II*, 171) ; *El Príncipe constante* : P.C. (*I*, 245) ; *El Purgatorio de San Patricio* : P.S.P. (*I*, 149) ; *La Sibila del Oriente* : S.O. (*IV*, 199) ; *La Virgen del Sagrario* : V.S. (*I*, 329) ; *La Vida es sueño* : V. Sñ. (*I*, 1). In each case the four-volume Hartzenbusch text of the B.A.E. edition has been used, the figures in brackets indicating volume and page. In order to facilitate consultation, references in footnotes have been made as detailed as possible. Where a secular play is cited its title is given in full.

[2] *Man's Unconquerable Mind.* Studies of English writers. London, 1939.

pervading the " democracia frailuna " and its strong nation-
alist spirit it is almost impossible to understand and appre-
ciate their manifestation in the drama. The art of the
theatre is above all a popular one and to be a success a play
must conform to public taste. A writer may set out to
indoctrinate his public but he cannot court disaster by
running counter to the spirit of the age. Calderón was in
every way a man of his age and country, sharing their
beliefs, prejudices, sentiments and emotions. Even his
Catholicism assumes specifically Spanish tints. Though,
with his fervent desire to utilize the theatre for inculcating
the Divine tenets of his creed, he developed and extended the
religious elements in the drama, yet even he was not insen-
sible to public favour.

To any detailed study, then, of Calderón's religious drama
a necessary preliminary will be an examination of points of
historical, theological and biographical interest which will
illuminate the dramatic production.

(i) THE HISTORICAL BACKGROUND

The poet's life, extending from 1600 to 1681, spanned the
greater part of the reigns of three monarchs—Philip III,
Philip IV and Charles II—a period in which Spain was still
animated by the spirit of the Counter-reformation but
already on the path of decadence : a nation, in short, living
to a great extent on past glories. That few at the time were
aware of the process of decay and its possible causes is no
reflection on human nature.

As student, soldier, courtier, dramatist and priest, Calderón
participated to the full in the manifold activities of his age,

> tomando, ora la espada, ora la pluma.

His was not the life of the recluse in the ivory tower—not, at
any rate, until, in later years, his natural reflectiveness, com-
bined with personal disillusionment, led him to a more
retired existence. But even in those last thirty years of
meditation and quietude he must often have heard the busy
rumours of the world outside.

Just two years before his birth the old King whom his
father had served sank into the grave, leaving Spain exhausted
after her prolonged effort as paladin of the Faith. The
dream of centralization and unity of belief had been achieved,
but at great cost. Spain had erected an almost impene-
trable barrier against the assaults of heresy. Not content
with the defensive activities of the Inquisition, she had taken
the war into the enemy's camp and become the supreme
champion of orthodoxy abroad, the spear-head of the
Counter-reformation. Material values had been sacrificed
on the altar of the spiritual. To his successor Philip left a
country of idle looms and untilled fields whose population
was slowly being taxed out of existence. The new King,
well-meaning but feeble, did little to remedy matters.
Government passed into the hands of the Duque de Lerma,
whose chief concern was to keep the monarch in ignorance of
his subjects' plight. A continuous round of entertainment,
joust, poetic academy, private theatricals and hunting was
calculated to make Philip forget the remonstrances of an
impatient Cortes. Pragmatics against luxury in dress and
the shifting of the capital from Madrid to Valladolid (in
which the Calderón family was involved) were sorry remedies
for a condition that had become chronic. A pompous
Court establishment of exorbitant cost kept up the pretence
of Spain's former greatness but meanwhile her bullion gal-
leons were the prey of the Dutch and attempts to assist
Catholic co-religionists in England and Ireland proved
abortive. The very year in which Calderón came of age saw
the sudden end of Philip III, and the King's pent-up resent-
ment against a favourite who had schooled him in ignorance
found bitter expression on his deathbed.

The reign of Philip IV began auspiciously. A clean sweep
was made of all officials connected with the former *régime*.
The storm of royal indignation burst on Lerma and on his
followers, one of whom, Rodrigo Calderón, the dramatist
may have seen publicly beheaded in the Plaza Mayor of
Madrid. The new King's determination to rule and his
feverish concentration on State business caused a sensation.
Many saw in the change the dawning of a new era for

Spain.   But such high hopes were soon to be shattered.   A
new favourite, the Conde-Duque de Olivares, promptly
installed, did not scruple to pander to the baser tendencies of
a monarch whose private amours were a subject of public
scandal, and whose nocturnal journeys through the streets
of his capital evoked the heated but unavailing protest of the
highest dignitaries of the Church.   Before long Olivares
became an object of general hatred, the butt of the Court
satirists.   While the saturnine, Machiavellian minister
occupied himself in the mazes of political intrigue, the talen-
ted, pleasure-loving King took delight in the patronage of
arts and letters, making his Court a *rendez-vous* for poets,
dramatists and painters.   In externals, Philip was the perfect
monarch—a master of courtesy and ceremonial, an expert
shot, an intrepid rider and a skilled hunter.   Among the
galaxy of talent adorning the Court were a Góngora as
chaplain, a Guevara as chamberlain, a Quevedo as secretary,
a Solís as minister, a Calderón as Court dramatist and a
Velázquez to chronicle on canvas the lineaments of its great-
est notabilities.   Such was the brilliant world that gave little
thought to the misery and poverty without, and heard un-
heedingly the tragic reports of the Cortes.   On the occasion
of Charles Stuart's visit to the capital it could outdo even its
own   prodigality   and   brilliance.   Meanwhile   Olivares'
policies were meeting with short-lived success.   Spinola had
captured Breda in one of the most brilliant military exploits
of the age, an opportunity for Calderón to express the
rejoicing of all Spain.   Further success attended Spain at
sea, where the Dutch fleet was destroyed off Gibraltar.   The
great day of Spain's glory seemed at hand.   But disaster
was not far distant.   The country's internal poverty could not
fail to have its effect on a policy of external adventure.
Trade and industry continued to decline and the neglect of
manual labour was everywhere prevalent.   Calderón fre-
quently refers to the monopoly of trade in the capital by the
Frenchmen masquerading under the name of Burgundians
for fear of popular resentment.   Olivares' attempt to offset
the successful intrigues of Richelieu had no other effect than
to cause a French invasion.   Resistance had been weakened

by the failure to silence the complaints of the Cortes made in the previous year. The French expedition under Condé gave Portugal an opportunity to proclaim its independence, while a revolt in Catalonia led to a long and costly campaign in which Calderón took part. The loss of the Roussillon[1] and the occupation of parts of Catalonia itself by the French troops was the last straw. National resentment could hold out no longer. Philip, at last brought to a sense of realities, dismissed Olivares in 1643 and the favourite ended his days in insanity shortly after.

Unfortunately earlier mistakes had taught Philip nothing. Matters continued as before with the nomination of a new favourite, Luis de Haro. Spain's calamities were not over. The Battle of Rocroy shattered the European prestige of Spanish arms. Despite the elevation to supreme command of army and navy of the brilliant but wayward Juan de Austria, the war dragged on and the condition of the country continued its downward path. The administrative bureaucracy extended its hold, as did the accompanying corruption. With the attack by England on Spain's overseas possessions dismay ran through the country. A hasty truce was signed with France but the depredations of Cromwell's fleets continued. To crown all, the attempt to reassert the Spanish hegemony over Portugal ended in the calamitous rout of Montesclaros. In 1665 this news reached Madrid. For Philip it spelled the end. With Christian resignation the oddly-named "Tercer Santo" accepted the inevitable, but his spirit was broken. A reign of brilliant promise but small achievement had come to an end. Within a decade the monarch not only witnessed the national ruin but also the collapse of his most cherished personal hopes. We can visualize Calderón the priest offering a Mass for the repose of the soul of his royal master.

Philip's second wife, the young plain-looking Mariana of Austria, ruled as regent during the minority of her son Charles

---

[1] Then a Spanish province. Calderón in his typically anachronistic manner relates that Ludovico Enio's father

> llegó a Perpiñán, un pueblo
> de España · . . . . (P.S.P., I, ii).

II, a child of four. To her the Austrian connection was all-important and once again Spain was dragged at the wheels of the Imperial Juggernaut. A period of consolidating peace might even at this late hour have saved the country, but instead, with a third of the country's revenue pledged, further costly commitments were undertaken.

Contemporary travellers all agree in painting an unattractive picture of the capital at this date, emphasizing the strange blend of luxury and squalor in a city whose mud-lined streets were thronged with a motley crowd of prostitutes and where the outward shows of religion went hand in hand with the utmost licentiousness and the most stringent code of marital ethics. From such scenes Calderón would gladly escape to the quieter seclusion of the neighbouring Toledo, where presumably the religious atmosphere of Spain's ecclesiastical centre somewhat softened the asperities and contradictions of life in the capital.

> Señor, aqueste retiro
> en que me ves . . .
> es natural condición
> mía, que gusto no tengo
> en la común vanidad
> de los públicos cortejos[1].

Madrid continued to be rent by the opposing factions grouped round Don Juan de Austria and the new director of affairs, the German Jesuit Nithard. Only when matters came to open blows in the streets of Madrid was the Queen-Regent prevailed on to dismiss her adviser. This national disunity could have only one outcome : a peace with France on the onerous terms dictated by Louis XIV.

But the system of *validos* had by now become an indispensable part of Spanish administration and the fall of one favourite simply implied the installation of another. This time the happy man was a fascinating but unstable Andalusian, Fernando Valenzuela, who also conveniently filled the *rôle* of the Queen's lover. The day of the King's coming of

---

[1] D.A.C., I, iv (Crisanto).

age was at hand and meanwhile Don Juan bided his time.
Unsuccessful attempts were made to force the weak, epileptic
lad to sign decrees exiling the favourite. But the mother's
influence proved too strong. Don Juan was exiled to Aragon
and favouritism continued unchecked. When, in 1675, the
King's minority ended, he became a virtual prisoner within
his palace and two years later a Court revolt put Don Juan
in power. But he had little administrative capacity and the
high hopes entertained of him were doomed to frustration.
The pusillanimous, almost imbecile King remained a pawn
in the game of intrigue. Once more the fickle mob[1]
changed its allegiance to the Queen's party. The sudden
death of Don Juan facilitated her return to the capital. In
the same year her young son married a French princess, whose
extravagant and dissolute manners soon scandalized the rigid
etiquette of the Spanish Court. Henceforth the reign was to
be characterized by an even more intense struggle of opposing
factions, for the Queen-mother spared no effort to minimize
her daughter-in-law's influence over her childish but adoring
husband, whose days seem to have slipped by in an endless
round of insignificant amusements and petulant bouts
of rage.

Thus the closing years of Calderón's life were spent amidst
scenes of courtly corruption, intrigue and incompetence
unparalleled in the annals of Spain. Even the staunchest of
traditionalists must have been saddened at this tragic spec-
tacle of a once great dynasty, which had raised Spain to the
peak of her splendour and was now expiring in the person
of an almost insane monarch. For the dramatist advancing
age can have brought only disillusionment, which, while it
seldom expressed itself openly, must have accentuated that
natural melancholy which broods over the severe features of
the only authentic portrait we possess. The simple words
" Desengaños del palacio "[2] contain a wealth of meaning.

---

[1] Calderón's hearty contempt for the mob has ample justification in the
chronicles of his time.

[2] E.C., I, ii (Anastasio). The reason given for Anastasio's long absence
from the Persian court. The play dates from 1648.

(ii) THE PHILOSOPHICAL AND THEOLOGICAL BACKGROUND

A comprehensive history of Spanish thought still remains to be written. Indeed, a certain school of criticism has denied the very existence in the Peninsula of any autonomous philosophic discipline, alleging in support of its theory that " philosophy " soon degenerated into a mere branch of theology, with all the attendant disadvantages that such an association implies. The phrase " la misère philosophique en Espagne " was at one time considered truistic : Spain was accused of having contributed little or nothing to the general store of ideas in Europe and inhibiting all progress by imposing through religious intransigence certain sanctions against what is termed fruitful and vivifying thought. In the light of such a conception, the *auto de fe*, the Inquisition, the expulsion of Morisco and Jew were seen as the expressions of a spirit of bigotry and intolerance and most forms of Spanish religiosity seemed morbid and fanatical exteriorizations of an outworn and barren creed. Despite its lack of foundation, the argument long maintained its plausibility. Only with the advent of a more impartial and scientific scholarship have certain positions now been abandoned. None the less, belief in the poverty of Spanish thought lingers on.

Unfortunately lack of authoritative works makes refutation difficult. Bonilla's *Historia de la filosofía española* stops at the thirteenth century. Menéndez y Pelayo's *Ciencia española* and *Historia de los heterodoxos españoles*, despite their great bibliographical value, are but a fragmentary collection of monographs containing many observations of merit but deficient in method and incomplete : it is as a preliminary contribution to the work to be done that they remain indispensable. A more recent writer, the Benedictine Dr. Alois Mager, who also comments upon the scarcity of reliable data in this field, considers that scholarship has touched only the fringes of a vast *terra incognita*.[1] From the scattered material available can be traced no more than the bare outlines of an evolution. Menéndez y Pelayo himself maintained that sheer ignorance of Spanish philosophical and religious thought has

[1] In *Handbuch der Spanienkunde*, Frankfurt a.M., 1932, pp. 358-83.

impeded and falsified literary criticism : the clues to many problems, he believed, lay hidden in the unread volumes of theologian, casuist and philosopher.[1]

The long though chequered career of philosophy in Spain can be held to date from the time of Seneca, the Cordoban whom with justifiable pride Spaniards claim as their own.[2] With his stoical outlook on life which emphasized the transitoriness of earthly things, the instability of fate and the inevitability of death, while advocating withdrawal from the world and its vain pursuits, the acceptance of voluntary poverty and the embracing of philosophy as a rule for conduct, later Christianity found many points of contact. The Fathers quote this pagan philosopher with approval and recognize in him an *anima naturaliter christiana*, a precursor of Divine truths. The later fusion of Senecan precepts with the evangelical dogmas exercised a deep influence on Spanish thought and fostered the spirit of disillusionment that characterized so many thinkers and justified Maeztu's dictum :

> No hay en la lírica española pensamiento tan repetidamente expresado, ni con tanta belleza, como éste de la insustancialidad de la vida humana y de sus triunfos.[3]

The Senecan elements in Calderón are not an isolated phenomenon but the result of a long tradition of so-called " pessimistic " thought reaching down through the ages and attaining its maximum development in the sixteenth and seventeenth centuries both in religious and in secular writers. The contemporary preacher, adorning his sermons with thoughts culled from the *Epistolae Morales*, the moralist like Quevedo ("el nuevo Séneca," in the words of Lope de Vega), openly acknowledging his indebtedness to Stoic philosophy, the lessons taught by a satirist like Gracián, all bear witness to the strength of the Senecan influence. With eminent reason could Menéndez y Pelayo term Seneca one of the three great masters of the Iberian race.

---

[1] The brief outline which follows avoids all side issues and consciously risks the charge of over-simplification by its exclusive concentration upon points of direct contact with Calderonian drama. Only in this way could the subject be even glanced at in this short essay.

[2] Cf. V. Sñ, I, vi, where Basilio refers to " el Séneca español."

[3] *Defensa de la Hispanidad*, Madrid, 1937, p. 50.

Between the age of Seneca and the rise of Scholasticism philosophy in the Christian West remained in thrall to the Platonic tradition, from which it was released only by the rapid development of the Judaeo-Arabic school whose greatest figure was Averroes. Henceforth Aristotle, from being one among so many expert logicians and systematizers, takes his rightful place as the master of those who know. His works, now revealed in their fullest extent through the exhaustive commentary of Jew and Arab, within a short time oust the Platonic writings from favour. Meanwhile the only indigeneous contribution to philosophy is made by an opponent of the new tendencies, Ramon Lull. Scholasticism has by now entered the Peninsula and is joining issue with Aristotle's non-Christian interpreters. The Spanish participation in the *philosophia perennis*, however, was not to make itself felt for at least two centuries, and the early stages of Scholasticism within the Peninsula are entirely derivative. Indeed, although Spain, as the home of the Dominican order, might have been expected to extend an enthusiastic welcome to the *Summa* of St. Thomas Aquinas, she did not in fact do so. During the first years of Scholasticism the basis of ecclesiastical learning was the *Libri quatuor Sententiarum* of Peter Lombard, the great Italian schoolman and pupil of Abelard. His manual, collated from the Scriptures and the works of the early Fathers, formed an encyclopædia of the whole system of Catholic ethics and theology and occasioned innumerable commentaries throughout Europe. Not till the middle of the fifteenth century can its hold be said to have relaxed, with the introduction of St. Thomas' main work into the schools. The real revival of Thomism dates from the first full-length commentary of the Italian Dominican, Giacomo Cajetan (1469-1534).

Within Spain that renaissance received its first impetus from the work of Francisco Vitoria, the great Thomist expositor at the University of Salamanca, during these years steadily increasing in prestige, and already rivalling the University of Paris, which till then had reigned supreme in the European world of learning. The advance of Salamanca and the propagation of Thomism go hand in hand, for the

University was early authorized by Papal decree to devote all its efforts to the study and commentary of the *Summa*. From Vitoria onwards the Spanish province of the Dominican Order yielded to no other in the zeal with which it published volume after volume illuminating and explaining the works of its own " Angelic Doctor," a task in which it was ably seconded by the rising but already powerful Society of Jesus. The Spanish Thomist-trained theologians who exercised such a preponderating influence in the deliberations of the Council of Trent, and whose aim it was, by securing a complete definition of dogma and the necessary internal reforms within the Church, to present a united front against the growing strength of the Reformist doctrines, must have been gratified to see lying side by side on the council table the complementary sources of authority, the Holy Scriptures, the Papal encyclicals and the *Summa*.

In addition to the purely theological work produced by the Orders during the sixteenth century and onwards there existed a corresponding activity in the field of exegetical, patristic and hagiographical literature. The innumerable " summæ " and " loci theologici " can be paralleled by the wealth of Biblical commentaries—in particular, by treatises on the Psalms, Job and Ecclesiastes, and collections of the lives of the Saints. Among the most noted of the Biblical scholars, Ribera at Salamanca, Prado at Córdoba and Pineda at Seville deserve mention. Exegetical scholarship of the day, however, was not of the modern scientific kind but followed the allegorical interpretation of the Scriptures as exemplified by St. Augustine.

Among the names of the chief Dominican theologians must be numbered those of Cano, de Soto, Báñez, Ledesma, de Lemos and Álvarez, while the best-known Jesuits include Azor, Vásquez, Ripalda—one of the earliest teachers at the " Colegio Imperial "—Francisco Suárez—the Society's greatest authority—and Luis de Molina, whose attempt to reconcile the Thomist doctrine of Free Will with the Augustinian views on Grace gave rise to the great theological controversy of the age.

Molina expounded the *Summa* for almost twenty years at

the University of Coimbra and his famous *Concordia liberi arbitri cum gratiæ donis* (Lisbon, 1588) became a bone of scholastic contention. It was violently attacked, not only by the Dominicans Báñez and de Lemos, but also by members of his own Order, and he published a defence of his syncretic theories in a revised edition of the *Concordia* (1589). Soon all Spain was ranged in opposing camps ; the book was denounced to the Inquisition ; and, in 1594, the Holy See, alarmed at the sudden threat to the unity so recently and so hardly achieved, intervened by forbidding further dispute till the case had been arbitrated in Rome. Not until 1598, however, was a " Congregatio de Auxiliis " set up, which proceeded with such embarrassing slowness that the final exoneration of Molina by Paul V took place only seven years after the great Jesuit's death, in 1607. The decision, none the less, disposed, once and for all, of the current notion that there existed an unbridgeable gulf between the Molinist and Augustinian positions and that the *Concordia* was in effect a covert attack upon the " Doctor of Grace." The repercussions of the controversy were clearly felt in the realm of literature : Tirso de Molina did not shrink from dramatizing one of its essential elements, the doctrine of predestination.[1]

The acute dissension, which had been maintained for well over a decade, in no way hindered the triumphal progress of Thomism ; by the end of the sixteenth century the Lombardian "Book of Sentences" had everywhere been replaced by the *Summa*, St. Thomas reigned supreme within Spain's universities and Salamanca reached the peak of its fame as the greatest centre of learning in Europe.

One of the earliest pictures of the young Murillo, commissioned for a Sevilian convent, depicts a monk troubled by theological doubt. To him in a vision appear the patroness of the convent, St. Francis of Assisi and St. Thomas Aquinas. St. Francis addresses the monk in these words :

> Crede huic, quia ejus doctrina
> non deficiet in aeternum.

---

[1] Calderón's " Aprobación " to the fifth part of Tirso's plays states that in them "no hallo cosa que disuene de nuestra santa fe . . .", a not unexpected tribute from the dramatist of the Divine Mercy.

The monk opens his copy of the *Summa* and all his difficulties are solved.

(iii) THE INTELLECTUAL FORMATION OF CALDERÓN.

Pedro Calderón de la Barca, born on January 17, 1600, was the fourth son of a comfortably-off middle-class family, whose head held a minor post in the Civil Service. Of the daughters, two early entered the religious life, while a maternal relative, Francisco Henao, was a member of the Society of Jesus, a fact which may have had some influence on the boy's later education.

Soon after his birth, the Court—and with it the Calderón family—was transferred to Valladolid, in which city Pedro learned his first letters. When the return to Madrid was made, the boy was sent to the Colegio Imperial, founded some years previously and under Jesuit direction. Among his teachers may have been a Father Ribadeneyra, whose works Calderón was to use for his plays.[1] During his five years at the Colegio, he obtained the grounding in Latin so necessary when University instruction was given in that tongue. There, too, were sown the seeds of his interest in Latin literature, more especially in Ovid.[2] It is doubtful whether he

---

[1] *E.g.*, Ribadeneyra's Life of St. Ignatius (G.P.F.) and his account of the martyr saints Crisanthus and Daria (D.A.C.). His *Historia Eclesiástica del Cisma del Reino de Inglaterra* (1588) provided material for Calderón's play on the same theme. Among other works of his are a translation of St. Augustine's *Confessions*, a Manual of Augustinian meditations and the better known *Tratado de la tribulación* (1589), in which he bitterly attacks the contemporary theatres as " patios de torpezas y pública profesión de maldades."

[2] D.A.C., I, viii (Cintia) :
>Quiero reclinarme aquí,
>donde en Ovidio, mejor,
>lêré el *Remedio de Amor*.

Cf. the secular play *No hay burlas con el amor* (I, vi), where the *précieuse* Beatriz says :
>Tray
>de mi biblioteca a Ovidio :
>no el *Metamorfosis*, no,
>ni el *Arte Amandi* pedí ;
>el *Remedio Amoris*, sí,
>que es el que investigo yo.

passed beyond the first stages in Greek, though a tractate of St. John Chrysostom was used as a college text. The Jesuits, the ablest Latinists of their time, saw to it that no pupil left them without a mastery of the language which gave access to most contemporary learning, especially in theology. Calderón's acquaintance with other languages is uncertain.[1]

In 1615, while he was an undergraduate at the University of Alcalá de Henares, the sudden death of his father and a subsequent costly lawsuit altered the family circumstances. Entrusted to the guardianship of an uncle, he was transferred to the more famous University of Salamanca.[2] Here he entered the Faculty of Civil Law and his plays reveal an

---

[1] Following a contemporary fashion, Calderón indulges in frequent etymologies, but no valid deductions can be made from such examples. Cf. S.O., I, iii (Salomón) :

Es mi nombre *Salomón*,
que es lo mismo que decir *Pacífico*.

However, in C.A., II, iv, David tells Solomon :

Que si amado de Dios, sois el querido,
conforme significa vuestro nombre . . . .

S.O., II, v (Salomón) :

Porque dice en hebreo
Moria, especulación.

C.D., I, v (Licanoro) :

El Génesis
se dice, voz que en hebreo
Creación quiere decir.

V.S., I, vi (Ildefonso) :

Toletot
quiere decir en hebreo
funadación de muchos.

A.C., III, i (Marañón) :

Faubro . . . . que significa
mes santo.

G.P.F., II, i. The Prince of Fez earns the Christian Balthasar's admiration because :

entre otras muy buenas prendas
que en él he reconocido,
una es saber varias lenguas,
fuera de que la toscana,
por lo mucho que comercian
con judíos de Liorna,
hay pocos que no la entiendan.

N.B.—The italics above are those printed in the Hartzenbusch text.

[2] Cf. E. Cotarelo y Mori : *Ensayo sobre la vida y obras de D. Pedro Calderón de la Barca* (Parte primera), Madrid, 1924, pp. 79–81.

excellent knowledge of current legislation and legal practice.[1] Their weakness, by comparison, in historical and geographical accuracy cannot be taken as proof of imperfect knowledge, for contemporary notions of exactness in these matters by no means tallied with modern views and in any case anachronisms were accepted as an integral part of dramatic technique.[2]   That Biblical figures appear in cambric and brocade,[3] fire muskets[4] and discourse learnedly on conceptions of honour,[5] or that characters of the second century allude to specifically Spanish religious practices[6] should cause no surprise.   Calderón himself was perfectly conscious of these lapses and on occasion did not hesitate to satirize the device :

> Señor crítico, chitón ;
> que nadie quita que en Grecia
> haya Vegas y Retiros.[7]

The dramatist's interest in astrology and certain occult practices must have received its initial impulse within the *aulas* of the University.[8]   Any philosophical training he might have been given would be entirely scholastic, as his former masters, the Jesuits, who maintained a flourishing ecclesiastical establishment alongside the official instruction, were, with the Dominicans, the chief expositors of St. Thomas Aquinas' *Summa*, the main text of the schools, commentaries

---

[1] Cf. H. Rojas de la Vega : *Juicio crítico de las obras de Calderón de la Barca, bajo el punto de vista jurídico*, etc., Valladolid, 1883.

[2] Cf. Cotarelo y Mori : *Op. cit.*, pp. 84–5.

[3] Cf. C.A., II, iii (Adonías) : " la holanda y el brocado."

[4] J.Mc., III, xiii (Jonatás).   [5] Cf. both the above plays, *passim*.

[6] M.P., I, i (Clarín) :
> no hay cosa más cansada
> que un día de procesión
> entre cofrades y danzas.

Cipriano enters dressed as a student and his servants as " gorrones."

[7] *Auristela y Lisidante*, II, xiv (Merlín).   The best known example in the religious plays occurs in D.A.C. (III, ii), where the *gracioso*, Escarpín, about to begin a story concerning a monk, stops short, exclaiming :
> Mas no es bueno ;
> porque aun no hay en Roma frailes.

[8] Cf. Cotarelo y Mori : *Op. cit.*, pp. 83–4.

on which abounded. The Thomist rationalism with its formal dialectical method and its use of "quaestiones disputatæ" as technique left a deep impression on the young student. The theological arguments of the religious plays are all conducted according to the syllogistic tradition of the schools and their phraseology is studded with the technical language of scholasticism.[1] Though civil law was Calderón's main concern, his intellectual development was essentially scholastic and theological. There may still be disputes as to the relative importance of the various influences undergone by him : Jesuit, through the neo-scholasticism of Suárez, or Augustinian, through later contacts with Neoplatonic Augustinian groups such as the Madrid society of secular priests known as the Congregación de San Pedro. As the Jesuit Baumgartner has pointed out, the scholastic training which he received in his early years was of paramount importance :

> El que quiera comprender y apreciar a Calderón ha de considerar que la filosofía y la teología escolásticas son el fundamento científico de su poesía ; y que, lejos de haber contenido su vuelo sublime, lo han favorecido sobremanera. En la escolástica fué precisamente donde Calderón adquirió aquella penetración intelectual tan clara y perspicaz que admiraba al mismo Goethe ; y de los tesoros de la escolástica sacó aquella riqueza inagotable de conceptos, alegorías y comparaciones ingeniosas y profundas que nos llenan de asombro y maravilla cuando repasamos sus *Autos*.[2]

Calderón never deviated from the religious paths marked out for him in his youth, though the knowledge which he acquired when young must have been enriched and deepened by a life of theological reading and study. Words which he gives to one of his characters are true of himself :

---

[1] *E.g.*, concedo la mayor ; la menor concedo ; evidencia es ; acepto la cuestión ; tomar la réplica ; la conclusión ; los principios ; por entrambas partes corre el silogismo ; tomar la contraria ; niego la mayor.

[2] A. Baumgartner, S.J. : *Calderón, poemita dramático*, etc., Madrid, 1882, *cit*. Cotarelo y Mori, *op. cit.*, p. 88.

> Crecí en fin, más inclinado
> que a las armas a las ciencias,
> y sobre todas me di
> al estudio de las letras
> divinas, y a la lección
> de los santos, cuya escuela,
> celo, piedad, religión
> fe y caridad nos enseña.[1]

Yet the period of preparation moulded the mind of the maturer man. He learned the invaluable truth :

> Discreto amigo es un libro.[2]

There is, it is true, an early stage of indecision, during which the young graduate, having, for reasons unknown, temporarily abandoned the prospect of a career within the Church, may have dreamed of purely secular triumphs and given free rein to the inclination of youth.

> ¿ No es mejor lograr primero
> los aplausos en la edad
> florida, y pasando el tiempo,
> en la decrépita y triste
> la soledad ?[3]

But that indecision was short ; for, ever present in him, partly by character and partly by training, was the latent priest. An incipient enthusiasm for the glories of the military life which was later to find expression in a famous passage of *Para vencer amor querer vencerle* (1650) soon gave way to disillusionment as far as he himself was concerned.

---

[1] P.S.P., I, ii (Patricio).   So Carlos, in *De una causa dos efectos* (I, i), spends

> todo el día
> encerrado con Platón
> y Aristóteles (que son
> luz de la filosofía) .   .   .   .

and Luis says of his friend Juan in *El Pintor de su deshonra* (I, i) :

> .   .   .   .   en libros suspendido
> gastabais noches y días.

The motif of the studious searcher after truth occurs frequently in both comedia and *auto*.

[2] ¿ *Cuál es mayor perfección* ?, II, ii (Beatriz).   [3] D.A.C., I, iv (Polemio).

¡ Ah cielos ! ¡ cuánto miente, cuánto engaña,
vista desde la corte la campaña,
al que nunca ha sabido
cuán pavoroso ha sido,
cuán terrible, cuán fuerte,
este cruel teatro de la muerte ! [1]

It is no surprise, therefore, to find that, once the first flush of
youth and vitality had passed, his task of composing the
autos set his thoughts once again on the early vocation.   It
can only be conjectured whether personal grief over the loss
of one brother and the insanity of another, together with a
breakdown in health due to the Catalan campaign in which
he had participated, may have been contributory factors to
the decision, arrived at when fifty years of age, to serve God
at the altar as well as in the theatre.   His gratitude to his
former masters can be deduced from a warm tribute which
he pays to the Society of Jesus :

. . . (d)esta suprema
religión (que siendo sola
una compañía, más guerra
hace al infierno que muchos
ejércitos) . . . . [2]

and the affection with which he so frequently recalls his
student days :

Bien os acordáis de aquellas
felicísimas edades
nuestras, cuando los dos fuimos
en Salamanca estudiantes,

says the young Félix to his companion in *Casa con dos puertas
mala es de guardar* (I, iv). With this reminiscence may be
compared a passage from *También hay duelo en las damas*
(II, iii), where Juan says to his friend Félix :

---

[1] E.C., II, x (Menardes). It is interesting to note that, even when praising
the military life, Calderón does not forget the claims of religion :
. . . . nunca es buen soldado,
quien buen cristiano no es.   (G.P.F., I, xii : Baltasar).

[2] G.P.F., III, xi (El Mal Genio).

> . . . . desde el tiempo
> que en Salamanca estudiando,
> amigos tan verdaderos
> fuimos, que con sola un alma
> animaban ambos cuerpos,
> y que la escuela dejamos
> por dos caminos diversos,
> vos de cortesano y yo de soldado . . . .

II

THE RELIGIOUS CONTENT OF THE PLAYS

(i) CALDERÓN'S CONCEPTION OF LIFE

When a thoughtful and deeply religious writer, with a sound theological training, has been brought up in an age, and writes for a public, whose interest in religion is paramount, certain bonds of sympathy may be presupposed between the dramatist and his audiences. Accepting the dramatist's creed, not only as a theoretical statement of belief but as a reality ever-present in their daily lives, the audiences were fully prepared to see its dogmas brought to life upon the stage. No other element in the national life, indeed, could have created such currents of sympathy between playwright and spectator. Deeply imbued with the Christian conception of life as a brief, fleeting interval separating man from his Maker, and of death, " la postrera línea fatal,"[1] as the true beginning of life, Calderón's audiences felt and suffered with his heroes and heroines as intimately as spectators have ever done. Just as, for the Greek, drama was a part of religion, so in seventeenth-century Spain religion, for a few brief hours, would come to life within the narrow limits of the *corrales*. The theatre being once again, as in mediæval days, the handmaiden of religion, the Catholic dramatist *par excellence* found it a unique medium for stressing the value of the great truths which he deemed essential to man's salvation.

[1] P.S.P., I, ii (Patricio). In the same play (II, vi) Ludovico **Enio** speaks of death as the " última línea de todos." Cf. D.C., III, xii, where Eusebio says :

> Ya llega el golpe más fuerte,
> ya llega el trance más cierto.

Whether or no Calderón's religious knowledge was, as I believe, only that of a well-educated man of his time, and not the specialist's intimate familiarity with its intricate problems is immaterial to a consideration of his main tenets. The simple catechism is often as faithful a guide to his thought as the most ponderous tome of ecclesiastical commentary.

Man, being placed in this " valle hondo, oscuro " only for a short time, must have ever present the thought of eternity with its possibility of salvation or damnation. Thus the whole religious drama becomes a gloss on St. Thomas' "Vita aeterna est ultimus finis humanæ vitæ." [1] Calderón's doctrine of life is " negative " in the sense that it advocates the *contemptus sæculi*, emphasizes the transitoriness of earthly things and depicts the world of sense as the realm of illusion. While St. Bartholomew refuses royal offers of worldly honours because he knows that

> es toda esa
> majestad y ostentación
> vanidad de vanidades,
> siendo la vida una flor,
> que con el sol amanece
> y fallece con el sol, [2]

the Roman Emperor Heraclius returning in triumph to the temple of Jerusalem with the true Cross is warned by the high-priest, Zacharias, to lay aside the imperial cloak and crown,

> los arreos
> de la vanidad humana. [3]

---

[1] *Summa*, P. 1-2, Q. 109, A. 5.

[2] C.D., III, ii. Cf. M.P., III, xiii, where the Skeleton says :
> Así, Cipriano, son
> todas las glorias del mundo.

Cf. V. Sñ., III, x (Segismundo) :
> . . . . ha de verse
> desvanecida entre sombras
> la grandeza y el poder,
> la majestad y la pompa . . .

[3] E.C., III, xxii.

It is this realization of the illusory nature of human pomps and glories that causes the disillusioned Segismundo to exclaim :

> ¿ Qué es la vida ? Un frenesí.
> ¿ Qué es la vida ? Una ilusión.
> Una sombra, una ficción
> y el mayor bien es pequeño :
> que toda la vida es sueño,
> y los sueños, sueños son.[1]

For Calderón, then, his characters are simply pilgrims on the road to eternity. All would agree with Segismundo when he pleads :

> Acudamos a lo eterno,
> que es la fama vividora
> donde ni duermen las dichas
> ni las grandezas reposan,[2]

because, like Cipriano, they are aware

> que sin el gran Dios que busco,
> que adoro y que reverencio,
> las humanas glorias son
> polvo, humo, ceniza y viento.[3]

Man cannot fail to arrive at such a conclusion when he realizes that birth for him merely signifies the entrance into an existence which is subject to the vagaries of fate and limited by the inevitability of death—

> nace el hombre
> sujeto a fortuna y muerte—[4]

and that for many each day brings its portion of tears and sorrow :

> Un día llama a otro día,
> y así llama y encadena
> llanto a llanto, pena a pena.[5]

Only a Job-like resignation, fortified by the knowledge of compensation in a future state, can help man to endure with patience the " slings and arrows of outrageous fortune " :

---

[1] V.Sñ., II, xix. Cf. P.S.P., III, vi (Polonia) :
> Siendo (¡ a quién no le asombra !)
> la vida breve una caduca sombra.

[2] V.Sñ., III, x. Cf. *ibid.* :
> ¿ Quién por vanagloria humana
> pierde una divina gloria ?

[3] M.P., III, xxi.

[4] P.C., II, xiv (Fernando).   [5] P.C., II, iv (Fernando).

> a la desdicha más fuerte
> sabe vencer la prudencia.
> Sufrid con ella el rigor
> del tiempo y de la fortuna.[1]

Life itself is but a trial, a time of suffering and temptation[2] for our " humano polvo "[3] and man's lot one of tribulation and unrest in this " golfo de los males."[4]   Such a condition calls for a Christian stoicism which bows before the will of God and accepts His decrees.   The true Christian will cause the non-believer to marvel at the calmness and faith with which he bears the heaviest yoke.

> ¿ Cómo con tanta paciencia
> llevas los trabajos ?

asks the magician Anastasio of the sorely-tried High Priest. The answer is exemplary :

> Como
> de mano de Dios los tomo
> por regalos.[5]

Nothing else will suffice.   The alternative to resignation, a concentration on worldly interests, must lead to discontent and vain endeavour :

> ¡ Oh ingrata y descontenta
> condición que tenemos
> los humanos, haciendo siempre extremos ![6]

[1] P.C., II, iii (Fernando).   Cf. J.Mc., I, i (Jonatás) :
> ¡ Oh venganzas de fortuna !
> ¡ Mil veces felice el hombre
> que ni teme tus amagos
> ni se sujeta a tus golpes !

[2] Cf. St. Augustine's *Confessions* (X, 28) : " Numquid non tentatio est vita humana super terram " and Seneca's " Tota flebilis vita est " and " Omnis vita supplicium est."   The " Militia est vita hominis super terram " of Job (vii, i) is a favourite text of the age, paraphrased and quoted by Gracián, Quevedo and Calderón himself in the *autos* (*E.g., Lo que va del hombre a Dios*). Ludovico Enio (P.S.P., I, ii) speaks of " la tormenta del mundo " and Fernando (P.C., III, viii) of " este confuso abismo."

[3] C.A., I, ii (David).   Cf. A.C., III, ii (Yupanguí) " . . . barro . . . . masa quebradiza del primer Adán."

[4] J.M., II, x (Eugenia).   Cf. E.C., II, xix (Anastasio) :
> . . . . el penoso
> golfo de calamidades,
> que en una y otra avenida
> son escollos de la vida . . . .

[5] E.C., II, xix (Zacarías).   Cf. " el divino príncipe mártir " (P.C., III, vi), thanking God for the sufferings imposed on him :
> ¡ Oh inmenso, oh dulce Señor,
> qué de gracias debo darte !

[6] C.A., I, i (David).

Can it be wondered at, then, that man, aware of his own nothingness, of the instability of human values and of the adversities laid up for him by fate, should display a sadness which is his from birth—

> una grave tristeza,
> pensión que trae la naturaleza—[1]

a sadness tinged by the melancholy certitude that every day of his existence is a relentless progress towards the grave.

> Pisando la tierra dura
> de continuo el hombre está,
> y cada paso que da
> es sobre su sepultura. [2]

Time, in varied metaphor, fills the *rôle* of a bird ever speeding by on swift wing, whose shadow nothing can escape, or of a conqueror whose attacks nothing can resist :

> a lo fácil del tiempo
> no hay conquista difícil. [3]

In a sense the gentle melancholy that invades the mind of man is understandable when he ponders the inevitability with which he is drawing nearer to old age, the very outpost of death, [4] and ultimately to the end which awaits all :

[1] C.A., I, i (Aquítofel). In the second scene of the same act David refers to
> la natural pensión
> deste nuestro humano polvo.

It will be seen that Calderón did not always follow consistently the distinction he draws in C.A. (I, vi : Amón) :
> Melancolía y tristeza
> los físicos dividieron,
> en que la tristeza es
> causada de un mal suceso ;
> pero la melancolía
> de natural sentimiento . . . .

[2] P.C., III, viii (Fernando). A commonplace of the Stoic philosophy.

[3] P.C., I, i (the song of the captive Christians). On occasion, however, Time can serve to assuage human grief : C.A., III, vi (David) :
> El tiempo que con la sorda
> lima de las horas llega
> a gastar nuestros afectos
> sin que su ruido se sienta,
> mi sentimiento ha gastado.

[4] J.Mc., I, vi (Chato) :
> La vejez . . . este mal
> que es la posta de la muerte.

> si para una jornada
> salió el hombre de la tierra
> al fin de varios caminos
> es para volver a ella. [1]

Even the very hours of repose which nature exacts for the refreshment of body and mind recall that sleep which is death :

> . . . el sueño . . . ¡ oh imagen de la muerte ! [2]

Yet for the believer all the terrors of death have been dispersed by faith : only for the wicked, to whom it comes not as gentle release but as stern retribution, does it retain its tragedy. Yet if man is at times tempted to exclaim bitterly with the imprisoned Segismundo (later to become for Calderón the symbol of erring human nature burdened with the chains of original sin) :

> el delito mayor
> del hombre es haber nacido. [3]

there is always an inducement to endure afflictions patiently in the expectation of a life to come in which toil will have ceased and peace be attained.

> la verdad
> sigue, que hay eternidad. [4]

[1] P.C., II, vii (Fernando).   Cf. *op. cit.*, III, vii (Fernando) :
> Bien sé que al fin soy mortal
> y que no hay hora segura.

[2] G.P.F., I, ii (El Príncipe).   Cf. S.O., III, vi (Sabá) :
> el sueño
> . . . . es pálida imagen de la muerte.

V. Sñ., II, xix (Segismundo) :
> el sueño de la muerte.

[3] V.Sñ., I, ii.   A comparison of the *auto* and the *comedia* which are both entitled *La Vida es sueño* will afford a striking example of the skill with which Calderón has deepened an idea already once developed, by endowing the incidents of his original treatment with a richer, symbolical meaning. Segismundo becomes the symbol of mankind, created in God's image and born to rule the earth, but destined to fall through pride to the snares of the tempter and have his former glory dimmed by the shadow of sin.   He then returns to his prison only to be redeemed by grace through the sacrifice of God-made-Man on the Cross.

In general, it may be said that the *comedias religiosas*, while composed of the same religious elements as the *autos*, lack their coherence and consistency.   It would seem that the shorter dramatic form was more congenial to Calderón's concise, architectonic genius.

[4] P.C., III, viii.

Thus, in this " gran teatro del mundo,[1] and in the presence of the great Author of the dramas, the frail human creature has to act his brief *rôle* and his future destiny will depend upon the manner in which he plays his part.   There can be no second chance.   A few short years decide the outcome—Heaven or hell.   To enable him to perform his task, man—a tiny world, to quote a favourite figure of Calderón's, launched into the greater macrocosm [2]—has been endowed with certain faculties and senses [3] :   Divine gifts, which, however, he must use warily, for in themselves they are but little.   The faculties can mislead and the senses delude.   Without help from above, man is only a puny weakling surrounded by powerful enemies, though that help will be forthcoming if he proves worthy of it.   All mankind suffers from the taint of original sin, which dims the faculties and throws the senses into bondage.   Thus man's greatest gift, the understanding, is a treacherous friend which easily leads astray, and which, even if controlled, can avail in the search for truth but little.   Human knowledge alone cannot hope to fathom God's mysteries :

> no es bien que se atrevan los humanos
> a secretos del cielo soberanos. [4]

Study without faith is useless :

> Que acá mientras más se estudia
> más se ignora. [5]

[1] Cf. V.S., II, x (Godmán) "al gran teatro del mundo " ; and V.Sñ., II, xviii (Segismundo) :

> La anchurosa plaza
> del gran teatro del mundo.

This is a Senecan concept which finds fullest expression in the secular play *Saber del mal y del bien* and the *auto*.

[2] J.M., I, xvii (El Demonio) :

> La circunferencia breve
> de aqueste mundo pequeño . . . .

Cf. V.S., II, vi (Luna) :

> Pues si el cuerpo es breve mundo,
> el alma es pequeño cielo.

V.Sñ., II, vii (Segismundo) :

> Era el hombre . . . . un mundo breve.

[3] C.D., I, ii (Irene) :

> Un alma con sus potencias
> y sus sentidos . . . .

[4] P.S.P., II, xix (Polonia).   [5] M.P., I, iii (Cipriano).

and wisdom, if salvation is lost, a mockery :

> Nada sabré, si yo no sé salvarme.[1]

Nor is a scrutiny of the world of sense more satisfactory. For in the Thomist sense of the word it is only the realm of the " accidental," and the instruments at man's disposal for perceiving its values are unsound :

> ¿ Eres sombra del deseo
> o del pensamiento sombra ?
> ¿ Qué quieres, forma fingida,
> de la idea repetida,
> sólo a la vista aparente ?
> ¿ Eres, para pena mía,
> voz de la imaginación ?
> ¿ Retrato de la ilusión ?
> ¿ Cuerpo de la fantasía ?

asks Julia, on seeing the sacrilegious intruder, Eusebio.[2]

---

[1] S.O., III, iv (Salomón).   The same character (loc. cit.) remarks :

> . . . . el mayor agravio
> de la ciencia es errar el hombre sabio.

[2] D.C., II, xi.   Cf. C.D., I, iii (Irene) :

> Aunque tengo
> en mal formadas especies
> retratados mil objetos
> que me llevan la atención . . . .

and I, xi (Irene) :

> Prodigio, ilusión y asombro,
> que ha bosquejado la idea
> de algún informe concepto
> de soñadas apariencias . . . .

Cf. V.Sñ., III, x (Segismundo) :

> Que hay cuestión sobre saber
> si lo que se ve y se goza
> es mentira o es verdad.

The whole of this play and also *Saber del mal y del bien* (*e.g.*, III, vi : Álvaro :

> . . . . tal vez los ojos nuestros
> se engañan, y representan
> tan diferentes objetos
> de los que miran, que dejan
> burlada el alma)

show how deeply Calderón was preoccupied by the philosophic problem of sense-perception.   The religious plays have only passing unimportant references. Cf., however, Ricardo's comment in D.C. (II, x), when Eusebio, about to make his sacrilegious entry into the convent, " sees " " un vivo fuego " threatening him :

> Alguna fantasía
> de su mismo horror fundada,
> en la idea acreditada,
> o alguna ilusión sería.

Julia, in the same play (II, xiv), finds that

> turbada la fantasía,
> en el aire forma cuerpos.

Man has no assurance that he is not living in a world of shadows. Reality must be sought elsewhere, but its truths can only come through faith, through a confession of ignorance, and the acceptance of Christ.

> A Cristo ha de confesar
> la ciega ignorancia mía
> por suma sabiduría.[1]

God alone embodies the sum of human knowledge and constitutes the fount of all arts and sciences. In Him alone can true peace be found. Man must subordinate all human activities to his chief end, and must recognize the primacy of the supernatural :

> no hay humana
> acción en que la divina
> más absoluta no manda.[2]

As ever with Calderón, the only remedy for human ills comes from above :

> Sospecho
> que la mejor medecina
> para el alma es la divina.[3]

Meanwhile, during the period of his exile, man has the consolations of a religion whose characteristics are the gentleness of its precepts and the rationality of its dogmas. The convert, asked :

> ¿ Cómo, prodigio divino,
> te va en nuestra religión ?

does not hesitate for an answer :

> Suaves sus preceptos son ;
> bien muestran que su ley vino
> de mano de Dios escrita.
> Cosa en ella no se lê
> que puesta en razón no esté.[4]

[1] E.C., III, xix (Anastasio). The same character exclaims (III, xx) :

> . . . . sabiendo
> que no sé nada, que vos
> lo sabéis todo.

[2] G.P.F., I, xiv (El Príncipe).

[3] D.C., III, xii (Eusebio).

[4] J.M., II, xi (Eugenia). Cf. A.C., III, viii (Andrés, the former Inca priest) :

> . . . . viendo las excelencias
> de ley tan en natural
> razón que para creerla,
> sin sus milagros, bastara
> la suavidad de sí mesma.

Faith will drive away all difficulties and bestow true contentment :

> La fe en todas cosas fué
> la que más facilitó
> la dificultad.[1]

But ere man arrives at that knowledge he may have to go through a period of aridity—days of fierce temptation and tormenting thought—for in him has been planted the seed of curiosity, the desire for truth :

> Este anhelo de saber
> que es el que al hombre le ilustra
> más que otro alguno.[2]

During those dark hours he is counselled to seek truth in the quiet solitudes of Nature. Here the wonder-working magician can consult his beloved books in peace, scrutinizing their mysterious texts with ever-increasing perplexity,[3] unaware that, once his doubts have been stilled, he will return to these silent retreats to contemplate the majestic creation of his Maker. For the contemplative mind, having arrived at truth, will discover in solitude philosophy, not only human

> —en la soledad se halló
> la humana filosofía—[4]

but Divine, and a sure refuge from life's disillusionments.

> Vengo a buscar seguros desengaños
> en estas soledades,
> donde viven desnudas las verdades.[5]

Those are the words of one who has abandoned the pomp of an episcopal palace and the vanities of human learning.

---

[1] D.A.C., II, xv (Carpoforo).

[2] This phrase, though not occurring in the religious dramas but in *La Estatua de Prometeo* (I, ii : Prometeo), aptly expresses the motive of the truth-seeking Calderonian protagonists.

[3] The device is constantly repeated and may well be a reminiscence of Acts viii, 27 ff., where an Ethiopian eunuch is perplexed by a passage in Isaiah and eventually converted by St. Philip.

[4] P.S.P., I, viii (Patricio). Cf. M.P., I, vii (Lisandro) :

> Dando a la imaginación
> la jurisdicción que tiene,
> con las soledades hice
> mil discursos diferentes.

[5] D.C., II, ii (Alberto).

(ii) GOD : THE BLESSED VIRGIN

God, the Cause of causes and the Science of sciences,[1] the
Supreme Being in Whom is neither beginning nor end,[2]
Who created man in His own image out of nothing—the
Biblical " emptiness " which Calderón was so fond of com-
paring with the Ovidian " chaos,"

> un Dios . . .
> poderoso, sabio, inmenso, ...
> Criador del cielo y la tierra.[3]

has foreseen all things, including the fate of man when he is
left without aid :

> la suma omnipotencia
> antevió todas las cosas
> desde que su misma esencia
> sacó esa fábrica a la luz
> del ejemplar de su idea.[4]

[1] J.M., II, i (Eugenia) :
> Discurriendo más atenta
> en la causa de las causas
> que la filosofía enseña.

C.D., I, iii, where the Devil refers to Licanoro as :
> Apurando y discurriendo
> quién es causa de las causas.

The last *auto* Calderón wrote, *La Divina Filotea* (1681), gives the same definition
of God.

E.C., I, vi (Anastasio) :
> Busquemos los dos . . . .
> esta ciencia de las ciencias,
> que tengo de hallar, si puedo,
> quién es causa de las causas . . . .

In the same play (II, iii), Zacarías, giving the reason why God is the " Science
of sciences," states that all learning is centred in Him.

[2] D.A.C., I, ii (El Espíritu bueno) : " Principio y fin *ab aeterno*." C.D.,
II, iv (Licanoro) : " Dios sin fin y sin principio."

[3] C.D., I, v (Licanoro).

[4] P.S.P., II, xiv (Patricio). The quotation refers to God's having foreseen
the particular case of Polonia, who had been " dead " and is then restored to
life. The subtle theological point then arises : Where was the soul during this
temporary period ? Calderón emerges from the difficulty by explaining that
the soul had remained

> . . . . suspensa
> sin lugar y con lugar.
> Teología sacra es ésta.

He goes further and affirms that even supposing the soul had been in Heaven
or hell God could have withdrawn it from either state, acting not by virtue of
" la potencia ordinaria " but by " la potencia absoluta." The whole question
is one of the academic problems so beloved of the schoolmen. A similar
situation is that of Eusebio's " death " in D.C. (III, xvii). Here the soul had
remained within the body.

If in mysterious fashion He embodies within His Godhead a
Triune Unity of Persons—

> ¿ Un Dios y tres
> Personas, con solo un mando,
> una sustancia, una esencia,
> y voluntad ?—[1]

of which the Father symbolizes power, His Divine Son love
and the Holy Ghost wisdom,[2] the aspect most emphasized is
the second, whereby the doctrine of forgiveness becomes the
corner-stone of His revelation.

> Saber saber perdonar
> dice tu Dios que es saber.[3]

Human frailty, ever liable to error, can always rely upon
the benevolence of the Creator, in Whose infinite mercy
Calderón sincerely believed.

> No tiene
> tantas estrellas el cielo,
> tantas arenas el mar,
> tantas centellas el fuego,
> tantos átomos el día,
> ni tantas plumas el viento,
> como Él perdona pecados.[4]

[1] D.A.C., I. xv (Crisanto). Cf. C.D., I, xi, where St. Bartholomew refers
to God as

> . . . . único en esencia,
> y trino en personas.

M.P., I, iii, where Cipriano seeks a God :

> Un Principio sin principio,
> una esencia, una sustancia,
> un poder y un querer solo.

[2] I have here given the usual qualitative attributes to each of the three
Persons of the Trinity, although Calderón in the plays does not always do so :
e.g., in J.M. (I, ii), Eleno assigns wisdom to Christ and love to the Holy Ghost.
In E.C., II, xix, Anastasio gives a further variation : the Father . . . .
Wisdom, the Son . . . . Power, and the Holy Ghost . . . Love. The division
in S.O., II, iv (Sabá), is yet again different : the Father . . . Unity, the Son
. . . . Death, and the Holy Ghost . . . , Love.

[3] S.O., II, ix (Sabá).

[4] M.P., III, xxiii (Justina). For similar statements, cf. D.C., II, xiv
(Julia) :

> . . . . pues creo
> de la clemencia divina,
> que no hay luces en el cielo,
> que no hay en el mar arenas,
> no hay átomos en el viento,
> que, sumados todos juntos,
> no sean número pequeño
> de los pecados, que sabe
> Dios perdonar,

Throned in Heaven is the Blessed Mother of God, supreme
advocate for sinners, whose intercession suffices to deliver
from earthly dangers and from temptation and sin :

> ¡ Virgen María !
> Vuestra gran piedad me valga. [1]
>
> El que pone en María
> las esperanzas,
> de mayores incendios
> no sólo salva
> riesgos de la vida
> pero del alma. [2]

She it is who, when the Prince of Fez, in grave danger of
shipwreck, invokes her name, appears in a radiant vision,
recalling by its details the traditions of Christian iconography
and more especially the dogma of the Immaculate Concep-
tion of Our Lady [3] so staunchly defended in the Spain of
Calderón's day :

> Una bellísima niña
> que coronada de estrellas,
> y rayos del sol vestida,
> con la luna por coturno
> la frente de un dragón pisa. [4]

and P.S.P. (III, v), where Ludovico Enio, the repentant sinner, expresses
his belief in

> . . . . un Dios
> tan divino y tan piadoso . . . .

Who will forgive his many crimes. Eusebio, in D.C. (III, xv), describes his
sins as being

> más que del mar las arenas,
> y los átomos del sol.

Criticism has frequently quite erroneously attributed Eusebio's redemption
to his devotion for the Cross. Whatever the title of the play may suggest,
it is obvious that his salvation was due to a strong belief in the power of the
Divine mercy. The antinomianism, too, which others have condemned cannot
be imputed to Calderón, who plainly states (in the auto ¿ Quién hallará mujer
fuerte ?) : " La fe sin obras no basta."

[1] A.C., II, ii (Pizarro).   [2] A.C., II, xiii.

[3] This dogma became the subject of controversy as early as the twelfth
century. St. Thomas' attitude is confusing : in the Summa he opposes it, but
there are certain passages in the Sententiae which suggest a revision of his views.
The Dominicans, however, as expositors of the Summa, mainly attacked the
belief, and the devotion to which it gave rise ; their chief opponents were
the Franciscans. The Council of Trent gave no definite ruling and controversy
continued till in 1617 Paul V forbade any public teaching against the belief,
though the Holy See made no definite decision until 1854. The Jesuits, in
general, favoured the devotion, which was always popular in Spain ; and
Calderón, in taking the popular line, departs from his usual allegiance to St.
Thomas.

[4] G.P.F., II, xxxi.

Similar in many respects is the vision appearing to save the
Spanish *conquistadores* :

> la nube, basa
> (guarnecida a listas de oro
> y tornasoles de nácar)
> es de una hermosa mujer,
> que de estrellas coronada,
> trae el sol sobre los hombros
> y trae la luna a sus plantas.[1]

In glowing terms Calderón pays homage to man's most
powerful intermediary in Heaven, to her who, in the words of
the Church which he himself utilizes, is the " refugium pec-
catorum " and the " consolatrix afflictorum."[2]   Indeed, so
profound is his devotion towards the Virgin that on one
occasion it approaches the hyperbolic and it is suggested that
she is incapable only of being a fourth Person of the Trinity.[3]

Man, in his constant struggle against adversity, whether
material or spiritual, is favoured by the help of God and of
His holy Mother.   Their intervention can always be relied
upon in the moment of fiercest temptation or greatest doubt.
The participation of the Divine in the sphere of action is an
integral part of the Calderonian scheme.   The miracle
becomes a commonplace.   God rules the world and His
main coadjutor is Mary.   As the principle of Evil receives
embodiment in the person of Satan, who in human form
conducts his nefarious designs, so Mary appears in visible

---

[1] A.C., II, xiv (Yupanguí). Both descriptions recall Luis de León's poem
to the Virgin, in which occur the lines :

> Virgen del sol vestida,
> de luces eternales coronada,
> que huellas con divinos pies la luna . . . . ;

in their turn a reminiscence of the Petrarchan *canzone* " Vergine bella, che di
sol vestita." The source of all these may well be Revelation xii, 1.

[2] At the close of V.S. (III, xv) he introduces a procession whose singers
mingle the salutations of the " Salve Regina " with the very words of the
Litany of the Blessed Virgin. Nor does he omit to make of his beloved flowers,
as in the *autos*, the symbols of her whom he called " Primera Flor del Carmelo."
Cf. G.P.F., III, xvii (El Príncipe) :

> Símbolo son de quien, de gracia llena,
> ni aun en primer instante vió el pecado.

[3] V.S., I, xi. The closing lines of San Ildefonso's sonnet to the Virgin :

> Mas si no os pudo hacer cuarta persona,
> después de Dios os hizo la primera.

form to thwart his plans or to console his victims. In addition God employs other agents for the confusion of His enemy ; the angels of His kingdom or those men of saintly life whom He has endowed with a supernatural power sufficient to baffle all the tempter's guile.[1]

(iii) THE EVIL ONE

The Calderonian world presided over by an Omnipotent God is by no means free from conflict, for, besides the enemies that lurk within man himself, the wayward faculties and the unruly passions, there is Satan, the rebel angel who fell through pride and whose stubborn spirit is incapable of self-amendment, seeking, as a solace to his offended pride, to steal souls from God.

> Obstinado
> mi espíritu que no ha sido
> capaz nunca de enmendarse,
> vencido puede mirarse,
> mas no darse por vencido.[2]

So there develops a drama which is a conflict between opposing forces, a struggle of Good with Evil, at times waged in visible form on the earth, at others in the mind of man, whose soul is the prize. This conflict between the powers of light and darkness is inherent in the Calderonian scheme, and in it Satan is a major actor—an instigator of confusion, enmity and intrigue, a relentless persecutor of the virtuous or a cunning snarer of the enquiring.

> De aquestas perturbaciones
> causa soy.[3]

---

[1] Calderón generally follows Christian tradition by making the heavenly visitants visible and audible only to the person favoured. Cf. P.S.P., I, ix : When the angel descends to hand St. Patrick the letter from God the *gracioso* remarks, " A nadie veo " ; G.P.F., II, xxxi : When the Virgin appears to the Prince, " Nada oímos . . . . nada vemos " is the cry of his companions. A.C., II, xiv : When the Virgin descends amidst a fall of snow the Incas are blinded.

[2] A.C., II, xvi (La Idolatría). Cf. C.D., III, iv (Irene) :
> no puedo arrepentirme
> de ningún delito yo.

[3] J.M., I, xvii.

His principal weapon is a subtle intellect :

> es cierto
> que aunque gracia y hermosura perdí
> no perdí el ingenio. [1]

He it is who when man, in his search for wisdom, tormented
by those mental conflicts which recall the " illa grandi rixa
interioris domus meae " of St. Augustine, [2] is approaching
the truth, hastily summons all his diabolic arts and interrupts
the trend of his thought or sets in motion the temptations
which he has always at his command. Ever fond, as in the
autos, of relating in allegorical guise the story of his fall [3] and
the secret of his knowledge, he can tempt man at his weakest
points, either through the flesh or through the intellect.
Thus he claims to come from

> una patria . . . .
> donde las ciencias más altas,
> sin estudiarse, se saben, [4]

in order to convince man of the validity of his credentials
and convince him that the key to life's deepest secrets is his
for the asking. He is, moreover, a subtle schemer, a plau-
sible meddler, a keen mind with great dialectical skill, a
master of disguise and impersonation, a tempter ever ready
to trap the doubter with intellectual and carnal snares.
The nearest point of triumph for him arrives when some
misguided or sorely tried creature is induced into signing a
pact bartering away life and soul. [5] In reality Satan is no

---

[1] G.P.F., III, xix. Cf. M.P., III, xv :

> La gracia sola perdí,
> la ciencia no.

The *auto La Primera Flor del Carmelo* (viii) has almost the identical words :

> yo . . . . aunque la gracia
> perdí, no perdí la ciencia.

[2] *Confessions*, VIII, viii.   [3] M.P., I, iii and II, vii.   [4] M.P., I, iii.

[5] Cf. M.P. (Cipriano), E.C. (Anastasio), A.C. (Tucapel), C.D. (Irene)
and J.M. (Eugenia) (*passim*).

The famous pact device derives from mediæval times and was employed
very effectively by Mira de Amescua, where the formula " Yo la aceto "
occurs. Calderón's indebtedness to Amescua, whom he specifically praises
in *La Dama duende* (I, i : Cosme) :

> Con que se hubiera excusado
> el doctor Mira de Mescua
> de haber dado a los teatros
> tan bien escrita comedia

match either for the unconquerable force of the will or for the supernatural powers aiding his victims.   The very title *Las Cadenas del Demonio* is highly significant.

> ¡ Oh si Dios, ...
> de la cadena cruel,
> que como a perro rabioso
> me tiene atraillado el pie,
> me alargará un eslabón ! [1]

Satan, released from his prison for a few brief hours and always controlled by God, can act only by the latter's express " permisión " or " licencia," a fact he never ceases to lament.

> ¿ Para esto abrirme dejaste,
> Señor, la prisión estrecha
> en que me tienes ?   Mas ¿ cuándo
> la libertad que me entregas
> no viene atada a las líneas
> de tu suma omnipotencia ? [2]

is well known, and manifests itself particularly in C.D.   The *gracioso's* comment on the pact is to be found in A.C. (III, v), where Tucapel says :

> hay otro yo que en mí reina
> a quien ofrecí alma y vida,

and his wife Glauca replies :

> Pues dile a ese señor diablo
> que tus acciones gobierna,
> que yo digo que es un tonto.

[1] G.P.F., III, iii.   Cf. A.C., II, iv (La Idolatría) :

> Dios la cadena me alarga.

A.C., I, ix :

> . . . . si Dios la acción no me limita
> y los poderes que me dió me quita.

[2] J.M., II, iii (Aurelio :   *i.e.*, El Demonio) and again in the same play (III, iv), where St. Bartholomew, when driving out Satan, exclaims :

> Rebelde espíritu que,
> por divina permisión,
> este sujeto atormentas . . . .

Cf. *op. cit.*, I, iii :

> Y es que tengo
> limitada la licencia
> de Dios, y así no me atrevo
> a más de lo que permiten
> sus soberanos decretos.

In G.P.F. (I, iii), the " réprobo genio " troubling the mind of the Prince can act only " con permisión de Dios."

The limited freedom granted to him includes the power to work miracles in order to stem the advance of truth—

> tengo
> con las mentidas grandezas
> de mis fingidos milagros
> toda esta gente suspensa—[1]

but little else.　He must seek to persuade the will but cannot employ *force majeure.*

> Pues yo no puedo hacer fuerza
> sino persuadir no más.[2]

Consent can always be withheld, even at the eleventh hour, by an exercise of the will.　The seeming triumph of Satan is a delusion :

> Tú no pudiste adquirir
> posesión segura y cierta
> de Irene, cuyo albedrío
> puede mejorar la senda.[3]

But even apart from resistance within man himself, Satan, following tradition, evinces a craven cowardice at the sight of the symbol of his greatest defeat of all, the Holy Cross. Before this he trembles and is stricken dumb.[4]　Fettered hand and foot, limited in his powers, and faced with the most formidable of coalitions, his defeat is inevitable.　Then

---

[1] C.D., I, ix, Cf. Satan's comment when he blinds Ceusis in the same play (I, iv) :

> me ha dado Dios
> permisión por sus decretos
> para usar de naturales
> causas.

[2] J.M., II, i (Aurelio : *i.e.,* El Demonio).

[3] C.D., II, xv (San Bartolomé).

[4] E.C., I, ii (Anastasio) :

> ¿ El pacto negáis a vista
> suya ?　(*v. gr.,* la cruz)

Cf. C.D., I, xi (El Demonio) :

> No puedo hablar . . . .
> porque cautivas y presas
> con cadena están de fuego
> mis acciones y mis fuerzas.

and A.C., I, ix (La Idolatría) :

> El cruzado madero
> a cuya vista pasmo, gimo y muero.

his self-pity knows no bounds and he bemoans the fact that
he is an " infeliz " who cannot be done to death.[1]   In-
capable of shaking invincible faith, he is reduced to
impotent rage :

> ¡ Qué horror ! ¡ Qué pena ! ¡ Qué rabia !
> ¿ Nada, invencible mujer,
> a hacerte tropezar basta ? [2]

When thus baulked of his prey at the moment of triumph he
degenerates, through his very rage, into a figure of comic
relief, the laughing-stock of the *mosqueteros*.   Calderón is well
aware of the " comicità " of this figure in the *comedia* for in
A secreto agravio secreta venganza a *gracioso* says :

> Echando chispas
> como diablo de comedia
> salgo huyendo de mi casa.[3]

On occasion, too, the Almighty, not content with routing
Satan, forces him publicly to confess his own vileness and
acclaim the truth he has so long combated.

---

[1] J.M., II, iv (Aurelio : *i.e.*, El Demonio) :

> . . . . es vana diligencia
> quererme dar muerte a mí,
> pues no es posible que muera
> un infeliz . . .

C.D., III, xiii (El Demonio) :

> ¡ Al cielo
> pluguiera, que fuera tanta
> mi dicha que yo pudiera
> morir !

A.C., III, xix (La Idolatría) :

> ¡ Quién no fuera inmortal para
> matarse antes que lo viera !

J.M., III, xix (Aurelio : *i.e.*, El Demonio) :

> ¡ Pluguiera
> al cielo divino y justo
> pudiera morir, y no
> viera el honor de su triunfo !

[2] J.M., II, xx. (Aurelio : *i.e.*, El Demonio). Cf. A.C., III, xx (La Idolatría) :

> ¡ Cielos !
> ¿ Qué fe es ésta deste indio . . . . ?
> Sufro, lloro, gimo y peno.

M.P., III, vi (El Demonio) : Mi pena, mi rabia fiera . . . .

[3] III, xix (Manrique).

> Oíd, mortales, oíd,
> lo que me mandan los cielos . . .
> Ésta es la verdad, y yo
> la digo, porque Dios mesmo
> me fuerza a que yo la diga . . . [1]

It is clear that, despite his many disguises, impersonations, learned arguments, wiles and temptations, Satan remains a forlorn figure, a comic caricature of the superb rebel depicted by Milton. The puny devil of Calderón hampered by his "chains" can avail nothing against those doughty allies Grace and Free Will. The mental conflict he inspires is never desperate or sustained nor are his temptations irresistible. The victims, moreover, have powerful intermediaries above who will fortify them and ultimately come to their assistance. The devil, a weakling fire-and-brimstone Lucifer, [2] is a pathetic and grotesque character struggling against impossible odds. From the outset the dice are heavily loaded against him.

(iv) MAN

Set midway between the opposing and warring principles of Good and Evil is the composite figure of man, a close union of body and soul, the one perishable, the other immortal. For the soul God has set apart His greatest gifts; for the body, only the heritage of original sin and the silence of the grave. Egerio, the pagan king of Ireland, puzzled as to the precise nature of the God Who claims to grant eternal life, asks how He can do so, since the body must die:

> El alma, destituída
> de un cuerpo ¿cómo pudiera
> tener otra vida allá
> para gloria o para pena? [3]

---

[1] M.P., III, xxvii. Cf. the "declaración pública" of C.D., III, xvi. This public confession of Satan's is to be met with in other dramas of the age—*e.g.*, in Luis de Belmonte's *El Diablo Predicador*, where it is logically justified.

[2] Cf. Clarín the *gracioso*'s references in M.P. (II, viii) to "humo" and "azufre."

[3] P.S.P., II, xiii.

St. Patrick's answer is succinct and clear :

> Desatándose del cuerpo,
> y dando a la naturaleza
> la porción humana, que es
> un poco de barro y tierra ;
> y el espíritu subiendo
> a la suprema esfera
> que es centro de sus fatigas
> si en la gracia muere.[1]

The problem for man, then, is how to secure entrance into the " celestial Sion "[2] which awaits him. For his struggle against Satan God has provided him with a powerful instrument to resist temptation, the faculty of Free Will, the Liberum Arbitrium of the scholastic philosophy.[3] But man also requires the aid of God through the medium of Grace, the " interiores auxilios " referred to by the Prince of Fez.[4] The relationship between the dual agencies of Grace and Free Will opens up the whole complex question of man's autonomy of action and the kindred problem of Predestination which so occupied the mind of contemporary theologians. In utilizing Thomist psychology, however, and introducing into it certain Augustinian modifications, Calderón was less concerned with exact definitions and logical arguments than with the dramatic possibilities of the theories which he adopted. Consequently the value of the faculty psychology for him lay, not in the subtleties by which it sought to reconcile God's omniscience with man's personal freedom but in the high place it gave to the will. Here, close to his hand, was an opportunity to emphasize a certain aspect of the Church's teaching and at the same time to take advantage of the superb

[1] *Ibid.*   [2] P.S.P., II, xvi (El Ángel Bueno).

[3] *Summa*, P. 1., Q. 83 (De libero arbitrio). A.4. : " liberum arbitrium nihil aliud est quam voluntas."

[4] G.P.F., III, ii. Cf. the specific reference to the doctrine of the " gratia efficax " in D.A.C., III, iv (Carpoforo) :

> . . . te olvidas de tan grandes
> auxilios de Dios, no sólo
> suficientes, sí eficaces.

P.S.P., III, v (Ludovico Enio) :

> (d)el cielo, que misterioso
> da auxilios al pecador.

P.S.P., III, viii (Ludovico Enio) :

> Auxilio fué, inspiración
> de Dios la que aquí me trajo.

dramatic possibilities which he saw in it.   Hence the domi-
nant *rôle* played in his drama by this psychological entity in
its contact with other factors.   Always Calderón unerringly
adopts the teaching of St. Thomas Aquinas and triumphantly
vindicates man's claim to be free.

The *Summa* depicts grace as the light of the soul, as that
without which it could not gain salvation.[1]   The soul is a
unity comprising three elements—the rational (*anima intellec-
tiva, vel rationale*), the sensitive (*anima sensitiva*), and the
vegetative (*anima nutritiva, vel vegetabile*).   The first of these
constituted man's outstanding characteristic, justifying the
Aristotelian definition of him as a " rational animal."[2]   The
second he shared with the brute creation ; the last, with the
world of Nature.[3]   To the all-important rational element
were assigned the three faculties—memory, understanding
and will.   The function of the will was to choose and decide
action : without such freedom of choice man would lose all
claim to rationality.   The *liberum arbitrium* or *voluntas* was the
king-pin of Thomist psychology.   It is to St. Thomas, and
to his contemporary commentators, such as Suárez, rather
than to St. Augustine, with his emphasis on the *rôle* of Grace,
that Calderón is primarily indebted.

Free will thus becomes man's great ally in his fight against
the powers of darkness.   The devil's liberty of action
includes permission to inflict temptation—

> y pues que tengo
> licencia de Dios, así
> desde hoy perseguirte pienso.[4]

---

[1] *Summa* P. 1—2, Q. 109. A.5 : " sine gratia homo non potest mereri
vitam aeternam." *Op. cit.*, Q. 110. A.1. : " gratia est quaedam lux animae."

[2] Calderón frequently employs the phrase " bruto racional."

[3] In the religious plays Calderón does not specifically deal with the three-
fold soul save in scattered references : *e.g.*, S.O., II, iv, where Sabá alludes
to

> el alma
> vegetativa que tiene (el árbol),

but it is clear from the *autos* that he followed the faculty psychology. Cf.
also *El Mayor Encanto Amor* (I, viii : Flérida) :

> Racional, vegetable y sensitiva
> alma, el cielo le dió al sujeto humano
> vegetable y sensible al bruto ufano
> al tronco y a la flor vegetativa.

[4] J.M., I, xvii.

But God will not permit man to be tempted beyond what he can bear, and, however persistently Satan may seek to influence him in a given direction, he always possesses the ultimate power of choice. The devil's sensual temptations can only lead the human will towards sin : they cannot force it.

> Que aunque el gran poder mío
> no puede hacer vasallo un albedrío
> puede representarle
> tan extraños deleites, que se halle
> empeñado a buscallos,
> y inclinallos podré, si no forzallos.[1]

For the very nature of free will would be falsified if it were subject to compulsion :

> No fuera libre albedrío
> si se dejara forzar.[2]

Satan is forced to recognize his impotence here and declares categorically :

> hallo
> que sobre el libre albedrío
> ni hay conjuros, ni hay encantos.[3]

Again, the action of the will is instantaneous, a fact which goes far towards accounting for deficiencies in the development of character. The human being is capable of arriving at lightning decisions in all spheres, be it in matters of love or of conversion.[4]

Seconding the will is the heart, an element of Calderonian psychology for the *rôle* of which no precedent can be found in the *Summa*. A possible source is the work of Judaeo-Arabic commentators of Aristotle which concede to the heart an important psychological function : in the *autos* Calderón goes so far as to make it the very centre of life and

[1] M.P., III, ii. Cf. *Summa* P. 1—2. Q.9. A.4 : " Voluntas violentiam pati non potest," and Q.6. A.4 : "Non ergo voluntas potest cogi ad agendum."

[2] M.P., III, vi (Justina). The whole scene is a *locus classicus* for an understanding of the problem.

[3] M.P., II, xix (Cipriano).

[4] *Summa*, P. 1—2, Q. 113. A.7 : " Motus autem liberi arbitrii, quia est velle, non est succesivus, sed instantaneus."

the ruler of the senses and faculties. In the plays under consideration it seems to fulfil an intermediary function between mind and matter. Receiving impressions from without, or at least having in some undefined and mysterious manner premonitions of forthcoming events, it transmits its messages to the understanding, and thence to the will, thus enabling the latter to decide upon its reaction. Its task is to act as sentinel

> —primera posta del alma—[1]

for the citadel of the soul guarded by the will and the understanding. Its messenger-like function is compared with some natural astrology possessed of a knowledge of future dangers :

> en un confuso extremo,
> al corazón parece que camina
> todo el alma, adivina
> de algún futuro daño.[2]

(v) THE CREATED WORLD : MAN AND THE STARS.

In the scene of man's struggle—the " fábrica gallarda del universo"[3]—Calderón seems to take a most restricted interest, save in so far as it is a manifestation of God's glory. A charming exception to this attitude is to be found in the pastoral scenes of *Los Cabellos de Absalón*,[4] which take place in flower-decked fields during the sheep-shearing in the poet's favourite month of May. They may well embody reminiscences of similar sights witnessed in Toledo and its neigh-

[1] D.A.C., II, xxi (Crisanto).

[2] D.C., II, iii (Eusebio). Cf. G.P.F., I, xviii, where Zara, fearing some evil, refers to the forebodings of

> la sabia
> natural astrología
> que sin estudios se alcanza.

Flora, in *El Sitio de Bredá* (I, viii), uses a similar phrase . . .

> Y astrólogo el corazón
> no sé qué le avisa al alma.

[3] M.P., I, i (Cipriano). Cf. C.D., I, v (Licanoro) :

> . . . . aquesta
> fábrica del universo.

E.C., II, iii (Zacarías) :

> . . . . esta fábrica opulenta
> del universo.

[4] II, xi, ff.

bourhood. Sometimes, on the other hand, Nature provides a terrifying background of mountain, boulder and crag to the heroes fleeing from persecution or seeking relief in solitude, much as supernatural interventions are heralded with storm, earthquake and deepest gloom. In this we need see no more than a skilful dramatist's desire to appeal to the more naif dramatic taste of the day. But when Nature is revealed to us suffused with the Divine glow, as the *décor* of a world created by God for His creatures, we cannot doubt that Calderón himself is speaking to us from the depth of his soul. Of this viewpoint the supreme expression in his drama is the magnificent paean of St. Patrick to the universe, which recalls the " Coeli enarrant gloriam Dei " of the Psalmist :

> Causa primera de todo
> sois, Señor, y en todo estáis.
> Esos cristalinos cielos,
> que constan de luces bellas,
> con el sol, luna y estrellas,
> ¿ no son cortinas y velos
> del empíreo soberano ?
> Los discordes elementos,
> mares, fuego, tierra y vientos,
> ¿ no son rasgos de esa mano ?
> ¿ No publican vuestros lôres,
> y el poder que en vos se encierra
> todos ?   ¿ No escribe la tierra
> con caracteres de flores
> grandezas vuestras ?   ¿ El viento,
> en los ecos repetidos,
> no publica que habéis sido
> autor de su movimiento ?
> El fuego y el agua luego
> ¿ alabanzas no os previenen . . . ?
> Luego aquí mejor podré,
> inmenso Señor, buscaros,
> pues en todo puedo hallaros.[1]

In small things as in great, God's immanence in His creation is a reality to him :

> el clavel más pequeño
> del pincel de Dios es rasgo.[2]

[1] P.S.P., I, viii.
[2] S.O., III, iii (Salomón).

Apart from the conventional Nature catalogues so frequent in the Spanish *comedia*,[1] the descriptions of natural beauty found in Calderón give a feeling of lightness and airiness and at the same time convey a sense of vagueness which never stoops so low as to particularize. Calderón is the poet of the starry skies, of trim gardens, sweet purling streams, crystalline fountains and multi-coloured flowers. His is the refined, delicate Nature of the court poet, accustomed to move within the gentle confines of surroundings entirely artificial. Thus he frequently pauses to depict the delights of some pleasant shady grove, or some garden bright with flowers, a fitting stage for the polite love-making or the poetic diversions of his high-born *dramatis personæ* :

> pienso que saldrá
> muy presto a la estancia bella
> dese jardín, porque en él
> está para hoy prevenida
> una academia lucida.[2]

But there are times, too, when he sees the flowers as symbols of man's fleeting earthly passage from cradle to grave,[3] just as, when he gazes on the heavens studded with

[1] Cf. M.P., II, xviii (Cipriano).

[2] J.M., I, vii (Capricho) and I, xi (Eugenia) :

> . . . . noble academia ilustre,
> en cuyo apacible duelo
> gala y hermosura hacen
> lid con el entendimiento.

Cf. D.A.C., I, vii *et seq.* and S.O., III, ii *et seq.* (Sabá) :

> Por divertirte no más
> hacer academia quiero
> este jardín.

These poetic tourneys in which music and verse were employed to treat a given theme set possibly by the host or hostess were a common contemporary entertainment.

[3] So Jonatás, on describing his brother's death in battle (J. Mc., I, i), comments :

> Y las que hoy lucientes son,
> mañana caducas flores.

Cf. the " cuna y sepulcro " of P.C., II, xiv (Fernando) :

> Flores, de la suerte mía
> geroglíficos, señora,
> pues nacieron con la aurora,
> y murieron con el día.

The symbolism derives originally from Job, the Psalms and Ecclesiastes, and is common in Golden Age writers, especially in the ascetics and mystics.

stars, " living torches " of the night,[1] he is tempted to see
in them the secrets of man's destiny.   In one favourite figure
he interchanges their functions :

> Que si estrellas del día son las flores . . .
> flores son de la noche las estrellas.[2]

The flowers become " stars " of the meadows, and the
stars, " flowers " of the heavens :

> estas selvas bellas
> que esmaltadas de primores
> son verde cielo de flores,
> son azul campo de estrellas.[3]

All his life through, Calderón was fascinated by the
" inquieta república de estrellas,"[4] and never laid aside his
longstanding interest in the astrological influences, remnants
of which still lingered on in his age.

In general, he follows in the wake of St. Thomas, who,
in treating of free will, refers in various places to astrology.[5]
The *Summa* includes a whole article entitled " De Super-
stitione divinativa " which deals, one by one, with all
the divinations forbidden by canon law.   His list—" nigro-
mantia, pythones, geomantia, hydromantia, astrologia,
augurium, auspicium, omen, chiromantia"[6]—recalls the
occult practices of the Calderonian magicians.[7] St. Thomas'
teaching is clear :   " omnis divinatio quae fit per invoca-
tiones daemonum est illicita."[8]   These words are echoed by

[1] M.P., I, vii. Lisardo's " tanta antorcha viviente."

[2] *Mejor está que estaba*, II, viii (Arnaldo).

[3] D.A.C., I, viii (Cintia).   [4] V.Sñ., II, vii (Segismundo).

[5] M. Choisnard, in an extremely plausible study entitled *Saint Thomas et
l'influence des astres*, has brought together all these passages, and proves, to his
own satisfaction, that the author of the *Summa* was a confirmed believer in the
legitimate use of the " science."   Modern Dominican commentators are
unable to accept either M. Choisnard's choice of texts or his interpretation of
them. I have followed their more objective analysis rather than a " practising
scientific astrologer " (his own words), whose *parti pris* makes his criticism
somewhat suspect.

[6] *Summa*, P. 2—2, Q. 95, A.3.

[7] Cf. E.C., I, ii, where Síroes, speaking of Anastasio's magic arts, includes
among them " la geomancia . . . . la eteromancia . . . la hidromancia . . . .
la piromancia," by means of which he conned the secrets of the four elements,
earth, air, water, and fire, and Cipriano's study of necromancy under Satan's
supervision (M.P., *passim*).   The rebuke of Fernando to his superstitious
brother Enrique over his belief in omens is another case in point. (P.C., I, vii).

[8] *Summa*, P. 2—2, Q. 95, A.4.

the King David of *Los Cabellos de Absalón* in his anathematization of the " etiopisa." :

> Pues has pensado que puedo
> tener por grandeza yo
> en mi palacio agoreros.
> Dios habla por sus profetas ;
> el demonio, como opuesto
> a las verdades de Dios,
> habla apoderado en pechos
> tiranamente oprimidos. [1]

Similarly, in *La Exaltación de la Cruz*, Zacarías warns Anastasio against the " diabólicas artes " which are the work of "dañados genios,"

> que, opuestos a Dios, intentan
> competir con sus milagros. [2]

All the characters which utilize the " dañados genios " are in the end convinced of the illegitimacy of the practice. The very impotence that seizes upon the diabolic agents when confronted with the heavenly powers is sufficient to convince the most doubting. By contrast, Calderón portrays the lawful use of divination in the inspired prophecies, whose source is uncontaminated and which foreshadow the great events of Christianity, of the Ethiopian queen and Oriental sibyl,

> que con espíritu ardiente
> de Dios merece alcanzar
> de sibila y profetisa
> nombre altivo e inmortal . . .
> Divinos misterios ve. [3]

The section of St. Thomas' treatise, however, which bears the closest relation to the Calderonian drama is that in which he deals specifically with astrology. [4] It should be noted that his treatment of the question closely follows the lines laid

---

[1] C.A., I, viii. In C.D. Satan assumes the disguise of a " fitonisa."

[2] II, iii.

[3] S.O., I, vi (Irífile). Cf. C.A., II, xiii, where Amón, being told of the " fitonisa," Teuca, says :

> Desta gente
> hacer caso es vanidad :
> tal vez dirá una verdad,
> y después mil veces miente.

[4] *Summa*, P. 2—2, Q. 95, A.5 : " Utrum divinatio quae fit per astra sit illicita."

down by St. Augustine, who, in the *De Civitate Dei*,[1] examines in detail the spurious claims of sorcerers and astrologers. As the whole body of mediæval comment is indebted to the Bishop of Hippo's penetrating analysis, it is hard to be sure whether Calderón's ideas derive from St. Augustine, with whose works he was undoubtedly familiar,[2] or at second hand from the *Summa*.

St. Thomas admits no *direct* influence of the stars on the rational part of the soul, thereby once more safeguarding that freedom of the will on which he placed so much value.[3] However, in accordance with the elementary state of medical knowledge in his days, he was willing to concede a possible connection between the heavenly bodies and the " vegetative " soul of man in the same way as a scientist places on record the interdependence of moon and tides. This fact accounts for the surprisingly extensive part played by astrology in his works. Calderón, who was interested in medical matters, and often used medical terminology,[4] follows him in allowing this concession. In spite of it, however, St. Thomas is a staunch defender of the autonomy of man, who, though his rational soul depends on God, in

[1] Liber V, Cap. vi.

[2] St. Augustine's abandonment of the astrological superstition is mentioned in the *Confessions* (X, 35), where he writes " Nec curo nosse transitus siderum." The Jesuit Ribadeneyra, to whom Calderón was so much indebted, had translated this book into Spanish. St. Augustine's classic refutation of astrology is based on the case of identical twins whose characters and futures are thereby by no means similar. Calderón frequently introduces the same motif—*e.g.*, the brothers Menardes and Síroes in E.C. and Ceusis and Licanoro in C.D. He dramatized the Saint's conversion in *El Sacro Parnaso* and quotes from the *Confessions* in *Lo que va del hombre a Dios*. Moreover, his use of pagan mythology to foreshadow the truths of Christianity finds its justification in a further passage of the *De Civitate Dei*. Cf. the use of the Aztec beliefs in A.C. (*passim*).

[3] *Summa* (*loc. cit.*) : " Impossibile est quod corpora caelestium *directe* imprimant in intellectum et voluntatem." And *ibid :* " Unde corpora caelestia non possunt esse per se causa operum liberi arbitrii."
Cf. Gregorio de Valentia's *Summa* commentary : " Coeli movent voluntatem *indirecte*," Lugduni, 1609, Vol. II, p. 156.

[4] Examples abound : *cuartana, parasismo, postema, antídoto, triaca, contrayerba, etc.* From the evidence of the plays Calderón possessed a firm belief in the curative properties of herbs and plants. Cf., V.Sñ., II, i (Clotaldo) :

> Y es cierto, que de secretos
> naturales está llena
> la medecina, y no hay
> animal, planta ni piedra
> que no tenga calidad
> determinada.

some mysterious fashion preserves freedom of action.　On that point he will brook no opposition.　In this defence of free will, he has in mind the cosmic determinism of the Arab scientists, particularly Averroes and Avicenna, with whose theories he connected the prevalent astrological beliefs, and against whose materialistic conceptions his arguments are chiefly directed.　So we find him grouping together and refuting Averroes, Avicenna and the astrologer Albumazar. A test of Ptolemy's which St. Thomas frequently cites and interprets summarizes his main conclusion :

> Sapiens dominatur astris. [1]

The text is well known to Calderón, whose plays abound in references to astrology, for he could appreciate the dramatic possibilities of the theme of man's struggle against external influences which seemed to possess the inevitability of fate.　He is continually preoccupied with the destiny of man as written in the stars :

> Lo que está determinado
> del cielo, y en azul tabla
> Dios con el dedo escribió,
> de quien son cifras y estampas
> tantos papeles azules
> que adornan letras doradas,
> nunca engaña, nunca miente. [2]

But, following St. Thomas, he never for a moment deviates

---

[1] Calderón translates this (*La Cisma de Inglaterra*, II, viii : Volseo) :
> sobre las estrellas
> alcanza dominio el sabio,

and in *Los Hijos de la fortuna*, I, xi (Cariclea) :
> Porque en fin el sabio tiene
> en las estrellas dominio.

Cf. V.Sñ., II, i (Basilio) :
> . . . . el hombre
> predomina en las estrellas

and again in the same play (III, xiii : Clotaldo) :
> . . . el prudente varón
> victoria del hado alcanza.

The whole theme is a vindication of free will.　Alarcón, in *El Dueño de las estrellas*, gives dramatic expression to the phrase in a play which demonstrates the ability of man to overcome the stars.　Filipo kills himself to disprove the truth of the " fated decree " that said he was to be the king's slayer, thus showing
> que el sabio, aunque más le inclinen
> es dueño de las estrellas.

[2] V. Sñ., III, xiv (Segismundo).

from the doctrine of the supremacy of the will. No matter however woefully the characters (like Julia in *La Devoción de la Cruz*) lament that the fault is not in themselves, but in their stars :

> Allí lloraré desdichas,
> de un hado tan inclemente,
> de una fortuna tan fiera,
> de una inclinación tan fuerte,
> de un planeta tan opuesto,
> de una estrella tan rebelde, ... [1]

or, like Ludovico Enio, that the planets reigned inauspiciously over their birth :

> sospecho
> que todos siete planetas,
> turbados y descompuestos,
> asistieron desiguales
> a mi infeliz nacimiento.
> La luna me dió inconstancia
> en la condición, ingenio
> Mercurio . . . .
> Venus lasciva me dió
> apetitos lisonjeros,
> y Marte ánimo cruel ; . . .
> el sol me dió condición
> muy generosa . . . .
> Júpiter me dió soberbia
> de bizarros pensamientos,
> Saturno cólera y rabia,
> valor y ánimo resuelto
> a traiciones ; y a estas causas
> se han seguido los efectos, [2]

[1] D.C., I, xi. Cf. E.C., I, ix (Clodomira) :

> De los hados hurtándome a la saña.
> de los astros huyéndome a la ira.

S.O., III, v (Candaces) :

> Todo con su estrella nace,
> todo con su inclinación . . . .

C.A., I, iii (Amón) :

> Mas ¡ ay ! en vano me opongo
> de mi estrella a los influjos . . . .

[2] P.S.P., I, i. Cf. C.A., I, iv (Amón) :

> Deste atrevimiento mío
> no tengo la culpa yo,
> porque en mí solo nació
> esclavo el libre albedrío.
> No sé qué planeta impío
> pudo reinar aquel día.

the fatalistic implications of the words last quoted are never accepted. In them lies the keynote to the very conception of the celestial influences that the dramatist sought to combat. The power he grants to the stars and to destiny is that accorded to Satan himself—a power which influences the will but leaves it perfectly free to make its choice :

> Si de un astro la violencia
> a una deidad me ha inclinado,
> no me ha forzado ; que no
> fuerzan, si inclinan, los astros.
> Libre tengo mi albedrío,
> alma y corazón . . . . [1]

Calderón's consistent defence of man's ability to overcome the stellar influences will serve to acquit him of any fatalistic tendencies which may be imputed to him.[2]

(vi) THE CROWN OF MARTYRDOM

In an age when the heroic missionary activities of the religious Orders and of the Society of Jesus[3] in the New World and in the Far East were fresh in the minds of all, it is not surprising that Calderón, whose family crest bore the proud words " Por la fe moriré," should have made martyrdom the central theme of his religious drama, allying it with the

---

[1] D.A.C., I, xiv (Crisanto). Cf. V.Sñ., I, vi (Basilio) :

> Porque el hado más esquivo,
> la inclinación más violenta,
> el planeta más impío,
> solo el albedrío inclinan ;
> no fuerzan el albedrío.

D.C., I, vii (Julia) :

> . . . . el hado impío
> no fuerza el libre albedrío.

[2] The only hint as to the source of Calderón's astrological knowledge is to be found, not in the religious plays, but in the comedy El Astrólogo fingido (1631), which, besides affording a convincing proof of his position in the controversy,

> Pues ¿qué astrólogo acertó
> cosa que dijo ?   (III. v : Antonio)

includes a direct reference to Juan Bautista Porta, an Italian writer who died in 1615 and was the author of several scientific works in addition to a drama called The Astrologer.

[3] The canonization, during Calderón's lifetime, of the Apostle of the Indies, the great Jesuit saint, Francis Xavier, found an echo in a play on his life by the dramatist, which unfortunately has not been preserved.

eternal quest for wisdom which Gracián made man's imperishable glory. The protagonists of the martyr-plays, the seekers after God, who vainly pursue earthly knowledge as a consolation for their restless minds, attain truth only after having made the supreme sacrifice for the Faith. Religion exorcises all the terrors of death, which becomes merely the happy moment of reunion, the culmination of suffering and persecution gladly borne. Anastasio, Cipriano, Crisanto, Daría, Licanoro, Irene, Eugenia and St. Bartholomew all greet the approach of death with joy and confidence. To the Moorish prince, Muley Mahomet, the honour of martyrdom is denied, but even he,

> si no es mártir por sangre,
> es mártir por el afecto.[1]

This attitude is the logical outcome of an outlook on life that centres in the eternal. In drawing upon the rich stores of hagiographical legend[2] to glorify those who had gained the crown of martyrdom, Calderón was only being true to his creed. To the religious poet the joy with which man greets his end and the prospect of heavenly reward was bound to be, of all topics, the most congenial. And to this " muerte más dichosa "[3] Calderón devoted no less than seven of his fourteen extant religious dramas.

[1] G.P.F., III, xix (El Buen Genio).

[2] E.g., Laurentius Surius : *De probatis sanctorum historiis* (Cologne, 1618) ; Alfonso de Villegas : *Flos Sanctorum* (1578-94) ; Pedro de Ribadeneyra : *Flos Sanctorum* (1601), *Vida de los Santos* and *Crisanto y Daría* (1600 ?) ; Ortiz Lucio : *Compendio de las vidas de los santos* (1597) ; Jacobus de Voragine : *Legenda Aurea sive Historia Lombardica.*

The first complete Spanish edition of the *Roman Martyrology*, revised by Dionisio Vásquez, S.J., dates from 1586 (Valladolid). (The *editio princeps* was issued in 1583). Calderón's indebtedness to Jesuit sources is shown in addition by his use of Ribadeneyra's Life of St. Ignatius (G.P.F.) and Pineda's Life of Solomon, 1609 (S.O.).

[3] V.S., II, iii (Doña Sancha) :

> Entonces será la muerte
> más dichosa, pues será
> por la fe.

Cf. P.S.P., I, ii, where St. Patrick, describing Ireland as the land of saints, says it was so called because :

> tantos fueron los que en ella
> dieron la vida al martirio,
> en religiosa defensa
> de la fe, que ésta en los fieles
> es la última fineza.

But the progress to martyrdom is a gradual one, involving
a period of initial doubt and a time of persecution and temp-
tation, during which God permits Satan to test man's con-
stancy :

> el oro no tiene
> segura su estimación,
> si no prueba sus quilates
> la experiencia del crisol. [1]

The mind, trammelled by pagan superstition, searches for a
way out of its difficulties and comes to realize the inconsisten-
cies and immoralities of ancient polytheistic belief.   For long
the mental conflict continues while the opposing forces
struggle for the supremacy :

> ¡ Oh, qué ciegas confusiones
> entre mí mismo padezco !
> Dos espíritus están,
> uno malo y otro bueno,
> luchando dentro de mí.
> Uno me inclina a creerlo,
> y otro me mueve a dudarlo,
> ambos totalmente opuestos. [2]

Nor is man allowed to continue his search undisturbed by
the trinity of watchful enemies—devil, world and flesh.

---

[1] D.A.C., III, ix (Daría).   Cf. in the same play (I, xvi) the heavenly voice
which says :

> quiero acrisolar
> la constancia de Crisanto.

[2] D.A.C., I, ii (Crisanto).   Cf. the same play, *loc. cit.* :

> Dos
> voces, si no dos afectos,
> que forma mi fantasía,
> sombras sin alma y sin cuerpo,
> a un tiempo están batallando
> dentro de mi mismo pecho.

In G.P.F., I, iii, the psychological warfare has developed into an actual
representation of the two presiding spirits representing on the stage the mental
struggle. Cf. :

> Representando los dos
> de su Buen Genio y Mal Genio
> exteriormente la lid
> que arde interior en su pecho.

This dramatization of mental conflict by the personification of mental
tendencies reaches its climax in the sphere of the *auto.*

The first utilizes every means to prevent recognition of the truth.   Knowing that

<blockquote>
es amor
homicida del ingenio. [1]
</blockquote>

he uses human love for the purpose of halting, even if only temporarily, the quest whose end he knows will be unfavourable to his own designs.   Thus, when at last slowly nearing the outskirts of truth, the truth-seeker finds himself assailed by the " rebelión de la carne," [2] which wrings from him the anguished cry :

<blockquote>
Dad, cielos,
nueva luz a mis sentidos ;
que entre un Dios y una belleza
anda delirando el juicio. [3]
</blockquote>

Temptations of the flesh are man's greatest affliction :

<blockquote>
La lid más sangrienta y fiera
de los hombres . . .
. . . . de mujeres buscado
de deseos combatido,
de lascivas oprimido
y de deleites cercado. [4]
</blockquote>

---

[1] M.P. I, xvi (Cipriano).   Cf. D.A.C., I, xiv (Crisanto) :

<blockquote>
¿Soy yo quien rendido aquí
al bellísimo milagro
de una hermosura, se olvida
de aquel primero cuidado
de sus estudios ?
</blockquote>

[2] G.P.F., II, xvi (San Ignacio).

[3] C.D., II, v (Licanoro).   In C.D., II, ii, Irene recognizes in the words of a song the same conflict of loyalties that she is undergoing :

<blockquote>
Sin mí, sin vos y sin Dios,
triste y confusa me veo ;
sin Dios, por lo que os deseo ;
sin mí, porque estoy en vos ;
sin vos, porque no os poseo.
</blockquote>

though here it is estrangement from a pagan deity that saddens her. Cf. the conflict between Love and Intellect in D.A.C., where Crisanto and Daría, from different motives, struggle against their mutual affections.   Justina, in M.P., resists the advances of Cipriano. In A.C. (II, xxi) Yupanguí is able to reconcile his allegiance to the Blessed Virgin and Guacolda :

<blockquote>
Que el vivir absorto no es
dejar de vivir amante.
</blockquote>

[4] D.A.C., II, xv (Carpoforo).

The struggle is the more desperate since, within the Calder-
onian psychology, the first surrender is instantaneous.[1]   But
resistance, through self-control, lies within man's power, and
the subsequent victory over the flesh is the greatest a human
being can obtain.

> Honrada victoria ha sido ;
> que la de más gloria es
> vencerse un hombre a sí mismo.[2]

The conflict of loyalties, both in the religious and in the
secular sphere, is constantly recurring.   But the dramatist
never forgets that man's animal instincts are controllable

[1] *E.g.*, D.A.C., I, xii (Crisanto) :

> Desde el instante que vi
> esta rara perfección,
> soy horror, soy confusión.

Cf. C.D., II, ii (Ceusis) :

> Desde el instante que os vi,
> toda el alma os entregué.

and A.C., I, xiv (Guascar Inga) :

> desde aquel mesmo
> instante que vi la rara
> hermosura sin ejemplo
> de aquella sacerdotisa . . .
> ni vivo, ni sé de mí.

The formula " yo vi, yo quise, yo amé " occurs in *Lances de amor y fortuna*
(I, vi : Aurora) and also the *gracioso* satire on the device (I, iii : Alejo) :

> ¿ En un punto, en un instante
> puede un hombre hablar amante ?

So Cipriano, as soon as he sees Justina, exclaims (M.P., I, ix) :

> Turbado
> estoy. ¡ Qué fuerte
> hielo discurre mis venas !

[2] J. Mc., III, ii (Tolomeo).   Cf. C.A., I, ii (David) :

> . . . imperio tiene
> el hombre sobre sí propio.

This same victory is often referred to in the secular plays and *autos*, e.g.,
El Segundo Scipión (III : Scipión) :

> A mí mismo me he vencido,
> siendo la mayor victoria
> el vencerse uno a sí mismo,

and *Mujer, llora y vencerás* (I, xiv : Laura) :

> Y así, que no hay, considera.
> quien venza con mayor fama,
> que el que a sí mismo se venza.

Cf. Seneca's " Imperare sibi maximum imperium est."

by the will, and, if resistance weakens, either in moments of doubt or of carnal temptation, recourse can always be had to supernatural help, which will not be denied.   The despairing cry of a doubt-tormented soul,

> ¿ Quién destas dudas podrá
> rescatar mi entendimiento ? [1]

is accompanied by the belief, which never deserts the oppressed, that

> los cielos han de abonarme. [2]

The insufficiency of human resources being once recognized, the appeal to Divine support is inevitable.   And Grace will infallibly reinforce the will's resistance, fortify the understanding and put Satan to flight.   An appeal of this kind never goes unanswered :

> A quien con fe le llama
> siempre socorre y nunca desampara. [3]

The appeal :

> ¡ Grande Dios de los cristianos !
> A ti en mis penas acudo. [4]

brings instant relief, the blinding flash of faith and the cessation of all doubt.

> En solo un instante he visto
> del Padre la omnipotencia,
> la sabiduría del Hijo,
> del Espíritu el amor. [5]

[1] D.A.C., I, ii (Crisanto).
[2] M.P., II, xvii (Justina). Cf. C.D., II, iv (Licanoro) :
> ¡ Valedme, cielos benignos !
> Que a tanto misterio falta
> la razón, fallece el juicio . . . .
[3] C.D., III, xv (La música celestial).
[4] M.P., III, xvi (Cipriano).
[5] E.C., II, xxi (Anastasio). Cf. G.P.F. (II, xxxi), where the Virgin informs the Moorish Prince :
> vuelve a Malta,
> donde te espera la dicha
> de que salgas de una vez
> de aquellas dudas antiguas ;
> pues el haberme invocado
> basta para que consigas
> librarte de esa tormenta,
> y saber con fe más viva.

The instantaneous conversion[1] inevitable after the Divine intervention destroys the seeds of doubt and substitutes the certitude of faith :

> Tú en fin los caminos ciertos
> del vivir y el morir ves. [2]

Henceforth the mind is at rest, comforted by faith's certainties :

> Todo es fácil al que cree, [3]

and seeks nothing so ardently as to die for the God Who has granted it abiding peace, and Whose own Son redeemed mankind :

> En fe suya mi deseo
> vivir y morir aguarda. [4]

There can be no way to recompense such a sacrifice like martyrdom.   But, before the goal is reached, heavenly aid will still be necessary : though the spirit is willing, the flesh may be weak :

> Pero ¡ ay de mí ! que no basto
> para mi defensa yo.
> Nuevo Dios que adoro, a quien
> la vida y el alma doy,
> en la confianza vuestra
> vivo, socorredme vos. [5]

And if previously, with the road to truth only half traversed, God did not fail to rescue the halting, He cannot fail to succour potential martyrs now.   With the crown almost within their

---

[1] Cf. C.D., III, v (Irene) :
> ¡ Cristo es el Dios
> verdadero !

and D.A.C., III, vii (Daría) :
> Pues digo a voces que vanos
> son los dioses que seguí,
> y que sólo crêr espero
> en Cristo Dios verdadero.

[2] J.M., II, xi (Eleno).

[3] D.A.C., II, xv (Carpoforo).

[4] E.C., III, iii (Anastasio).

[5] D.A.C., III, ix (Daría).   Cf. J.M., II, xv, where the converted Eugenia, subject to fresh trials, exclaims :
> Mi esperanza tengo en Dios.

and M.P., III, vi (Justina) :
> Mi defensa en Dios consiste.

grasp, they must not lack essential grace. So all advance joyfully towards death chanting the praises of Him for Whom they die and through Whom they have attained their desire. Like swans, they go to their death singing :

> quien por él padece,
> muere con tal regocijo
> que como cisnes, celebran
> su muerte en esos caistros.[1]

Their agony has no bitterness and with rejoicing heart the chalice can be drunk to the lees.

> De nada desconfío
> beber tu cáliz ofrecí, Dios mío,
> el fuego del amor el pecho labra ;
> feliz voy a cumplirte la palabra.[2]

What Christian but can contemplate with exceeding joy the prospect of meeting God face to face and receiving the eternal reward ?

> ¡ Dichoso mil veces yo
> este día ! pues es cierto
> que siendo a morir será
> a tener mi fe su premio.[3]

---

[1] E.C., II, xx. The admiring comment of Anastasio, not yet himself converted, on hearing the joyful psalms of the Christians who think the end is near.

[2] C.D., III, xi (San Bartolomé).

[3] E.C., III, xx (Anastasio). Cf. D.A.C., III, xix (Crisanto) :
> ¡Oh qué alegre a morir voy !

J.M., III, xi (Eugenia) :
> ¡Qué alegre voy a morir !

Ibid. :
> ¡Dichosa yo que a ver llego
> persecuciones tan fuertes !
> . . . mi mayor consuelo
> librado tengo en mi muerte.

M.P., III, xxvi, where the *gracioso* Moscón, on seeing Justina and Cipriano being led to their death, remarks :
> ¡Qué contentos a morir
> se van !

It is interesting to note that even the hardened sinner, Ludovico Enio (P.S.P., I, ii), was willing to lay down his life for the Faith :
> Pero con todo, en defensa
> de la fe que adoro y creo,
> perderé una y mil veces
> (tanto la estimo y precio)
> la vida.

III

OTHER ASPECTS OF THE PLAYS

The preceding examination of the religious dramas of Calderón has aimed at presenting a coherent and ordered account of their main theological content. Since the plays in question belong to very unequally spaced periods of Calderón's life they have been considered *en bloc* and no attempt has been made to trace any evolution of thought in them. In general, they are seen to have been strongly influenced by the poet's *milieu* and education : Calderón's conception of life, like his attitude to its problems, is essentially that of contemporary Spanish Catholicism.

But drama is above all a popular art and these plays of Calderón's show traces of the controversies and restrictions which affected the stage during his career as a writer. During the time when secular love and passion were proscribed, Spanish playwrights naturally tended to circumvent legal enactments and to palliate the monotony of exclusively religious fare by introducing in a thinly disguised form the very *motifs* condemned. Calderón must have deliberately chosen those Biblical themes that would have a popular appeal : *Judas Macabeo*, for example, though Biblical in its sources, is entirely secular in treatment and it is of interest to compare *Los Cabellos de Absalón* with Tirso de Molina's *La Venganza de Tamar*. It is quite clear that these plays are not purely religious and that they embody traditional elements of the *comedia*—the complex plot of the *capa y espada* type ; the code of "honour"; the monarchist spirit ; and, above all, the *vis comica* of the *gracioso*. To that last traditional figure not even the most sacred theme can forbear to pay tribute.

Moreover, there are indications in the plays of Calderón's attitude to more worldly matters than the fate of man's soul : we can gather, if only fragmentarily, his views on life's secular aspects, and thus once again form a mental picture corresponding to our previous one. For the dramatist's traditionalism has expressed itself, not only through a rigid orthodoxy in matters of faith, but also by a stubborn conservatism in the field of politics and social relations.

Criticism has not been slow to attribute inconsistency to Calderón, the dramatist of the vanity of human wishes who was at the same time court poet and royal favourite and hastened to acquire patents of nobility. A disconcerting episode, yet one quite in keeping with the attitude of the man who accepted the social code of his day as firmly as he did its religious beliefs. In neither field does he seem ever to have questioned the established order. Tradition, the accumulated experience of centuries, handed down from generation to generation, is the repository of truth :

> no hay
> que buscar lugar más cierto
> que la opinión heredada
> de nuestros padres y abuelos ;
> pues la voz de unos en otros
> son los anales del tiempo.[1]

An illustration of this position is Calderón's attitude to the Divine right of kings. Human kingship, for him, is only a shadow and a symbol of the Divine—

> viene a ser la majestad humana
> sombra de aquella Reina soberana—[2]

and in itself possesses titles to admiration and homage :

> Eres rey a quien respeto,
> porque, al fin, la majestad
> por sí sola admiración
> tiene y no por el lugar.[3]

No wonder, if Calderón reflected the sentiments of his times, that Madame d'Aulnoy could describe it as impossible to find " une soumission et une obéissance plus parfaite ni un amour plus sincère que celui des espagnols pour leur roi."[4]

---

[1] V.S., I, vi (Ildefonso).

[2] V.S., I, vi (La Reina). Cf. P.C., III, vii (Fernando) :

> Rey te llamé, y aunque seas
> de otra ley, es tan augusta
> de los reyes la deidad,
> tan fuerte y tan absoluta,
> que engendra ánimo piadoso.

[3] S.O., I, vi (Irífile).

[4] Madame d'Aulnoy : *Relation du voyage en Espagne*, ed. R Foulché-Delbosc, Paris, 1926, p. 467.

Loyalty to the king was paramount over the things that a man prizes most highly :

> La lealtad del Rey ¿ no es antes
> que la vida y que el honor ? [1]

The King's status and authority were supreme :

> Nadie iguala con el Rey ;
> Él solo es igual consigo. [2]

Unlike many of his contemporaries, notably Lope de Vega, Calderón shows little liking for the common people, of whom he normally thinks as the " hydra-headed multitude,"

> desagradecido monstruo,
> que eres compuesto vestiglo
> de cabezas diferentes. [3]

They are fickle and treacherous—" monsters " of irresponsibility :

> Como se ve en tus diversas
> opiniones, vulgo, que eres
> monstruo de muchas cabezas ; [4]
>
> el vulgo, monstruo, despeñado y ciego ; [5]
>
> 　　　　es en su condición
> el vulgo un disforme monstruo. [6]

To him, as to Gracián, [7] the voice of the people is certainly not the voice of God :

> 　　　　la plebe
> monstruo es desbocado : no hay
> prevenciones que la enfrenen,
> cuando su mismo furor
> la obliga a que se despeñe.
> La novedad al principio
> la alimenta, y fácilmente,
> dejándose llevar della,
> de instantes a instantes crece. [8]

[1] V. Sñ., I, iv (Clotaldo).　　　　[2] P.C., II, xvii (Fernando).
[3] *La Hija del aire*, Segunda parte, I, x (Semíramis).
[4] C.A., III, iv (David).　　　　[5] V. Sñ., III, vii (Clotaldo).
[6] *La Gran Cenobia*, I, ii (Astrea).
[7] *El Criticón* (ed. Romera-Navarro, Philadelphia, 1938-40, Vol. III, p. 202) : Que por ningún acontecimiento se diga que la voz del pueblo es la de Dios ; sino de la ignorancia, y de ordinario por la boca del vulgo suelen hablar todos los demonios.
[8] C.A., III, xvii (Joab).

The principal characters in his plays are almost invariably drawn from the higher ranks of society and express themselves in a language which is cultured to the point of affectation.   Rustic speech merits only a disdainful reference :

> ¡ Villano al fin ! El lenguaje
> rústico claro lo da
> a entender, porque los nobles
> hablan más cortado y más
> político.[1]

Remembering his own humble origin, he goes so far as to defend acquired as against inherited nobility :

> Porque no es más la heredada
> que la adquirida nobleza,[2]

a distinction which his Ludovico Enio remembers when saying of Filipo :

> Es mucho mayor que yo
> en la nobleza, que aquí
> le dió la naturaleza ;
> mas no en aquella nobleza
> que ha merecido por sí.[3]

But, whatever the source of nobility, it entails certain responsibilities from which not even poverty, which to Calderón seem to have been remarkably like a crime

> —no sabe cuanto yerra
> quien, por excesivos gastos,
> pobres a sus hijos deja ;[4]

> es delito la pobreza—[5]

can absolve :

> la necesidad,
> aunque ultraje la nobleza,
> no excusa de obligaciones
> a los que nacen con ellas.[6]

Chief among these obligations is that of preserving inviolate the family honour, which, according to the punctilious code of the times, assumed an almost religious significance.

[1] S.O., I, v (Libio).   [2] D.C., I, iii (Eusebio).
[3] P.S.P., II, i.   [4] D.C., I, iii (Lisardo).
[5] Ibid.   [6] Ibid.

13

The elaborate unwritten laws which existed for the safe-
guarding of honour and which Calderón in his dramas went
so far towards standardizing, rested on the extremely delicate
nature of the concept :

> el honor,
> es de materia tan frágil,
> que con una acción se quiebra
> o se mancha con un aire. [1]

Among the well-born, the reputation of woman's virtue is a
treasured possession to which harm can be done by the
slightest rumour : suspicion need not wait upon proof for
condemnation.

> Mas quien tiene sangre hidalga
> no ha de aguardar a creer,
> que el imaginar le basta. [2]

Nor does the passage of time serve to eliminate the memory
of a fancied insult. Vengeance is long-suffering and patient :

> El agravio nunca duerme. [3]

---

[1] V. Sñ., I, iv (Clotaldo).   Cf. P.S.P., II, iii (Ludovico Enio) :
> no hay humano respeto
> que importe más que mi honor.

Here the phrase justifies one of the breaches of the code—viz., the drawing
of the sword in the king's presence.

Amid the multitude of crimes committed by Ludovico Enio, the hardened
sinner who rejoiced in his transgressions of the Decalogue, it is characteristic
of Calderón to make his " hero " rate as most shameful the selling of a woman's
virtue. Cf. P.S.P. (I, ii) :
> Si hubiera de cuanto he hecho
> de tener vergüenza alguna,
> sólo lo tuviera desto ;
> porque es la última bajeza,
> a que llega el más vil pecho,
> poner en venta el honor,
> y poner el gusto en precio.

[2] D.C., I, viii (Curcio).

It is interesting to find the same character (*ibid.*) uttering a protest against the
conventional and strict observance of the honour precepts which he qualifies
as :
> (. . . ¡oh ley tirana
> de honor ! ¡oh bárbaro fuero
> del mundo !)

Cf. V. Sñ., I, viii (Clotaldo) :
> Un hombre bien nacido
> si está agraviado, no vive ;
> que vida infame no es vida.

[3] P.S.P., II, x (Ludovico Enio).

But in the end it must be avenged by blood :

> ceniza: . . .
> no quitan la mancha de honra :
> sangre sí, que es buen jabón.[1]

Just as, within the State, authority is vested in the person of a monarch with absolute sway over his subjects, so, within the family, it devolves, as according to the Roman tradition, upon the father.   He it is who rules and whose commands must be obeyed : rarely, and only by the most independently minded, is any protest made against paternal control :

> Bien, señor, la autoridad
> de padre, que es pieferida,
> imperio tiene en la vida ;
> pero no en la libertad.[2]

In the final words of this passage Calderón hints at his interest in a problem which in fact continually preoccupied him—the exact place to be assigned to freedom in the formation of the human being.   Naturally such a concern led, in its turn, to a consideration of the best method of education.   The hymns to liberty intoned by characters zealously guarded or protected reveal a thorough understanding and a surprisingly modern conception of the psychological principles involved.   The theory that it was possible rigidly to seclude the young from the dangers and difficulties of life or completely to ignore them and yet to develop the human personality finds no support whatever in Calderón.   Freedom, he holds, is the truest master.   If the environment is controlled in any way which excludes temptation, the curiosity of the victim of such control is provided with an added incentive to seek after the very thing forbidden. Restraint and repression lead only to disaster.

So, despite his adherence to the code of honour, Calderón stands by his ideas on personal freedom sufficiently to appreciate the dangers of its suppressive tendencies.   There is a

---

[1] C.A., II, v (Tamar).   The whole magnificent speech of the dishonoured heroine is a glorification of the honour code.

[2] D.C., I, vii (Julia).

doubly significant remark by Llocía in *El Purgatorio de San Patricio* :

> Y en queriéndome celar
> me tengo de enamorar
> de todo el género humano.[1]

The remark is made, not by one of the main characters, but by the wife of the *gracioso* : the explanation may well be that Calderón was safeguarding himself in this way against any possible criticism that he was attacking one of the most cherished of contemporary principles.

We come next to Calderón's position in one of the controversial questions of the time, the place of women and the part they might be allowed to play in society. He seems to have defended their full participation in all life's activities : indeed, his women, not without reason, have been dubbed " hombrunas." The adjective " varonil," applied to women, is a compliment in Calderonian drama. That he dramatized the story of Eugenia, the female prodigy of learning, is significant. Her lament will be remembered :

> ¡ Oh, nunca mi vanidad . . .
> me hubiera puesto en aquesta
> estudiosa obligación
> de darles a entender cuanto
> más capaz, más superior
> es una mujer el día
> que, entregada a la lección
> de los libros, mejor que ellos
> obran, discurre veloz ![2]

Nor does his interest stop short at the world of books : woman, he holds, can rival man in the military sphere and compete like an Amazon on the field of battle :

---

[1] P.S.P., I, vii.

[2] J.M., I, i. Cf. D.A.C., II, xii (Cintia) :
> Yo, que dada a mis estudios,
> no hay ciencia en que no me esmere,
> y en la poética, que es
> arte que enseña y divierte,
> les hago ventaja a muchos
> ingenios que ahora florecen.

Y yo, que entre los viles
adornos vanos, galas mujeriles,
en los campos he dado
a la hacienda doméstico cuidado,
hoy en la guerra quiero,
vistiendo mallas y tocando acero,
publicar lo que intenta
mujer determinada.[1]

As might be expected of a religiously-minded man of conservative tendencies, Calderón disliked all the artificial aids to beauty to which women of his days were so much addicted. For him external beauty was primarily a reflection of the internal beauty of the soul and should therefore appear in its natural state :

Bien haya quien la belleza
debe a la naturaleza,
no al afeite y compostura.[2]

Indeed, a special department of purgatory is reserved for those women who during this life devoted excessive time to the cultivation of their physical charms—

las mujeres
que en esotra vida fueron,
por livianos pareceres,
amigas de olores y aguas,
unturas, baños y afeites.[3]

Another contemporary touch is the frequent reference to the habit of sending portraits of young princesses to their prospective husbands, who were expected to choose their wives without seeing them.[4] The custom is repeatedly satirized by the matter-of-fact *gracioso*, who finds such a method of choosing a mate a somewhat hazardous one.

[1] J.Mc., I, viii (Zares). Cf. the warlike sentiments of Queen Clodomira in E.C., III, x,

Hoy verá el mundo si saben
las mujeres manejar
acero y gobierno iguales,

Julia in D.C., II, vii and Deborah, in the *auto* ¿ *Quién hallará mujer fuerte* ? Barbara Matulka, in her monograph, *The Feminist Theme in the drama of the Siglo de Oro* (New York, n.d.) has analysed the anti-feminist conclusion of the *comedia palaciega* entitled *Afectos de odio y amor*.

[2] C.A., II, xiii (Amón).   [3] P.S.P., III, x (Ludovico Enio).

[4] *E.g.*, E.C., I, vii, and (an example of the inverse proceeding) P.C., I, iv.

More needs to be said of the *gracioso* of Calderón's religious plays than of their other leading types of character, for his utterances comprise the greatest wealth of idea and sentiment, other than theological, that they contain. To modern readers the inclusion of this burlesque figure in religious drama may savour at times of irreverence. But it must be admitted as a concession to the taste of the time and to dramatic convention. No dramatist would have dared to leave the comic element out of his plays. Moreover, despite its artistic incongruence, the character possesses compensating features. Through the *gracioso* the audience was brought into touch with the humdrum existence of the ordinary person. To a great extent his comments present the standpoint of the average man as contrasted with the exalted notions of aristocrats, saints and martyrs. He gives us hints of local colour, speaks the language of the people, voices the habits, foibles and prejudices of ordinary folk. He supplies those homely touches which could not be provided by the complex interplay of speech and action of the upper classes, intent upon their own problems of love, jealousy and honour.[1]

Calderón, the dramatist of religion, honour and allegiance to the king, who had little time for the populace he so much despised, makes use of the *gracioso* for the expression of his views on the most diverse of subjects. Among these are the principles of art. In the *gracioso's* humorous sallies we shall find the *disjecta membra* of the " Arte nuevo de hacer comedias " which Calderón never wrote. An educated man and a skilled playwright, he was always a conscious artist, and a complete collection of such comments culled, not from one group of plays, but from the whole body of his works, would constitute an invaluable commentary on the dramatic technique of the *comedia*.

The *gracioso* stands in marked contrast to his fellow-characters. He is the Sancho Panza of the *comedia*, the materialistic figure of the common man set over against the

[1] I purposely refrain from touching upon the vexed question of the *gracioso's* " comicità," concerning which there have been as many opinions as critics. Humour, though in essentials the same, is apt to change its form with the times.

idealistic noble, intellectual or saint.   In him are to be
found the cowardice, the cupidity, the fondness for wine,
the gaming instincts,[1] the mendacity, the diminutives of
popular language, the malapropisms of the uneducated, the
topical allusions, the puns, the anecdotic inserts, the occa-
sional Latin tags, the social satire or the skits at the devices of
the *comedia*, the slapstick, the dirt, the sensual asides which
mar the plays so little.   Here, too, occurs the parody of the
main plot and its motifs, which serves to lighten dramatic
tension.   A few examples will suffice.

The predominant trait of cowardice is based on a *terre
à terre* philosophy which values the preservation of human
life above all, and shuns physical danger :

> es dislate
> digno del hombre más loco,
> que haya quien morirse quiera
> por no dar una carrera.
> ¡ Cosa que cuesta tan poco ![2]

The proper place for his sword, he always considers, is the
scabbard : how, if it is anywhere else, can he be sure of
avoiding any fatal consequences that may attend his master's
adventures ?   The only *gracioso* to meet his death, it may be
added, is Clarín of *La Vida es sueño*, one of the few comic
characters to achieve any depth or dignity of thought.

It is interesting to find that drunkenness, a vice of such
rare occurrence in Spain, is never attributed to Christian

---

[1] Turín, the rough and ready soldier-*gracioso* of G.P.F., who is upbraided
by his master for an unbecoming lack of devotion, ultimately finds himself
penniless owing to gambling losses. (III, vii).   The prevalence of gaming
houses in contemporary Spain is a well attested fact, evidence for which is
supplied by many of the secular plays : *e.g.*, *El Médico de su honra* (II, xi) and
El Astrólogo fingido (II, viii).

[2] P.S.P., III, i (Paulín).   Cf. P.C., I, ix (Brito) :
> El cuartel de la salud
> me toca a mí guardar siempre ;

J.Mc., III, xii (Chato) :
> ¡ Miedo, miedo !
> ¿Adónde estaré seguro ?

A.C., II, i (Tucapel) :
> Si no hubiera un coronista
> que huyera de las batallas,
> no hubiera como saberlas . . .

What Américo Castro elegantly terms " el chiste maloliente," so frequent
both in the Cervantine work and the *comedia*, usually accompanies references
to cowardice.

characters, but usually to another familiar figure, the
Moorish servant who speaks a sort of pidgin-Spanish and
takes delight in violating the supposedly rigid precepts of the
Koran.[1]   Calderón took this means of availing himself of a
theme which has been a common mirth-provoker throughout
the ages and, at the same time, of poking fun at the " com-
mon enemy," for whose religion, incidentally, he showed a
tolerance unusual in his day.

> Aunque es religión cerrada,
> ya es religión por lo menos.[2]

In the Christian characters inclination for strong drink
expresses itself in a constant invocation of Bacchus :

> ¡ Gracias
> a Baco, opíparo Dios
> de las cepas y las parras,
> (Que es el que invoco yo en todas
> buenas y malas andanzas) . . . ![3]

Of the more obvious characteristics of the *gracioso*, his
possession of a certain rudimentary culture calls for comment.
For this somewhat surprising feature there is a perfectly
plausible explanation.   The servant to a young man of
good birth who attended courses at the university,[4] or of a
military master who saw foreign service in Flanders or Italy,
could not fail to pick up during his wanderings certain
scraps of knowledge which he was only too pleased to display
on every possible occasion.   Further acquisitions of the kind
would result from constant intercourse with his social betters.

[1] Cf. the Alcuzcuz of G.P.F. and Alí in V.S.   (The negro Mandinga in S.O.
also uses a similar distorted manner of speech).   The same stock figure under
the identical name (Alcuzcuz) appears in the secular play *Amar después de la
muerte*.

[2] G.P.F., I, xi (El Buen Genio).

[3] E.C., III, ii (Morlaco).   Cf. D.A.C., II, vi (Escarpín) :

> Por Baco (que éste es el Dios
> por quien todos los pícaros ruegan),

and J.M., II, viii (Capricho).

The Velázquez picture " Los Borrachos " (c. 1629) provides a parallel.   The
classically-draped Bacchus and the ragamuffin topers of this drinking-piece
are obviously posed studio models.   The picture, painted under the influence
of Rubens, does not correspond to an observed social reality.

[4] Clarín and Moscón in M.P. serve their student master at the opening of the
play dressed as " gorrones."

Thus the *gracioso* can generally be relied upon to produce a Latin quotation or an item of legal jargon.[1] In fact, it is the exception to find a *gracioso* who does not understand Latin.[2]

But the relative freedom assumed by the *gracioso* does not lead to any serious criticism of contemporary social evils : even on the very few occasions when this does appear, it concerns itself, not with any established principles or institutions but with the delinquencies of particular individuals. The *gracioso's* most daring exploit of this kind is to poke fun at the court-hanger-on, the " sabandija palaciega," whose chief duty is " comer y holgar."[3]

In the history of the *comedia* the work of Calderón marks the culminating point of a long process of evolution : he can certainly not be termed an innovator. He took the *genre* as he found it, deviating hardly at all from its traditional formula, but perfecting and re-polishing it with all the technical skill at his command. The merit of the plays under consideration derives no less from a mastery of construction

[1] Thus in E.C. (III, xii), after a Latin hymn has been sung, Morlaco, the servant of a learned master, shows he has understood the last verses by asking a pertinent question. The same character voices his cowardice in Italian (III, ii) :
          . . . una bella ritirata . . . tutta la vita onora.
Even a woman, Livia in M.P. (II, iii), recalls a famous definition of justice taken from the " Corporis Juris " in the line
                    dar
          a cada uno lo que es suyo
(*e.g.*, Justitia est constans ac perpetua voluntas ius suum cuique tribuendi). Krenkel points out that the same definition is given in the *Legenda Aurea*, Calderón's main source for the play.

[2] *E.g.*, Capricho in J.M., II, ix, who, on hearing Eugenia exclaiming " Deo gratias," asks " ¿Qué lengua es ésta ? "

[3] G.P.F., II, iv (Alcuzcuz). Calderón puts these phrases into the mouth of a non-Christian. Cf. also E.C., I, x (Morlaco) :
                    ¿No es
          mejor llegar ahora ? pues
          entre tanta confusión
          podremos dar a entender
          que en la guerra hemos estado
          y fuertemente peleado,
          como lo suelen hacer
          otros, que en la corte están
          vestiditos de color ;
          y no se sabe, señor,
          ni cuándo vienen ni van.

and stage technique than from the intrinsic interest of their theological content. At the same time, it is not in the *comedias religiosas* that his best work is to be found and from the technical standpoint many of them are open to severe criticism.

Preoccupied as Calderón was with other considerations, he found little time for flights of the imagination. The invention of new plots he hardly conceived to be his task at all ; and in this respect he was like his contemporaries. So short was the stage-life of the ordinary play that the busy dramatist was forced to adapt the works of his contemporaries,[1] to refurbish old legends[2] and to dramatize incidents from the Bible[3] or episodes from the lives of saints.[4]

These varied sources provide the basic elements for the plot which are worked into the traditional framework of the *comedia*. But the religious material employed is all too frequently given a secular treatment which detracts from the general artistic unity. Further defects arise from the intercalation of irrelevant and incongruous incidents and motifs. Nor is compensation for these defects to be found in the skill with which the dramatist handles such disparate elements and combines them into intricate patterns. Excessive ingenuity and complexity of plot mar the directness and forcefulness which the clear-cut religious truths require. The extent of the harm done varies from the insertion of such elements as the Florio and Lelio episodes in *El Mágico prodigioso* and the Sergio and Aurelio complication in *El José de las mujeres* to the complete transformation of a so-called Biblical play like *Judas Macabeo* into a mere *comedia de enredo* with a love interest as its main theme. Of all the

[1] C.A., for example, is a re-handling of Tirso de Molina's *La Venganza de Tamar* ; M.P. and C.D. are considerably indebted to Mira de Amescua.

[2] V.S. is a blending of Toledan legends and hints from the *Romancero*. D.C., though apparently based on no one particular work, must have drawn upon the rich stores of pietistic legend, as well, it seems, as on a contemporary event of some note.

[3] The apocryphal Book of the Maccabees and Josephus would have supplied most of the material in J.Mc., though there was also in existence a widely circulated anonymous *Historia de Judas Macabeo y sus esforzados hermanos*. Neither here nor in C.A., however, does Calderón follow his Biblical originals closely : contrast, for example, C.A., III, xxv with 2 Kings, xvi, 9.

[4] Cf. p. 175, above.

comedias religiosas, only *La Devoción de la Cruz* can be said to preserve both structural unity and singleness of purpose.

The dramatic device most frequently employed is that of the long *romance* narrative, such as Clodomira's in *La Exaltación de la Cruz* (I, x), Joab's in *La Sibila del Oriente* (II, i)and the lengthy passages in *El Purgatorio de San Patricio* (I, ii), in which both St. Patrick and Ludovico Enio relate the histories of their respective lives. [1] The almost invariable purpose of these narrations is to inform spectators of the life-stories of the *dramatis personæ* or to relate events not represented on the stage.   And Calderón, it seems, shared Lope de Vega's opinion :

> Las relaciones piden los romances. [2]

Even allowing for the known rapidity with which the lines were delivered by the actors, the excessive length of some of these narratives, especially when the dramatist took advantage of them to display his lyric skill, must have placed a great strain on the spectator's patience.   Calderón evidently recognized the abuses to which the device might lead.   Once he makes a character cut short his *relación,*

> para que en pinturas
> no se vaya todo el tiempo. [3]

Similarly the *gracioso* finds a continual butt for his wit in the

---

[1] Here an added interest is given to the device by the element of antithesis the key-note of the narrations being the opposition of good and evil.   The *gracioso* Calabazas in *Casa con dos puertas mala es de guardar* (I, iii) casts ridicule on the convention :
> En tanto que ellos se pegan
> dos grandísimos romances,
> ¿ tendréis, Herrera, algo que
> se atreva a desayunarme ?

Cf. also *Hombre pobre todo es trazas* (I, ii : Diego) :
> ¿ No has visto en una comedia
> verse dos, y en dos razones
> hacerse mil relaciones
> de su gusto y su tragedia ?
> Pues imitemos aquí
> su estilo : que en esta parte
> tengo mucho que contarte.

[2] *Arte nuevo de hacer comedias*, Liverpool, Institute of Hispanic Studies, 1935, p. 8.

[3] P.S.P., I, iii.

convention of the soliloquy which is used to express doubt in deciding upon a course of action :

> Pero sepamos : ¿ a quién
> le cuento yo todo esto ?
> ¿ Hay semejante locura ?
> ¡ que hablando conmigo venga, . . .
> diciendo mil necedades . . . ! [1]

Linked to these devices is the clever handling of the trick of narrative suspense—the interruption of the story at its crucial point to sustain dramatic interest—as during the argument between Zacarías and Anastasio in *La Exaltación de la Cruz*, Lisardo Curcio's conversation with Julia in *La Devoción de la Cruz* and the breaking-off of Lisandro's account of Justina's life-history in *El Mágico prodigioso*. [2] Conventional though it be, the device is extremely effective and must often have caused audiences to follow these plays with heightened interest.

In the sphere of incident the outstanding characteristic of these plays is the care which the dramatist takes to safeguard himself from any possible charge of impiety when the exigences of plot require him to introduce scenes that might give occasion for scandal. Twice—in *El Purgatorio de San Patricio* (1627) and in *La Devoción de la Cruz* (1633)—a convent sacrilege is dramatized and on each occasion the delicacy with which this dangerous theme is handled merits attention. Incidentally, both these plays belong to Calderón's youth and possess certain dynamic qualities for which in his later work we may search in vain.

On the first occasion when Calderón presents the " lance sacrílego " he insists upon making his position with regard to it perfectly clear. The incident is not depicted, but merely reported, and extreme emphasis is placed upon the heinousness of the crime which the character who describes

---

[1] J.M., II, viii (Capricho). Cf. G.P.F., III, vii (Turín) :
> nadie a un pícaro quita
> el don de los soliloquios.

[2] In many respects this incident recalls Prospero's narrative to Miranda in *The Tempest*.

it professes diffidence even about relating :

> Me atreví . . . Turbada aquí . . .
> muda fallece la voz . . .
> Triste y absorto, no tengo
> ánimo para decirlo,
> si le tuve para hacerlo.
> Tal es mi delito en fin
> de detestable, de feo,
> de sacrílego, de profano
> (harto así te lo encarezco),
> que de haberle cometido,
> alguna vez me arrepiento.[1]

Though the very recital makes the culprit tremble with horror and the dramatist spares no effort to depict the episode as detestable, he advances a step farther when next dealing with the theme, dramatizing the incident in all its details and even showing the intruder scaling the convent walls and entering the nun's cell :

> he atropellado
> el respeto del sagrado
> y la ley de la clausura.[2]

But once more the dramatist seeks to disarm criticism by suggesting that a secret marriage invalidated Julia's vows, thus excusing, if not condoning, Eusebio's crime. Despite this artificial expedient, which is wholly unprepared, Calderón did not escape a reproof from the ecclesiastical censorship, which demanded a radical modification of the scene.

The desire, even when introducing the *escabroso* into a drama, not to present it in too favourable a light is clearly the preoccupation of a poet intent upon spiritual values. Unlike some other masters of the *comedia*, Calderón rarely descended to the portrayal of licentious scenes or allowed his comic characters excessive licence. In this respect his plays are beyond reproach.[3]

When dealing with the subject of a woman's loss of her

[1] P.S.P., I, ii (Ludovico Enio).

[2] D.C., II, xi (Eusebio).

[3] Only some half-dozen cases have been noted in the whole of these dramas and all of them come from two plays, P.S.P. (I, v and vi) and D.C. (*passim*), which belong to the early period.

honour Calderón never describes the misfortune, but suggests it as modestly as possible. Thus a character bringing a false accusation of an attempt on her virtue simulates diffidence and stops short of entering into details about the dishonourable proposals made to her :

> Aquí la voz
> se pasma, aquí se entorpece
> la lengua, y el labio aquí
> se tropieza balbuciente. [1]

The secular plays, it may be added, afford many parallel examples, especially where the dramatization of Classical themes necessitated the introduction of the unchaste. In Act I of *Eco y Narciso*, for example, Liriope, after being dishonoured by Céfiro, excuses herself thus :

> .... Entendedlo vosotros,
> y a mi vergüenza suplid
> cosas, que para saberse
> no se han menester oír.

and Leonor, in *No hay cosa como callar* (II, iv), avoids the *mot propre* with great delicacy :

> ¿ Qué frase habrá más decente
> que lo refiera ? Ninguna,
> porque la más elocuente
> es la que, sin decir nada,
> el más rústico la entiende.

Even in his descriptions of woman's beauty, it would seem, Calderón's restricting of himself to conventional lyrical comparisons springs from his desire not to trespass on dangerous ground :

> No quiero detenerme
> en retóricas pinturas ;
> que peligra lo decente
> donde hay baños y beldades. [2]

In this connection it may be recalled that a similar Catholic puritanism influenced the development of Spanish painting : Velázquez's only nude is the discreet Rokeby Venus.

Modern Catholic theory inclines to the view that the Catholic writer should not be exclusively pietistic, but treat

---

[1] J.M., III, xi (Melancia). The seduction of Tamar in C.A. takes place, off the stage, after the close of Act I.

[2] *Fineza contra fineza*, I, iii (Anfión).

of any subject, moral or immoral, as he may desire. Every phase of human life is material for the literary artist and religious ends are not served by its falsification. To ignore life's darker aspects is to betray truth. The differentiation between use and abuse becomes the artist's personal problem : the purity of his own life will guarantee the integrity of his literary product. Such, in brief, is the latest solution to an age-old problem ;[1] but its acceptance has to a large extent been facilitated by modern conditions. It would be unfair to judge Calderón by modern standards. Apart from the moral reservations which were dictated by the age in which he lived, his disinclination to treat life in its fullness is the result of a natural sensitiveness and reticence. In the convention which dictated the elimination of the immoral and the prosaic his religious muse found a congenial ally.

In the sphere of characterization we meet a similar difficulty. Our natural tendency to-day is to condemn the Calderonian *comedia* for its poverty in life-like figures and to draw the inevitable but hackneyed comparison with the complex protagonists of Shakespeare. This analogy clearly underlies much denunciatory criticism in the past. Though the *comedias religiosas* contain few of Calderón's finest characters, because (to go no farther for reasons) their schematic theological framework and simplified psychology make for monotony of character-drawing, there is undoubtedly foundation for the charge that in general Calderón's personages are all cast in the same mould. No matter how subtly the dramatist's ingenuity rings the changes on plot and situation, his human beings lack vigour and vitality.

But the Spanish *comedia* never pretended to attain richness of characterization. Its strength lay elsewhere. In Spain, the mainspring of drama has always been plot—and here, once again, Calderón is faithful to tradition. Like his predecessors, he set but little store upon the exact portrayal of character. His short-lived conflicts afford small opportunity for intricate psychological analysis. His men

---

[1] It is outlined more fully, and treated critically, in Charles du Bos's *François Mauriac et le problème du romancier catholique* (1933).

and women are not creatures of flesh and blood who lived
in his own day, but purely subjective and often symbolic
creations incarnating their author's beliefs and ideals. It
is by preference that Calderón deals in abstractions and in
his religious plays the human element cedes pride of place
to the spiritual values it is intended to personify. Thus even
the non-religious characters tend to become social types
rather than individuals. It would be a generalization
not far from the truth to say that whereas in the *autos*,
which chronicle the whole of man's spiritual history, he
attained the height of his abstract art, and in the secular
plays dramatized the predominant social tendencies of his
age, in the *drama religioso* he produced an intermediate *genre*
in which all the elements of his characterization are blended.

An examination of the stylistic traits of these plays
involves some consideration of the meaning of the word
" Baroque," which in recent years has found such favour
with literary critics and historians both in the Peninsula
and elsewhere.

Long employed very loosely in architectural manuals,
the word acquired a well-defined and modern significance
with the publication of Wölfflin's *Kunstgeschichtliche Grundbe-
griffe* in 1915. This book, as Wölfflin declares, arose from
the need of establishing on a firmer basis the classifications
of art history. Its main concern was the analysis of the
development of post-Renaissance art, the study of which led
Wölfflin to the theory that in addition to a personal style
which is the expression of a certain temperament there
exists also a period counterpart, the result of the limited
choice of formal possibilities open to each epoch. Not all
artistic attempts are possible at all times. The transition
from Renaissance to seventeenth-century art is the classic
example of how a new *Zeitgeist* enforces new forms. Follow-
ing a five-fold scheme of differentials the characteristics of
the Baroque were established. [1]

---

[1] The work is a modification of the original theory first expounded by
Wölfflin in an early book on the same subject, *Renaissance und Barock* (Munich,
1888). I have consulted the English translation by M.D. Höttinger (*Principles
of Art History*, 1932) from the seventh German edition (1929).

Wölfflin's exhaustive analysis and re-definition at once commended themselves to German literary critics, who hastened to apply his criteria to their own seventeenth century. The rehabilitation of the Baroque had begun. Spain soon followed suit, and Gracián, Quevedo, Góngora and Calderón became the supreme Baroque artists.

As used to-day, the term denotes not only "a profusion of ornament irrelevant to the work as an organic whole," but also the employment of certain rhetorical devices, such as antithesis,[1] parallelism, allegory, accumulated metaphor, etc., as well as an internal dynamism that expresses itself in feverish action. The static, the immobile and the perspicuous have given place to the dynamic, the restless and the obscure. However, the latest examination of the concept and its use in modern criticism finds the art-literature analogy, so far as Germany is concerned, lacking in validity, and insists on the absence of agreement among the various theorists of the Baroque. At best the term can only be legitimately retained as a convenient label, implying a certain use of technique occurring predominantly at a certain time.[2]

No attempt, therefore, will be made to draw conclusions from the discussion which follows of certain outstanding features of Calderón's style and the presence in it of what are commonly called Baroque elements. We have as yet no basis for generalization ; and, until a full and comparative study has been made of the language of the seventeenth century, it would be hazardous to declare which of the characteristics of a writer's style are the result of contemporary trends and which are due to personal taste.

---

[1] Thus, for example, in P.S.P., the antithesis between Saint Patrick and Ludovico Enio :

> Los dos, somos tan opuestos
> que distamos cuanto va
> desde ser malo a ser bueno.   (I, ii).

and the exact parallelism of their respective " relaciones " would be termed Baroque characteristics, and so with the other elements of contrast, the *gracioso* parody of the main plot, or the occurrence of the twin motif.

[2] Cf. J. Marks : " The use of the term Baroque," in *Modern Language Review*, October, 1938 (XXXIII, 546-63). The article deals especially with German literature, but it is important for its bearing on general critical theory.

14

As an educated man of his day and a practising play-wright, Calderón could not fail to be interested in the writings of his contemporaries. Some of his debts to fellow-dramatists have already been noted. Following an established fashion, he frequently alludes to contemporary plays,[1] while also citing several non-dramatic authors. Interspersed with his lyric flights are some well-known lines by Garcilaso de la Vega. Such are the opening lines of the famous sonnet :

¡ Oh dulces prendas, por mí mal halladas !. . . [2]

and the refrain from the First Eclogue :

Salid sin duelo, lágrimas, corriendo.[3]

Góngora, however, is the author who figures most prominently in his work, and, both verbally and structurally, contributes most to the formation of his style. Not only does Calderón on occasion borrow from him directly but he resembles him in diction, and particularly in his use of metaphor. A careful reader of the *Metamorphoses*, he was no doubt attracted by the Ovidian sources of the *Polifemo*. The long conversation between Don Fernando and Muley (P.C., I, xi) is a gloss on Góngora's " Romance de los Cenetes" [4] and the description of the mysterious cave by Polonia (P.S.P., II, xix) owes several of its details to a similar passage in the *Polifemo*. The fondness of Calderón's characters for comparing themselves with Biblical or mythological figures—

[1] E.g., the references in M.P. to Alarcón's *La Verdad sospechosa* and Mira de Amescua's *La Esclava del demonio*. Among his own plays the most often mentioned is probably *La Dama duende*. Cf. Restori's *Piezas de títulos de comedias* (Messina, 1903).

[2] C.A., I, i (David) :
¡Ay, dulces prendas, por mí bien halladas !
P.S.P., II, xiii (El Rey) :
¡Ay, bella
prenda por mí mal hallada !

[3] C.A., III, xxiii (David) :
Salid sin duelo, lágrimas, corriendo.
The same character repeats the line in the next scene.

[4] In *Las blancas manos no ofenden* (III, xv), the *gracioso* Patacón, after quoting several lines from the same ballad, states :
(*Textus in Gongora*, en el
romance de los Cenetes).

> Icaro seré sin alas
> sin fuego seré Faetón—[1]

and the continual references to the Greco-Roman deities derive from the same Gongoristic source. However, where the influence of the " culto " style evinces itself most clearly is in the bombastic flights of descriptive lyricism. An account of a shipwreck enables a captain to allude to the sea as

> Ese monstruo nevado
> que en sus ondas dilata
> a espejos de zafir marcos de plata[2]

and again a ship becomes

> . . . . un delfín que es pájaro sin pluma,
> . . . una águila que es pez sin escama,
> monte de velas, huracán de pino,
> selva de jarcias, vecindad de lino.[3]

But it is the horse that supplied Calderón with the best opportunity for indulging his descriptive powers.

> Cuando en veloz caballo, cuyo aliento
> jeroglífico ha sido de la guerra,
> sierpe del agua, exhalación del viento,
> volcán del fuego, escollo de la tierra,
> caos animal . . .[4]

Even the *gracioso* cannot forbear to parody his betters in his account of the animal.

> (Perdóname, que fuerza es el pintallo
> en viniéndome a cuento).[5]

---

[1] D.C., II, x (Eusebio). In P.S.P., I, i, Egerio calls himself " segundo Nembrot." The Nimrod comparison is very frequent.

[2] P.S.P., I, i. Cf. the accounts of the storm by St. Patrick, Ludovico Enio and Polonia.

[3] S.O., I, iii (Candaces). Cf., in the same play (I, x), Sabá's " e terano " description of a ship, and A.C., I, iii, where Guacolda terms it in turn : " un escollo que navega, preñada nube, marino pez, velera ave, aborto de mar y viento."

[4] S.O., I, iii (Hirán). Cf. Fernando's description (P.C., I, xi) where he alludes to the horse as " hijo del viento " and V. Sñ, I, i (Rosaura) : " Hipogrifo violento . . . . pájaro sin matiz, pez sin escama."

[5] V. Sñ., III, ix (Clarín).

Apart from the Góngora sources, a precedent for the description can be found in Job xxxix, 19-25, where the sacred author sings the praises of the steed in battle. It may also be that Calderón's interest was aroused by his own participation in military campaigns and then whetted by the spectacle of the magnificent specimens in the royal stables of the hunting monarch, Philip IV,[1] which are so superbly portrayed in the equestrian canvases of Velázquez. Pliny (one of the dramatist's favourite Classical authors), in Book VIII of the *Historia naturalis*, treats of the animal kingdom in detail and mentions cases of conceptions by the wind in terms which recall Calderón's " parto del viento."

In his emotional scenes Calderón prefers to employ a conventional language in which " Etna, volcán, basilisco, áspid " and the ever-recurring " fénix " serve to depict anger, jealousy and love. In his use of the latter he follows Góngora, while the asp and the basilisk, though elements of *culto* style, may also be reminiscences of the Oriental symbolism of the Old Testament. The Gongorine partiality for elaboration and complexity of metaphor finds a parallel in Calderón's favourite rhetorical device : the enumeration of a series of metaphors to describe the same object and their final accumulation in the closing verses.[2] Of extreme syntactical innovations there are few traces save in the *Purgatorio de San Patricio* ; and it is only fair to point out that the bulk of the evidence which its author provides of *culteranismo* in all its forms is to be met with in the plays of the early years. The *Purgatorio*, the *Príncipe constante* and the *Sibila del Oriente* are cases in point, to which may be added many minor indications, such as the scene of the " Academia poética " in *El José de las mujeres* (I, xi) and several passages in *Los Dos Amantes del cielo* (I, xi), such as the conversations of Crisanto and Daría and the scene between Licanoro, Ceusis and Irene, in which the last-named accuses her suitors of using " cortesanos estilos."

---

[1] Many of Calderón's female characters are accomplished horsewomen fond of hunting. Cf. P.C., II, i (Fénix) ; D.A.C., II, vii (Daría).

[2] Cf. M.P., II, xviii : Cipriano's praise of Justina's beauty.

In the present state of research, it is impossible to pronounce definitely upon many other conjectural stylistic influences such as those of the casuists and of contemporary preachers. Of *conceptismo* in these plays I have been unable to find any evidence, apart, of course, from the theological refinements of Scholasticism, which could be termed a " conceptismo a lo divino." Calderón invariably preferred the complexities of verbal imagery to the paradoxical interplay of thought.

INDEX

INDEX